Temperament in Context

Temperament in Context

Edited by

Theodore D. Wachs
Purdue University

Gedolph A. Kohnstamm
University of Leiden

2001

LAWRENCE ERLBAUM ASSOCIATES, PUBLISHERS

Mahwah, New Jersey   London

Lawrence Erlbaum Associates, Inc., Publishers
10 Industrial Avenue
Mahwah, NJ 07430

Cover design by Kathryn Houghtaling Lacey

Library of Congress Cataloging-in-Publication Data

Temperament in Context / edited by Theodore D. Wachs,
Gedolph A. Kohnstamm.
p. cm.

Includes bibliographical references and index.
ISBN 0-8058-3019-7 (hardcover)
1. Temperament—Congresses. 2. Temperament in children
—Congresses. I. Wachs, Theodore D., 1941-
II. Kohnstamm, Gedolph A., 1937-
BF798.T443   2001
155.2'6—dc21

00-057285
CIP

Books published by Lawrence Erlbaum Associates are
printed on acid-free paper, and their bindings are chosen for
strength and durability.

Printed in the United States of America
10 9 8 7 6 5 4 3 2 1

Contents

Introduction

Temperament is traditionally defined as relatively stable, early appearing, biologically based individual traits (Rothbart & Bates, 1998). Individual differences in temperament along such dimensions as reactivity and self-regulation are viewed as an essential first step to individual variability in later personality patterns. Individual differences in temperament are thought to be related to individual genetic differences (Goldsmith, 1989; Plomin & Saudino, 1994), which in turn lead to individual differences in those aspects of central nervous system structure and neurochemistry that act to mediate individual differences in temperament (Calkins & Fox, 1994; Kagan, Reznick, & Snidman, 1989; Strelau, 1994).

Although an emphasis on the biological roots of temperament can be traced back to the early centuries of the present millennium (Diamond, 1974), historically there has also been speculation on the role played by nonbiological *contextual* influences such as climate and education (Jacques, 1881). For the purposes of this volume we define *context* as "organized conditions or patterns of external stimuli that impinge upon and have the probability of influencing the individual" (Wachs, 1992, p. 39). It is important to recognize that this broad definition of context can encompass both psychosocial (e.g., the family, culture) and biological conditions (e.g., physical ecology, diet, environmental toxins). The focus of this volume is primarily on the psychosocial context, given that there is only limited evidence available on the behavioral consequences associated with variability in the biological context. Summarization of evidence on issues involving the measurement of the biological context in behavioral research can be found in a recent chapter by Evans (1999); summarization of evidence on diet and temperament can be found in a chapter by Wachs (in press).

The relative neglect of psychosocial contributions to the study of temperament in part reflects the historical tradition of viewing temperament as a biologically rooted phenomena. In addition, as pointed out by Matheny and Phillips (chap. 6, this volume), the longstanding assumption that temperament is a highly stable phenomena hindered the search for psychosocial contextual variables that might lead to discontinuity in temperament over time or across situations. However, as pointed out by other contributors to this

volume (e.g., Arcus, chap. 4) the modest level of predictability of temperament variability from purely biological predictors, as well as the modest level
of predictability of developmental outcomes from temperament per se, has
emphasized the need to go beyond main effect theories concerning temperament and development. Even among temperament theorists who have a
strong biological orientation there is nonetheless agreement that temperament is more than just a biological phenomena (Buss & Plomin, 1984;
Rothbart, 1989). Conceptually, the importance of linking temperament to
psychosocial context has been most often emphasized in the writings of
Chess and Thomas (1991, 1999), with specific reference to the concept of
"goodness of fit." As defined by Thomas and Chess (1977): "Goodness of fit
results when the properties of the environment and its expectations and demands are in accordance with the organism's own capacities, characteristics
and style of behaving" (pp. 11–12). When there is a good fit the individual is
able to adapt and function effectively in his or her environment; under conditions of poor fit ("discrepancies and dissonances between environmental opportunities and demands and the capacities of the organism," Thomas &
Chess, 1977, pp. 11–12) maladjustment and deviations from normal developmental trajectories are more likely to occur. The critical point is that development is a function of neither the individual's environment nor of their
temperament but rather of the nature of the interaction (fit) between individual and environmental characteristics.

While cognizant of this historical tradition, the genesis of this volume de-
rives directly from a previous volume designed to summarize and integrate
current knowledge on biological contributions to individual differences in
temperament (Bates & Wachs, 1994). Interestingly, one of the conclusions
that repeatedly emerged in many of the chapters in this previous volume was
the importance of context for understanding both biological contributions to
individual variability in temperament and the developmental consequences
of such variability.

Whereas the potential importance of context for temperament has been
repeatedly discussed by temperament researchers there has been all too little
systematic research on the unique role specific aspects of context play in the
development and impact of temperament. The goal of this volume is to sys-
tematize current knowledge and theory on the role played by specific aspects
of context in the etiology, expression, and influence of temperament. It is our
hope that such a summarization will act as a springboard to generate more research on the question of temperament and context.

This volume is organized around four approaches to dealing with the
question of temperament and context. Although it may seem strange in a
book devoted to temperament and context to have the first approach propose the hypothesis that temperament and context are unrelated, nonetheless this is a traditional view that is held by many temperament and

personality researchers and it deserves consideration. In their chapter, Costa and McCrae present a provocative theoretical analysis arguing that although the individual's adaptations to the world may be potentially influenced by context, temperament itself is basically independent of contextual influences viewed either at a personal or a cultural level. The second approach is also based on a traditional view of the nature of temperament-context relations, namely that temperament acts to influence the nature of the individual's context. Based on the concept of reactive covariance (Plomin, DeFries, & Loehlin, 1977) it is assumed that the individual's temperament characteristics act to structure how others react to them. Such differential reaction is the basis for different contexts for individuals with different temperaments. Looking at longitudinal relations among infant reactions to stress, infant temperament, and patterns of mother–child relations this second approach is reflected in the chapter by Ramsay and Lewis.

The third approach illustrates the bidirectional nature of temperament-context relations. Without denying that temperament can influence context, in their respective chapters Arcus, Halverson, and Deal, and Matheny and Phillips present evidence showing how parent–child transactions, family characteristics, and characteristics of the physical environment can act to modify both the child's temperament and changes in the child's temperament over time. The final approach found in this volume emphasizes the nature of underlying processes whereby individual differences in temperament act to influence individual differences in behavioral–developmental variability. Common to the various chapters in this section is the argument that the predictive value of temperament can only be understood by taking into account the nature of the child's context. Using classroom and cultural data both Goldsmith et al. and Kerr present evidence in their respective chapters showing how our ability to predict developmental outcomes from temperament is context dependent. Looking at temperament in both adulthood and childhood, and coming from very different research traditions, both Strelau and Bates present evidence suggesting that the interaction between individual differences in temperament and context is an essential mechanism for understanding the role temperament plays in individual behavioral development. This volume closes with a chapter by the editors that integrates the various approaches presented in this volume, agrees or disagrees with specific conclusions, and presents directions for future research in the study of temperament and context.

ACKNOWLEDGMENTS

A number of the chapters presented in this volume were initially presented at a conference on temperament and context held in 1996 at the Netherlands Institute for Advanced Study in the Humanities and Social Sciences (NIAS). We are grateful to NIAS for providing both facilities and financial support for this conference. In addition, financial support for the conference and for initiation of this volume also came from the Netherlands Organization for Scientific Research and the Royal Netherlands Academy of Arts and Sciences, and we wish to acknowledge and thank these organizations for their help. The authors also wish to acknowledge our editor at Lawrence Erlbaum Associates (Judi Amsel) for her patience and encouragement during the writing of this volume.

REFERENCES

Bates, J., & Wachs, T. D. (Eds.). (1994). *Temperament: Individual differences at the interface of biology and behavior*. Washington, DC: American Psychological Association.

Buss, A., & Plomin, R. (1984). *Temperament: Early developing personality traits*. Hillsdale, NJ: Lawrence Erlbaum Associates.

Calkins, S., & Fox, N. (1994). Individual differences in the biological aspects of temperament. In J. Bates & T. D. Wachs (Eds.), *Temperament: Individual differences at the interface of biology and behavior* (pp. 199–218). Washington, DC: American Psychological Association.

Chess, S., & Thomas, A. (1991). Temperament and the concept of goodness of fit. In J. Strelau & A. Angleitner (Eds.), *Explorations in temperament* (pp. 15–28). New York: Plenum.

Chess, S., & Thomas, A. (1999). *Goodness of fit: Clinical applications from infancy through adult life*. New York: Brunner/Mazel.

Diamond, S. (1974). *The roots of psychology*. New York: Basic Books.

Evans, G. (1999). Measurement of the physical environment as stressor. In S. Friedman & T. D. Wachs (Eds.), *Measuring environment across the life span* (pp. 249–278). Washington DC: American Psychological Association.

Goldsmith, H. (1989). Behavior-genetic approaches to temperament. In G. Kohnstamm, J. Bates, & M. Rothbart (Eds.), *Temperament and childhood* (pp. 111–132). New York: Wiley.

Jacques, D. (1881). *The temperaments*. New York: Fowler & Wells.

Kagan, J., Reznick, J., & Snidman, N. (1989). Issues in the study of temperament. In G. Kohnstamm, J. Bates, & M. Rothbart (Eds.), *Temperament in childhood* (pp. 133–144). New York: Wiley.

Plomin, R., DeFries, J., & Loehlin, J. (1977). Genotype environment interaction and correlation in the analysis of human development. *Psychological Bulletin, 84,* 309–322.

Plomin, R., & Saudino, K. (1994). Quantitative genetics and molecular genetics. In J. Bates & T. D. Wachs (Eds.), *Temperament: Individual differences at the interface of biology and behavior* (pp. 143–174). Washington, DC: American Psychological Association.

Rothbart, M. (1989). Biological processes in temperament. In G. Kohnstamm, J. Bates & M. Rothbart (Eds.), *Temperament in childhood* (pp. 77–110). New York: Wiley.

Rothbart, M., & Bates, J. (1998). Temperament. In W. Damon (Series Ed.) & N. Eisenberg (Vol. Ed.), *Handbook of child psychology: Vol. 3. Social, emotional, and personality development,* 5th ed. (pp. 105–176). New York: Wiley.

Strelau, J. (1994). The concepts of arousal and arousability as used in temperament studies. In J. Bates & T. D. Wachs (Eds.), *Temperament: Individual differences at the interface of biology and behavior.* Washington, DC: American Psychological Association.

Thomas, A., & Chess, S. (1977). *Temperament and development.* New York: Brunner/Mazel.

Wachs, T. D. (1992). *The nature of nurture.* Newbury Park: Sage.

Wachs, T. D. (in press). Linking nutrition and temperament. In D. Molfese & T. Molfese (Eds.), *Temperament and personality development across the life span.* Mahwah, NJ: Lawrence Erlbaum Associates.

1   A Theoretical Context for Adult Temperament

Paul T. Costa, Jr.
Robert R. McCrae
*National Institute on Aging, National Institutes of Health**

In this chapter we sketch a theory of temperament, its development, and its influence on the individual's adaptation. In keeping with the theme of this volume, we emphasize the role of context in all these issues. Because theorizing properly begins with a description of the phenomena the theory is intended to explain, we first present some illustrative empirical findings. Many students of temperament, personality, and development will be surprised by these findings, which is why a new theory is needed.

The theory is based on research on adolescents and adults. In the final section of this chapter we speculate on how it might be applied to infants and children, on whom most temperament research has focused.

ADULT TEMPERAMENT AND PERSONALITY

The formal definition of temperament we propose makes sense only in terms of the theory, so we must begin informally. Most psychologists agree that the term *temperament* refers to individual differences that are in some sense innate, biologically based, and perhaps shared with other primate species. Although many researchers focus on temperament in infants and children (a point to which we will return), others—including Buss and Plomin

*Official contribution of the National Institutes of Health; not subject to copyright in the United States.

(1975), Strelau (Strelau, Angleitner, Bantelmann & Ruch, 1990), and Zuckerman (1979)—have developed instruments to assess aspects of temperament in adults. These scales provide a provisional operational definition of what we mean by temperament.

Although the specific temperament variables measured in these systems vary, some common themes emerge clearly when they are factored together. In one such analysis, Angleitner and Ostendorf (1994) found five factors. The first was defined by general emotionality and poor inhibition; the second by sociability, approach, and positive mood; the third by experience seeking, flexibility, and low rhythmicity; the fourth by anger and boredom susceptibility; the fifth by tempo, vigor, and persistence scales. To anyone familiar with recent research in personality psychology, these factors are unmistakable: They are the dimensions of the Five-Factor Model (FFM) of personality. This interpretation is supported by loadings on the same factors of both adjective and questionnaire measures of the FFM itself. Similar results were reported by Strelau and Zawadzki (1995), except that they also found a specific sixth factor defined by rhythmicity variables.

The first surprise, then, is that the domains of adult temperament and personality appear not only overlapping, but essentially isomorphic. A decade ago, it would have seemed reasonable that Neuroticism and Extraversion factors would be related to temperament; both, after all, are heritable (Eaves, Eysenck, & Martin, 1989), and both are intimately tied to emotions (Costa & McCrae, 1980). But Openness to Experience sounds too humanistic to be classed as temperament, and Agreeableness and Conscientiousness are clearly related to character, long considered the nurtured complement to temperament's nature.

But there are three powerful lines of evidence that support the notion that all five factors are biologically based. First, the same five factors are found in every culture in which they have been sought (McCrae, Costa, del Pilar, Rolland, & Parker, 1998), including those with non-Indo-European languages such as Estonian, Filipino, and Chinese; thus, the factors are likely to be characteristic of the human species itself. Second, and even more dramatically, there has recently been a report that the same factors—along with Dominance—have been found in consensually validated observer ratings of chimpanzees (King & Figueredo, 1997), suggesting that human and primate personality factors may have common evolutionary precursors. Third and finally, there is now solid evidence that all five factors are strongly heritable (Jang, McCrae, Angleitner, Riemann, & Livesley, 1998), with measurement-corrected estimates that genetic influences account for more than two thirds of the variance in each of the five factors (Riemann, Angleitner, & Strelau, 1997). Empirically, at least, it seems difficult to distinguish adult temperament from personality.

DYNAMIC INTERACTIONISM AND PERSONALITY STABILITY

Perhaps personality is closely related to temperament because temperament is the raw material of personality, the starting point from which adult personality is shaped through interaction with life experience. This is akin to the view of *dynamic interactionism,* a theoretical perspective in which person and environment codevelop through mutual and reciprocal effects (Magnusson, 1990). In contrast to the one-sided environmental determinism of radical behaviorism, dynamic interactionism acknowledges that persons bring something to their encounters with the world, and that both are likely to be modified by the experience.

Asendorpf and Wilpers (1998) recently tested this theory in a sophisticated longitudinal study of students entering the university. Over the course of 18 months they measured personality traits four times and social relationships seven times. Diary methods supplemented questionnaires on two occasions. Growth curve analyses were used to assess effects of personality traits on relationships and vice versa. The effects of personality on social relationships were clear and consistent: Extraverts made friends sooner, agreeable people had fewer conflicts with peers. But as Asendorpf and Wilpers (1998) showed, contrary to the hypothesis, personality was quite stable throughout the course of the study:

> Whether students' peer network grew quickly or slowly, whether they experienced increasing or decreasing conflict with parents or peers, whether they fell in love or not, whether they began a serious romantic relationship or not, and whether their perception of available support from parents or peers increased or decreased had no effect on their personality. (p. 1541)

Asendorpf and Wilpers (1998) argued that theirs was a fair test of dynamic interactionism, at least as applied to adults, because entry into college is an important life transition at an age when traits may still be malleable, and they regarded their results "as a warning against the naive environmentalism that has for a long time dominated the literature on personality development" (p. 1543).[1]

Although this study was the one of the most direct and ambitious tests of dynamic interactionism, its finding that individual differences in personal-

---

[1]Child developmentalists (see Halverson & Wampler, 1997) may be less naive than personality psychologists in this regard, having recognized for some time the important influences that children bring with them to their own development. Clinical psychologists are often uncritically environmentalistic (see Bowman, 1997).

ity traits endure despite important life events and changing circumstances is not new: Many longitudinal studies conducted over much longer time intervals have reported very similar results (Costa & McCrae, 1997). Relatedly, Costa, McCrae, and Zonderman (1987) showed that changes in marital status, employment status, and state of residence had no long-term effect on psychological well-being. Within fairly broad limits, personality traits in adulthood appear almost impervious to environmental influences (McCrae & Costa, 1984).

CULTURE, HISTORY, AND ADULT DEVELOPMENT

Perhaps the basic premises of dynamic interactionism are correct, but they operate on a larger scale than Asendorpf and Wilpers studied. Perhaps only wars, economic depressions, and mass movements (Agronick & Duncan, 1998) are powerful enough to shift ingrained personality traits. Perhaps only when aggregated across large groups of people will environmental effects on personality be found. A large ($N = 7,363$) cross-cultural study of age differences in adult personality recently addressed these issues (McCrae et al., 1999). We will describe the cultural and historical context of the samples in some detail to convey the scope and power of this natural experiment.

Cross-cultural studies of personality development are informative because different cultures represent systematic variations in the environment. There are differences in language, child-rearing styles, educational and economic systems, religious beliefs, dietary habits, and so on; but perhaps more important, all these aspects of culture are thought by anthropologists to cohere at some level to define an ethos (Benedict, 1934; Triandis, 1996). Most individuals are immersed in this total environment for their entire lives; effects on personality development ought to be clearly seen when diverse cultures are contrasted. Our collaborative group examined personality in five cultures.

It is impossible in the space of a chapter to describe fully the cultures and histories of five nations, but brief sketches give some notion of the diversity of background in the five samples studied. These necessarily selective sketches are based on general sources (e.g., Federal Statistical Office, 1995; Manzel, 1994; Marques, 1977; McHenry, 1993) and on accounts from psychologists native to each culture.[2]

Germany is perhaps culturally nearest to the United States. Linguistically, German and English are closely related, and the two countries share a signifi-

---

[2]For background sketches of their nation's culture and history we thank Margarida Pedroso de Lima and António Simões, University of Coimbra, Portugal; Fritz Ostendorf and Alois Angleitner, University of Bielefeld, Germany; Iris Marušić and Denis Bratko, University of Zagreb, Croatia; Gian Vittorio Caprara and Claudio Barbaranelli, University of Rome, "La Sapienza," Italy, and Joon-Ho Chae, Sogang University, South Korea.

cant religious influence from Protestantism. Like the United States, Germany is a highly industrialized modern secular democracy, with most of its population living in cities. On a collectivism–individualism rating scale from 1 (Bangladesh) to 10 (United States), Germany was rated 8 (see Table 1.1). In Germany as in the United States, members of the older generation generally prefer to live apart from their adult children, and economic and medical support is provided by the government.

Italy is also a modern Western nation, but somewhat less individualistic than Germany. Compared to Americans and Germans, Italians have strong family ties, with older parents tending to live with their adult children. The divorce rate in Italy, a Roman Catholic country, is about one fourth of that in Germany.

Portugal shares with Italy a romance language and a Catholic tradition, but differs in a number of respects. After half a century of dictatorship, its democratic government was restored only in 1974, and it lags behind most Western European nations in educational level, economic prosperity, and urbanization. Portuguese culture is family centered. Although there is some economic support from the government, older individuals sometimes must depend on the support of their adult children. With modernization, however, reverence for older family members is diminishing, and Portuguese share with Americans some negative stereotypes about older people in general, including the perceptions that they are withdrawn, rigid, and limited in their capacity to learn (Simões, 1985).

Croatia was part of the former communist federation of Yugoslavia; since 1992 it has been an independent state. Croatian is a Slavic language, but as a former part of the Austro-Hungarian Empire, Croatia shares its cultural heritage with the West. Most Croatians live in cities. Croatians traditionally have

TABLE 1.1   Urbanization and Individualism in Five Cultures

Culture	Urban Population	Individualism
Germany	86%	8
Italy	67%	6
Portugal	36%	5
Croatia	64%	6
South Korea	81%	3

Note. Collectivism-Individualism ratings by H. Triandis, reported in Diener, Diener, & Diener, 1995, Factors predicting the subjective well-being of nations. Journal of Personality and Social Psychology, 69, pp. 851–864. Entry for Croatia taken from the rating of the former Yugoslavia.

strong family ties, with multigeneration families, but are described as being somewhat more individualistic than the Portuguese.

A very different cultural context is provided by South Korea. Unlike German, Italian, Portuguese, and Croatian, Korean is not an Indo-European language (it is in fact not usually classified in any language family). Historically, Korea was heavily influenced by Chinese thought and customs, including Confucianism, with its emphasis on filial piety, a strictly hierarchical social structure, and a strong family orientation. Older people are esteemed for their wisdom and have considerable influence in family affairs; parents tend to live with their adult children. More recently, Western Christian and secular influences in this highly urbanized country have moderated Korean traditions, but South Korea does not yet have a strong democratic tradition. It is the most collectivist of the five cultures compared here.

In each of these countries, a translation of the Revised NEO Personality Inventory (NEO-PI-R; Costa & McCrae, 1992a) was administered to a sample of men and women ranging in age from 18 to more than 50. The NEO-PI-R is a widely used measure of the FFM, assessing six specific traits or facets for each of the five factors. Factor analyses provided provisional evidence of construct validity for all these translations. If our interest had been in comparing cultures on the mean levels of personality traits, we would have been faced with the arduous task of demonstrating that our personality measures were strict parallel forms (McCrae, Yik, Trapnell, Bond, & Paulhus, 1998).[3] Instead, we were concerned here only with patterns of adult development across cultures. Cross-sectional analyses of age differences in personality within each culture were compared across cultures.

But cross-sectional studies compare people who differ not only in age, but also in the time period when they were born and the unique experiences of their generation. In other words, age differences are inextricably bound to historical context, so a consideration of the recent histories of these five nations is also essential to an understanding of our findings.

Table 1.2 provides a brief summary of historical events in the five cultures for three historical periods. The oldest respondents in the study were born in the first period and experienced events in all three. The youngest groups of respondents were born in the third period described in Table 1.2.

Table 1.2 suggests both similarities and differences across the five countries. In general, the second half of this century has seen more peace and prosperity than the first, and other influences not discussed in the table (including the mass media, technological innovation, and improvements in medical treatment) have been shared to some extent by all these cultures. But

---

[3]In fact, that article did show rough equivalence between American and Hong Kong Chinese versions of the NEO-PI-R, and also provided evidence that acculturation experiences may affect the mean levels of some personality traits. The latter findings suggest possible limitations to the thesis developed in this chapter.

TABLE 1.2 Three Periods of History for the Five Cultures

Country	1915–1945	1945–1965	1965–1995
Germany	Defeat in WWI; Great Depression; decline of democracy and rise of Third Reich (Hitler); territorial expansion; the Holocaust; defeat in WWII	Marshall Plan and postwar reconstruction; Soviet blockade of Berlin and division of Germany; Cold War, nuclear threat, Berlin Wall; economic prosperity; television	Student movement and liberalization of values; peace and prosperity; East/West rapprochement and reunification. Current concerns: Unemployment, AIDS, environmental pollution
Italy	Social and labor unrest, postwar nationalistic discontent leads to rise of fascism (Mussolini); conquest of Ethiopia and occupation of Albania; alliance with Germany brings Italy into WWII; defeat and civil war of liberation	Marshall Plan and postwar reconstruction; industrialization and urbanization foster rapid transformation of society and economic growth	Center left coalition; social conflict, student movement, and strong unionization; legalization of divorce; escalation of political conflict; terrorism; fighting mafia and political corruption; emergence of new parties
Portugal	Brief democracy; WWI; 1926 military coup and dictatorship (Salazar); restrictions on free speech and social development; neutrality but hardships in WWII	Initial industrialization in 1950s; beginning of colonial wars in Africa, 1961, and return of colonists; continued dictatorship; widespread emigration to Europe	Increasing political opening; end of colonial war and massive immigration of ex-colonists; student movement in 1960s; restoration of democracy, 1974; enters EEC; social liberalization: divorce legalized, women's rights
Croatia	Austro-Hungarian Empire dismantled; multiethnic Yugoslavia formed under Serbian King; Croatian independence movement; occupation by Axis powers and creation of independent Croatia under fascist puppet dictator	Nonaligned Communist government (Tito) reunites Yugoslavia; gradual economic recovery; continued nationalist sentiment	Economic boom, then decline in 1980s; democracy restored in Yugoslavia, 1990; war of Croatian independence, recognized in 1992; continuing Balkan conflict
South Korea	Japanese Occupation; social discrimination against Koreans and Korean culture, severe economic hardship, widespread starvation, continued through WWII	Intensive efforts at economic recovery; Korean War and the partition of Korea; military dictatorship and social repression	"Economic Miracle" introduces prosperity; continued military threat from North Korea; continuing dictatorship sporadically resisted by demonstrations; civilian democracy established in 1990s

profound differences are also evident. In particular, young people in Germany, Italy, and Portugal (as well as the United States) have been fortunate in comparison to the young people of Croatia and Korea. And although the oldest generation in every culture suffered some degree of hardship, conditions in Korea were far worse than Americans or most Europeans faced.

The attentive reader may wonder what we could possibly have hoped to learn by comparing samples from such diverse cultures and histories. Almost any pattern of results might have appeared, and so many contextual variables were confounded that interpreting the different patterns of adult development would have been hopeless.

Fortunately for us, we did not find many different patterns. In each country very similar trends were seen for the five factors, and the pattern is precisely what had previously been described in American samples (Costa & McCrae, 1994): From adolescence to old age, Neuroticism, Extraversion, and Openness declined modestly, whereas Agreeableness and Conscientiousness increased. Figure 1.1 illustrates these findings for one of the factors, Conscientiousness, demonstrating that older cohorts in each culture are more competent, dutiful, and deliberate than younger cohorts.

Similar patterns were also seen across cultures when the 30 NEO-PI-R facet scales were examined. For example, in each country, the Excitement

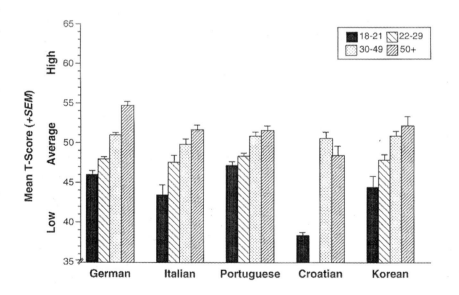

FIG. 1.1. Mean levels of Conscientiousness factor scores in five cultures. None of the Croatian respondents were aged 22–29. *T*-scores are based on the mean and standard deviation of all respondents over age 21 within each culture. SEM = estimated standard error of the mean. Adapted from McCrae et al. (1999).

Seeking facet of Extraversion decreased rapidly, whereas the Activity facet of Extraversion changed little. Analyses of the facet scales were also conducted controlling for the five factors; the residual specific variance unique to each facet scale also showed cross-culturally consistent age trends.

Cross-sectional analyses have also been conducted on data from other countries, including Russia, Japan, Estonia, Spain, Turkey, and the Czech Republic, with similar results (Costa et al., 2000; McCrae et al., 2000). Unless one is prepared to believe that those historical changes shared by all these cultures profoundly affect personality, whereas those historical changes unique to each country have virtually no effect, then it appears that history hardly matters, and that cross-sectional age differences are more a matter of maturation than of generational cohort effects. And maturation, it seems, takes much the same course in vastly different cultural contexts.

These, then, are some of the facts that a theory of adult temperament and personality must address: That the structure of temperament is isomorphic with the structure of personality; that personality traits, like temperaments, are heritable, universal, and shared with other species; that individual differences in personality influence social relationships and other life outcomes but are themselves stable; and that adult development can be characterized in terms of intrinsic maturational changes that appear to transcend the contexts of culture and history.

FIVE-FACTOR THEORY AND TEMPERAMENT

There are, however, other facts that a theory of temperament must also accommodate. The theory must explain how life changes for the undergraduate introvert who falls in love, and how the same intellectual curiosity is expressed differently in Berkeley and Tehran, and why the German people of today think, feel, and act so differently from the German people of the 1930s. Temperament may transcend context, but people most assuredly do not, and personality psychology must account for the actions and experiences of people. A model of temperament cannot constitute a complete psychology of personality, which must also explain how temperament is expressed in particular times and places. Our approach to that task is called Five-Factor Theory (McCrae & Costa, 1996, 1998).

Figure 1.2 illustrates the personality system proposed by Five-Factor Theory as it operates over time.[4] Most of the components are long familiar. At the top left is a circle representing *biological bases* of personality—genetic, neuroanatomic, psychophysiological, and so on. On the right is an ellipse representing the entire range of *external influences,* from the complete cultural

---

[4]Compare Murray and Kluckhohn's (1953) summary definition: "Personality is the continuity of functional forms and forces manifested through sequences of organized regnant processes and overt behaviors from birth to death" (p. 49).

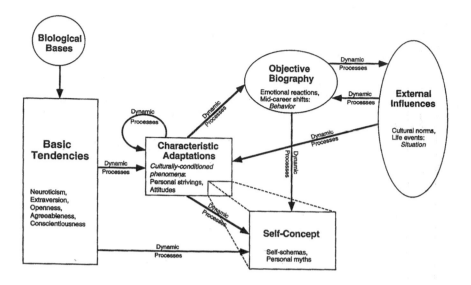

FIG. 1.2.   A model of the personality system as conceived by Five-Factor Theory. Selected examples of contents are listed to illustrate each component. Adapted from McCrae & Costa (1999).

ethos to peer group influences (Harris, 1995), down to the demands and opportunities of the immediate situation. The remaining ellipse, *objective biography,* is the output of the system, the cumulative stream of actions and experiences that transpire over a lifetime. These three components correspond roughly to nature, nurture, and behavior, and the overall layout of the figure suggests that the personality system is located somewhere between biological and sociocultural systems (Mayer, 1999).

The three rectangles are components of personality per se. *Basic tendencies* are the psychological raw materials of personality, the capacities and dispositions that the individual brings to his or her encounter with the world. Out of that interaction, another category of variables arises called *characteristic adaptations*. These include skills, habits, beliefs, defenses, interests, values, roles, and relationships. They also include a subcomponent of beliefs, feelings, and stories about the self, of sufficient psychological interest to warrant a box of its own (the *self-concept*). Note that the three rectangles are similar to the three levels of analysis in personality psychology proposed by McAdams (1998): traits, adaptations, and narratives.

It should be fairly obvious that temperament falls within the category of basic tendencies, because temperament consists of biologically based, content-free dispositions that give rise to contextualized adaptations. The figure, however, does not mention temperaments among its contents. Instead, it lists the five personality factors. What this implies is that in our view, there is no useful distinction between personality traits and temperament; the two are not merely isomorphic, they are equivalent. All of the major features of temperament—its stability, heritability, intrinsic maturation—characterize personality traits equally. It is in a sense an accident of intellectual history that some personality traits are regarded as temperaments whereas others are not. The theory of temperament that we promised at the beginning of this chapter is, therefore, neither more nor less than the Five-Factor Theory of personality.[5]

Many psychologists would argue that temperament consists of early appearing individual difference variables, which can thus be distinguished from adult personality. These early temperaments might be qualitatively different from the traits in the FFM (as perhaps rhythmicity is), or they may be precursors to them (Kohnstamm, Halverson, Mervielde, & Havill, 1998). But from the perspective of Five-Factor Theory, temperaments are formally similar. They are basic tendencies; when Fig. 1.2 is used to describe the personality system of infants and children, temperaments occupy the box that is filled by personality traits in the adult personality system.

For example, shyness might be construed as a temperament, whereas the attachment bond is a characteristic adaptation. The quality of infant/caregiver attachment might depend both on the natural shyness of the child (a basic tendency) and on the parenting skills of the caregiver (an external influence). Because characteristic adaptations are built on prior adaptations, early bonding may facilitate or disrupt later interpersonal relationships. Five-Factor Theory, however, would not predict that bonding would directly affect shyness itself.

Personality and temperament are inferred from characteristic adaptations and the behaviors to which they give rise. The cognitive capacities and behavioral repertoire of infants and young children are very different from those of adults, and in consequence, the assessment of personality must be different, normally relying on adult observations rather than self-reports. This marks an important technical difference between research on child temperament and on adult personality, but it is of no real substantive significance.

Researchers who identify with the temperament tradition may take umbrage at this assimilation of their preferred variables into Five-Factor Theory. But if they have lost the battle for a unique niche in psychology, they have

---

[5]If temperament is consigned to basic tendencies, is character to be included among characteristic adaptations? A case might be made for that; we could regard a person's values, manners, good or bad habits as that person's character. But if one considers strength of will or generosity of spirit as its true essence, then character would better be assigned to basic tendencies, associated especially with Conscientiousness and Agreeableness. Perhaps it would be wisest to heed Allport's dictum that "character is personality evaluated," and leave it altogether outside a scientific description of the person.

won the war of scientific explanation of individual differences. What are typically called personality traits and assessed by personality questionnaires, are best conceptualized in the terms long familiar to temperament theorists.

Temperament theorists typically seek to understand individual differences in terms of biologically based psychological processes (Strelau & Zawadzki, 1995). Ahadi and Rothbart (1994), for example, described Extraversion in terms of "a sensitivity to signals of reward in the environment and an active engagement of the environment" (p. 191). Interpreting traits as manifestations of basic processes is useful in understanding their psychological essence and can guide efforts to identify the underlying biological mechanisms. For example, systems in the brain that govern reward (such as the dopaminergic system) are likely involved in Extraversion. A process orientation is also useful because analogous processes can be sought in infants and children and in other species.

Researchers outside the temperament tradition typically conceptualize personality in terms of content. Murtha, Kanfer, and Ackerman (1996), for example, wrote that "extraversion is composed of behaviors such as talking, laughing, and feeling positive emotions" (pp. 193–194). Five-Factor Theory would recast that assertion; such behaviors are regarded here as part of the objective biography. But it is from these behaviors that characteristic adaptations and, ultimately, personality traits are inferred. The item "Are you a talkative person?" would probably work well in a scale to measure Extraversion, whereas the item "Are you sensitive to signals of reward in the environment?" probably would not.

One advantage to the identification of personality traits with temperaments is that the questions usually posed by temperament theorists can now meaningfully be asked with regard to a much wider range of individual difference variables. Within Five-Factor Theory, it is appropriate to ask whether altruism is heritable (Jang, Livesley, & Vernon, 1996), to look for signs of Conscientiousness in dogs and cats (Gosling & John, 1998), or to relate brain activation to Openness to Experience (Costa & McCrae, 1997). It also makes sense to try to define the full range of personality traits in terms of basic psychological processes as part of a complete theory of personality traits (McCrae & Costa, 1999).

TEMPERAMENT, DEVELOPMENT, AND CONTEXT

The context in which temperament develops is time. A good deal is known about the course of personality development from adolescence to old age. Between age 18 and age 30 there is continuity in individual differences, but also significant change (Siegler et al., 1990). After age 30, there is predominant stability, with a gradual decay in predictability noticeable after several decades (Costa & McCrae, 1992b). Superimposed on this picture of individual rank order stability are shared maturational changes in the mean levels of personality traits, as illustrated in Fig. 1.1. These changes are most rapid before age 30, but apparently continue at a very slow rate thereafter.

What is the cause of these changes? Five-Factor Theory offers an answer. The arrows in Fig. 1.2 represent the causal paths that show the principal ways in which the components of the system interact. Our formulation is called Five-Factor Theory not so much because the five factors are located in one of its boxes, as because the decision to include or exclude specific arrows is based on research on these five factors. Most significantly, there is no arrow from external influences to basic tendencies: Personality traits are postulated to be endogenous dispositions whose origin and development are independent of environmental influence.

Radical as that position may seem, it is consistent with a substantial body of evidence. Why is personality stable in the face of changing life circumstances (Asendorpf & Wilpers, 1998)? Why do variations in culture and history have so little impact on personality structure or development? Why is there so little evidence that childrearing practices affect adult personality (Rowe, 1994)? Perhaps because there are few psychological mechanisms by which external influences can affect personality traits. There will surely be exceptions to that generalization—including perhaps traumatic events (Engdahl, Harkness, Eberly, & Page, 1993) and acculturation (McCrae et al., 1998)—but they are far fewer and less important than psychologists have usually imagined, and we believe it is worthwhile to develop the implications of a theory that ignores them.

The adult development of personality appears to be a natural unfolding, presumably regulated by unknown biological clocks. It is, of course, possible that this developmental process requires an environmental context. A 30-year-old who emerged from a 12-year coma might still be psychologically adolescent, high in excitement seeking and low in self-discipline. The nature of the environment, however, seems to matter rather little; any encounter with life, it would seem, has much the same result.

If context is more or less irrelevant to the maturation of personality traits, it is all-important for the development of characteristic adaptations. Every directly observable feature of the adult's psychological being has taken shape in interaction with the environment. Languages spoken, fashions worn, political sentiments, friendships, and phobias are all imposed by, selected from, or created out of the requirements and opportunities of the social environment.

Characteristic adaptations may express personality traits, but they must do so in context, and at least three different contexts can be distinguished. The first and most obvious is that provided by external influences. Consider, for example, religious affiliation. Throughout most of history, human beings practiced the religion of their ancestors without question, and religious affiliation gave no scope for personality expression. In modern times, however, people often choose a religion that seems congenial to them; here in the United States, people high in Openness to Experience gravitate toward liberal, nonfundamentalist denominations (Streyffeler & McNally, 1998). They may even opt for more nontraditional religions, such as Baha'i or Scientology. Most Americans, however, no matter how open, will never become Siberian shamans. The external environment is unlikely ever to support the development of that adaptation.

A second form of context for the expression of personality traits is provided by basic tendencies, including other personality traits—that is, the manifestation of one trait may be conditioned by other traits or tendencies. Open individuals may aspire to become musicians, but unless they are also high in Conscientiousness, they may not practice enough to succeed. An extraverted altruist may volunteer to entertain nursing home residents, whereas an introverted altruist may prefer to donate crafts made at home. Ahadi and Rothbart (1994) stress the influence of Effortful Control (a proposed precursor of Conscientiousness) on the expression of Approach and Anxiety systems (proposed precursors of Extraversion and Neuroticism), noting that "infant and child temperamental dimensions may interact with each other ... to create variation in personality" (p. 202).

A final context for development is provided by the body of characteristic adaptations already in place, as indicated in Fig. 1.2 by the reflexive arrow. New habits, skills, and relationships build on established habits, skills, and relationships, just as learning calculus draws on prior knowledge of algebra. The extravert who expresses assertiveness by running for public office draws on previously acquired social skills in public speaking, glad-handing, and networking; the open person who takes up painting as a hobby uses manual skills transferred from handwriting and aesthetic preferences formed by education and experience. By adulthood, in fact, almost every new characteristic adaptation is enmeshed in a lifetime of prior adaptations, and personality traits have been concretized in a myriad of interlocking adaptations.

That phenomenon provides the basis for an alternative explanation for the stability of personality. Instead of isolating personality from environmental influences as Five-Factor Theory does, some theorists propose that personality traits are sustained by the life circumstances individuals choose and create. Caspi, Elder, and Bem (1987) showed that children prone to temper tantrums became adults prone to lower socioeconomic status and divorce, and they proposed that "maladaptive behaviors are sustained through the progressive accumulation of their own consequences" (p. 308). This *cumulative continuity* theory can explain both the stability of personality and the persistence of maladaptive lifestyles.

Note that two radically different hypotheses have now been offered to account for the remarkable fact that traits remain basically unchanged by a lifetime of experience. Five-Factor Theory holds that traits continue because they are influenced solely by biological features—neurological structures, DNA sequences—that themselves change little; cumulative continuity theory holds that traits are sustained by a self-perpetuating interaction with the environment. Biological and environmental explanations, of course, are not mutually exclusive, and it would be easy to dismiss the issue by saying that both are probably correct. But the implications for intervention of the two rival hypotheses are enormous, and they merit closer attention.

It is surely the case that characteristic adaptations follow a pattern of cumulative continuity. A hostile relationship leads to acts that provoke further hostility; a defeatist attitude contributes to poor performance. Interventions that break these cycles sometimes alter the underlying adaptation. But do such interventions truly alter personality? Making friends with an old enemy does not necessarily make one a friendlier person in general, for an aggressive person can always find new targets.

Under most circumstances people carry with them both their self-perpetuating characteristic adaptations and their biologically based traits, confounding any attempt to understand which is causally prior. Dramatic shifts in the external environment like that experienced by prisoners of war (Engdahl, Harkness, Eberly, & Page, 1993) can create massive changes in characteristic adaptations and sometimes leave lasting effects on personality traits, but these exceptional experiences may tell us little about the effects of more typical environments.

What would happen if basic tendencies were altered directly? If levels of Neuroticism in a psychiatric population were substantially lowered, would the patients remain trapped by the long-standing characteristic maladaptations they have created? Experience with Prozac (Kramer, 1994) and other antidepressants suggests that this is not the case. Once the biological basis is altered, it seems to be relatively easy to change irrational beliefs and self-defeating behaviors.

A natural experiment in changing basic tendencies occurs with the process of aging. Between age 18 and age 30 there are predictable decreases in Neuroticism and Extraversion, and increases in Agreeableness and Conscientiousness. One of the most socially significant consequences of this is a decline in criminal behavior ("Serious crime," 1997). Even individuals diagnosed with Antisocial Personality Disorder, whose early lives are characterized by a poor work history, crime, and drug use—circumstances that could easily perpetuate an antisocial lifestyle—tend to remit as they grow older, "particularly by the fourth decade of life" (American Psychiatric Association, 1994, p. 648; cf. Costa, McCrae & Siegler, 1999). Personality disorders can be seen as characteristic (mal)adaptations that express, among other things, the influence of personality traits; when the underlying traits change, these behavioral expressions often change as well. Such facts suggest that personality stability and change are both best regarded as endogenous processes.

PERSONALITY AND TEMPERAMENT
IN INFANCY AND CHILDHOOD

Five-Factor Theory was designed to account for personality in adults, and it remains to be seen how useful it may be in describing personality in children. There is by now considerable evidence that versions of the five factors themselves are found in school children (Digman & Inouye, 1986; Halverson, Kohnstamm, & Martin, 1994; Kohnstamm, Halverson, Mervielde, & Havill, 1998), and there is no good reason to think that the personality system described in Fig. 1.2 is substantially different. In newborns, however, it might be argued that the category of characteristic adaptations is empty, and thus, personality is directly expressed in behavior.

That argument has persuaded many people that temperament is seen in its purest form in infants, and that adult personality differs from temperament only because of the cumulative influence of childhood and adolescent experience. As Wachs (1994) pointed out, however, this presupposes a rather primitive view of genetic determinism, in which genes operate continuously from birth on. A more sophisticated view is that gene systems switch on and off during the course of development. Even if infant temperament and adult personality were each entirely due to genetic influences, it is possible that they would be unrelated to one another. That possibility is hinted at by studies of the continuity of temperament and later personality. Although such studies are rare, it appears that measures of temperament in infancy and childhood show limited stability even over short intervals and very modest ability to predict adult personality traits (Wachs, 1994). Considering the growth of the brain itself during this period—the corpus callosum continues to grow until the mid 20s (Pujol, Vendrell, Junqué, Martí-Vilalta, & Capdevila, 1993)—this is hardly surprising.[6]

In fact, there are some reasons to think that personality becomes more clearly rooted in biology with increasing age. Every experience is new for the infant, and environmental influences may overwhelm basic tendencies in early childhood. With increasing maturity, the impact of any single experience is diluted by a lifetime of sometimes competing experiences; basic tendencies may perhaps grow stronger, and the adaptations of the child gradually come to be more and more characteristic. Evidence for this scenario is provided by studies that show higher heritability for personality in adults than for temperament in infants (Loehlin, 1992).

By at least the second year, however, genetic influences can be seen in children's temperament, and with that comes the possibility of intrinsic maturational trends. It is possible that the developmental trends in personality found in adulthood also extend back from age 18. For example, Measelle

---

[6]Could this explain why personality is "set like plaster" only at age 30?

and John (1997) reported that Conscientiousness increased from age 5 to age 7, as it does from 20 to 70. Few would be surprised, however, if researchers were to find that Conscientiousness declines during early adolescence. Charting such developmental trends will be a difficult task, because different items and perhaps altogether different methods will be needed to assess personality at different ages, and establishing metric equivalence (Butcher & Han, 1996) of these alternate forms will be daunting. The cross-cultural studies of development that will be so useful in assessing the universality of developmental trends will add another layer of complexity. At least, however, we now have a good idea of what child temperament ought to develop into: The adult Five-Factor Model of personality.

CONCLUSION

In this chapter we have argued for a new theoretical context for interpreting temperament. We have reviewed empirical parallels with adult personality traits and argued that the same biologically based, process-oriented approach that typifies traditional studies of temperament should be applied to the full range of traits. We have also offered a different causal perspective, seeing traits not as products of the environment, nor as dispositions that codevelop in dynamic interaction with it, but as independent forces that follow their own intrinsic course of development. Traits or temperaments and the characteristic adaptations they give rise to provide a crucial context in which human beings adapt and live their lives.

REFERENCES

Agronick, G. S., & Duncan, L. E. (1998). Personality and social change: Individual differences, life path, and importance attributed to the women's movement. *Journal of Personality and Social Psychology, 74,* 1545–1555.

Ahadi, S. A., & Rothbart, M. K. (1994). Temperament, development, and the big five. In C. F. Halverson, Jr., G. A. Kohnstamm, & R. P. Martin (Eds.), *The developing structure of temperament and personality from infancy to adulthood,* (pp. 189–207). Hillsdale, NJ: Lawrence Erlbaum Associates.

American Psychiatric Association. (1994). *Diagnostic and statistical manual of mental disorders* (4th ed.). Washington, DC: Author.

Angleitner, A., & Ostendorf, F. (1994). Temperament and the Big Five factors of personality. In C. F. Halverson, G. A. Kohnstamm, & R. P. Martin (Eds.), *The developing structure of temperament and personality from infancy to adulthood,* (pp. 69–90). Hillsdale, NJ: Lawrence Erlbaum Associates.

Asendorpf, J. B., & Wilpers, S. (1998). Personality effects on social relationships. *Journal of Personality and Social Psychology, 74,* 1531–1544.

Benedict, R. (1934). *Patterns of culture.* Boston: Houghton Mifflin.

Bowman, M. (1997). *Individual differences in posttraumatic response: Problems with the adversity-distress connection*. Mahwah, NJ: Lawrence Erlbaum Associates.

Buss, A. H., & Plomin, R. (1975). *A temperament theory of personality development*. New York: Wiley.

Butcher, J. N., & Han, K. (1996). Methods of establishing cross-cultural equivalence. In J. N. Butcher (Ed.), *International adaptations of the MMPI-2: A handbook of research and clinical applications* (pp. 44–63). Minneapolis: University of Minnesota Press.

Caspi, A., Elder, G. H., Jr., & Bem, D. J. (1987). Moving against the world: Life-course patterns of explosive children. *Developmental Psychology, 23,* 308–313.

Costa, P. T., Jr., & McCrae, R. R. (1980). Influence of extraversion and neuroticism on subjective well-being: Happy and unhappy people. *Journal of Personality and Social Psychology, 38,* 668–678.

Costa, P. T., Jr., & McCrae, R. R. (1992a). *Revised NEO Personality Inventory (NEO-PI-R) and NEO Five-Factor Inventory (NEO-FFI) professional manual*. Odessa, FL: Psychological Assessment Resources, Inc.

Costa, P. T., Jr., & McCrae, R. R. (1992b). Trait psychology comes of age. In T. B. Sonderegger (Ed.), *Nebraska symposium on motivation: Psychology and aging* (pp. 169–204). Lincoln, NE: University of Nebraska Press.

Costa, P. T., Jr., & McCrae, R. R. (1994). Stability and change in personality from adolescence through adulthood. In C. F. Halverson, G. A. Kohnstamm, & R. P. Martin (Eds.), *The developing structure of temperament and personality from infancy to adulthood* (pp. 139–150). Hillsdale, NJ: Lawrence Erlbaum Associates.

Costa, P. T., Jr., & McCrae, R. R. (1997). Longitudinal stability of adult personality. In R. Hogan, J. A. Johnson, & S. R. Briggs (Eds.), *Handbook of personality psychology* (pp. 269–290). Orlando, FL: Academic Press.

Costa, P. T., Jr., & McCrae, R. R. (1997, July). *The FFM as a universal passport to understanding personality*. Paper presented at the Eighth Biennial Meeting of the International Society for the Study of Individual Differences, Aarhus, Denmark.

Costa, P. T., Jr., McCrae, R. R., Martin, T. A., Oryol, V. E., Senin, I. G., Rukavishnikov, A. A., Shimonaka, Y., Nakazato, K., Gondo, Y., Takayama, M., Allik, J., Kallasmaa, T., & Realo, A. (2000). Personality development from adolescence through adulthood: Further cross-cultural comparisons of age differences. In V. J. Molfese & D. Molfese (Eds.), *Temperament and personality development across the life span* (pp. 235–252). Mahwah, NJ: Lawrence Erlbaum Associates.

Costa, P. T., Jr., McCrae, R. R., & Siegler, I. C. (1999). Continuity and change over the adult life cycle: Personality and personality disorders. In C. R. Cloninger (Ed.), *Personality and psychopathology* (pp. 129–153). Washington, DC: American Psychiatric Press.

Costa, P. T., Jr., McCrae, R. R., & Zonderman, A. B. (1987). Environmental and dispositional influences on well-being: Longitudinal follow-up of an American national sample. *British Journal of Psychology, 78,* 299–306.

Digman, J. M., & Inouye, J. (1986). Further specification of the five robust factors of personality. *Journal of Personality and Social Psychology, 50,* 116–123.

Eaves, L. J., Eysenck, H. J., & Martin, N. G. (1989). *Genes, culture, and personality: An empirical approach*. New York: Academic Press.

Engdahl, B. E., Harkness, A. R., Eberly, R. E., & Page, W. F. (1993). Structural models of captivity trauma, resilience, and trauma response among former prisoners of war

20 to 40 years after release. *Social Psychiatry and Psychiatric Epidemiology, 28,* 109–115.

Federal Statistical Office. (1995). *Im Blickpunkt: Familie heute [In focus: The family today].* Stuttgart: Metzler-Poeschel.

Gosling, S. D., & John, O. P. (1998, May). *Personality dimensions in dogs, cats, and hyenas.* Paper presented at the 10th Annual Convention of the American Psychological Society, Washington, DC.

Halverson, C. F., Jr., Kohnstamm, G. A., & Martin, R. P. (Eds.). (1994). *The developing structure of temperament and personality from infancy to adulthood.* Hillsdale, NJ: Lawrence Erlbaum Associates.

Halverson, C. F., Jr., & Wampler, K. S. (1997). Family influences on personality development. In R. Hogan, J. Johnson, & S. R. Briggs (Eds.), *Handbook of personality psychology* (pp. 241–267). San Diego: Academic Press.

Harris, J. R. (1995). Where is the child's environment? A group socialization theory of development. *Psychological Review, 102,* 458–489.

Jang, K. L., Livesley, W. J., & Vernon, P. A. (1996). Heritability of the big five personality dimensions and their facets: A twin study. *Journal of Personality, 64,* 575–591.

Jang, K. L., McCrae, R. R., Angleitner, A., Riemann, R., & Livesley, W. J. (1998). Heritability of facet-level traits in a cross-cultural twin study: Support for a hierarchical model of personality. *Journal of Personality and Social Psychology, 74,* 1556–1565.

King, J. E., & Figueredo, A. J. (1997). The five-factor model plus dominance in chimpanzee personality. *Journal of Research in Personality, 31,* 257–271.

Kohnstamm, G. A., Halverson, C. F., Jr., Mervielde, I., & Havill, V. L. (1998). *Parental descriptions of child personality: Developmental antecedents of the big five?* Mahwah, NJ: Lawrence Erlbaum Associates.

Kramer, P. (1994). *Listening to Prozac.* New York: Basic Books.

Loehlin, J. C. (1992). *Genes and environment in personality development.* Newbury Park, CA: Sage.

Magnusson, D. (1990). Personality development from an interactional perspective. In L. A. Pervin (Ed.), *Handbook of personality: Theory and research,* (pp. 193–222). New York: Guilford.

Manzel, J. E. (1994). *Reaktionen jugendlicher auf gesellschaftliche bedrohung [Reactions of adolescents to social threats].* Munich: Juventa.

Marques, A. H. O. (1977). *História de Portugal [History of Portugal].* Lisbon: Palas Editores.

Mayer, J. D. (1998). A systems framework for the field of personality. *Psychological Inquiry, 9,* 118–144.

McAdams, D. P. (1998). Trick or treat: Classifying concepts and accounting for human individuality. *Psychological Inquiry, 9,* 154–158.

McCrae, R. R., & Costa, P. T., Jr. (1984). Personality is transcontextual: A reply to Veroff. *Personality and Social Psychology Bulletin, 10,* 175–179.

McCrae, R. R., & Costa, P. T., Jr. (1996). Toward a new generation of personality theories: Theoretical contexts for the five-factor model. In J. S. Wiggins (Ed.), *The five-factor model of personality: Theoretical perspectives* (pp. 51–87). New York: Guilford.

McCrae, R. R., & Costa, P. T., Jr. (1999). A five-factor theory of personality. In L. Pervin & O. P. John (Eds.), *Handbook of personality* (2nd ed., pp. 139–153). New York: Guilford.

McCrae, R. R., Costa, P. T., Jr., del Pilar, G. H., Rolland, J. P., & Parker, W. D. (1998). Cross-cultural assessment of the five-factor model: The Revised NEO Personality Inventory. *Journal of Cross-Cultural Psychology, 29,* 171–188.

McCrae, R. R., Costa, P. T., Jr., Lima, M. P., Simões, A., Ostendorf, F., Angleitner, A., Marušić, I., Bratko, D., Caprara, G. V., Barbaranelli, C., Chae, J. H., & Piedmont, R. L. (1999). Age differences in personality across the adult lifespan: Parallels in five cultures. *Developmental Psychology, 35,* 466–477.

McCrae, R. R., Costa, P. T., Jr., Ostendorf, F., Angleitner, A., Hřebíčková, M., Avia, M. D., Sanz, J., Sánchez-Bernardos, M. L., Kusdil, M. E., Woodfield, R., Saunders, P. T., & Smith, P. B. (2000). Nature over nurture: Temperament, personality, and lifespan development. *Journal of Personality and Social Psychology, 78,* 173–186.

McCrae, R. R., Yik, M. S. M., Trapnell, P. D., Bond, M. H., & Paulhus, D. L. (1998). Interpreting personality profiles across cultures: Bilingual, acculturation, and peer rating studies of Chinese undergraduates. *Journal of Personality and Social Psychology, 74,* 1041–1055.

McHenry, R. E. (1993). *The new encyclopedia Britannica.* Chicago: Encyclopedia Britannica.

Measelle, J., & John, O. P. (1997, May). *Young children's self-perceptions on the big five: Consistency, stability, and school adaptation from age 5 to age 7.* Paper presented at the Biennial Meeting of the Society for Research in Child Development, Washington, DC.

Murray, H. A., & Kluckhohn, C. (1953). Outline of a conception of personality. In C. Kluckhohn, H. A. Murray, & D. M. Schneider (Eds.), *Personality in nature, society, and culture* (2nd ed., pp. 3–49). New York: Knopf.

Murtha, T. C., Kanfer, R., & Ackerman, P. L. (1996). Toward an interactionist taxonomy of personality and situations: An integrative situational-dispositional representation of personality traits. *Journal of Personality and Social Psychology, 71,* 193–207.

Pujol, J., Vendrell, P., Junqué, C., Martí-Vilalta, J. L., & Capdevila, A. (1993). When does human brain development end? Evidence of corpus callosum growth up to adulthood. *Annals of Neurology, 34,* 71–75.

Riemann, R., Angleitner, A., & Strelau, J. (1997). Genetic and environmental influences on personality: A study of twins reared together using the self- and peer-report NEO-FFI scales. *Journal of Personality, 65,* 449–475.

Rowe, D. C. (1994). *The limits of family influence: Genes, experience, and behavior.* New York: Guilford Press.

Serious crime decline attributed to aging of baby boomers. (1997, October 5). *The Baltimore Sun,* p. 3A.

Siegler, I. C., Zonderman, A. B., Barefoot, J. C., Williams, R. B., Jr., Costa, P. T., Jr., & McCrae, R. R. (1990). Predicting personality in adulthood from college MMPI scores: Implications for follow-up studies in psychosomatic medicine. *Psychosomatic Medicine, 52,* 644–652.

Simões, A. (1985). Estereótipos Relacionados com os Idosos [Stereotypes related to the elderly]. *Revista Portuguesa de Pedagogia, 19,* 207–234.

Strelau, J., Angleitner, A., Bantelmann, J., & Ruch, W. (1990). The Strelau temperament inventory—Revised (STI-R): Theoretical considerations and scale development. *European Journal of Personality, 4,* 209–235.

Strelau, J., & Zawadzki, B. (1995). The Formal Characteristics of Behaviour—Temperament Inventory (FCB—TI): Validity studies. *European Journal of Personality, 9,* 207–229.

Streyffeler, L. L., & McNally, R. J. (1998). Fundamentalists and liberals: Personality characteristics of Protestant Christians. *Personality and Individual Differences, 24,* 579–580.

Triandis, H. C. (1996). The psychological measurement of cultural syndromes. *American Psychologist, 51,* 407–415.

Wachs, T. D. (1994). Fit, context, and the transition between temperament and personality. In C. F. Halverson, Jr., G. A. Kohnstamm, & R. P. Martin (Eds.), *The developing structure of temperament and personality from infancy to adulthood* (pp. 209–220). Hillsdale, NJ: Lawrence Erlbaum Associates.

Zuckerman, M. (1979). *Sensation seeking: Beyond the optimal level of arousal.* Hillsdale, NJ: Lawrence Erlbaum Associates.

2 Temperament, Stress, and Soothing

Douglas Ramsay
Michael Lewis
Institute for the Study of Child Development
Robert Wood Johnson Medical School

Considerable work has focused on the behavioral manifestations of temperament in infancy. How infants react to and cope with stressful events is an important aspect of temperament. It is generally believed that differences in maternal behavior play an important role in differences in infant temperament and stress responsivity. In particular, it would seem that differences in maternal soothing behavior in response to infant distress would impact on infant temperament and stress responsivity. In this paper, we examine the relation between infant temperament and stress responsivity and the relation of infant temperament and stress responsivity to maternal soothing.

ISSUES

There are four major issues discussed in this chapter. First, we consider whether differences in infant temperament involve differences in two dimensions, emotional valence, and reactivity level. *Emotional valence* refers to negative or positive emotional tone, whereas *reactivity level* refers to high or low intensity regardless of the direction of emotional tone. Such a distinction is reached by observing that there is not a strong relation between positive and negative emotionality, suggesting that valence is not a sufficient dimension of temperament and that both dimensions are needed to adequately assess differences in temperament. Second, we examine the relation between infants' behavioral and cortisol responses to stress and the two dimensions of temperament. The relations found indicate the importance of considering both dimensions in assessing differences in temperament and their relation

23

to stress responsivity. Third, we assess whether mothers' soothing behavior in response to their infants' distress is related to the dimensions of temperament and/or stress responsivity. Our findings provide no evidence that maternal soothing is efficacious in ameliorating infant temperament or reducing infant stress responsivity. Moreover, maternal soothing was not a factor in the relations found between infant temperament and stress responsivity. Thus, our findings are inconsistent with the prevailing view that emphasizes a strong role for maternal responsivity to infant distress in infant socioemotional development. Finally, in light of these findings, we conclude by discussing various roles for maternal behavior in age change and individual differences in infant temperament and stress responsivity.

Infant Temperament and Dimensions of Emotionality

Infant temperament involves individual differences in the expression of emotion. In their pioneering work, Thomas, Chess, and Birch (1968) described nine dimensions of temperament: rhythmicity, mood, activity, adaptability, distractibility, persistence, threshold, intensity, and approach. Based on these dimensions, infants have been characterized as difficult or easy in temperament (e.g., Bates, 1980; Thomas & Chess, 1977), that is, as predominately high in negative or high in positive emotional tone. Similarly, Buss and Plomin (1984) identified three temperamental traits in infancy that showed evidence of heritability: emotionality, sociability, and activity. Buss and Plomin's construct of emotionality involves negative affective responses including distress, anger, and fear, and therefore, is not unlike the notion of difficult temperament (cf. Bates, 1980). This suggests that differences in infant temperament involve differences in the expression of predominately negative as opposed to positive emotions.

Nonetheless, Thomas et al.'s (1968) dimensions of intensity and threshold involved reactivity independent of the emotion shown. That is, some infants may be high or low in both negative and positive emotional tone. More recent views on infant temperament (e.g., Goldsmith & Campos, 1986; Lewis, 1989; Rothbart & Derryberry, 1981) also suggest that there may be individual differences in reactivity level. In adults, there is evidence that positive and negative affect are independent aspects of mood or personality (e.g., Larsen & Ketelaar, 1991; Watson & Tellegen, 1985) and that affect intensity is a stable individual characteristic (Larsen & Diener, 1987). Thus, in infants, to the extent that there is not a strong inverse relation between positive and negative emotion (cf. Goldsmith, 1986, 1996), individual differences in temperament may well involve differences in reactivity level as well as emotional valence.

To address this question, we examined the relation between positive and negative emotion during the 2- to 6-month period. Maternal ratings on the Rothbart (1978) Infant Behavior Questionnaire (IBQ) were obtained for a longitudinal sample ($N = 62$) at 2 and 6 months of age. There is a large literature showing that maternal report provides a valid assessment of infant temperament (Bates, 1987; Goldsmith, 1996). The IBQ consists of six scales: smiling and laughter; duration of orienting; soothability; distress to novelty; distress to limitations; and activity level. To obtain a positive valence score, the smiling, orienting, and soothability scales were summed, whereas to obtain a negative valence score, the novelty and limitations scales were summed (see Rothbart, 1986; Worobey, 1990; Worobey & Blajda, 1989).[1] The relations among the separate scales provided support for considering positive versus negative valence as an important aspect of temperament. The smiling, orienting, and soothability scales were related to each other (rs between .29 and .47 and between .23 and .36 at 2 and 6 months, respectively). The novelty and limitations scales were related to each other ($r = .29$ and .26 at 2 and 6 months, respectively). There was no relation between any positive and negative scale at either age.

In order to see if there was a relation between the positive and negative valence scores at each age, correlational analysis was used. At 2 months, there was a moderate inverse relation between the positive and negative valence scores ($r = -.26, p < .04$), whereas, at 6 months, there was no relation between the two scores ($r = .03$). The lack of a strong correlation indicates that although some infants show predominately positive or negative emotional tone, most infants show a mixture of both. Because of this, at each age, four groups of infants were formed using the positive and negative scores and dividing subjects at the median: (a) Positive Valence group (high positive scores, low negative scores); (b) Negative Valence group (low positive scores, high negative scores); (c) Low Reactivity group (low positive scores, low negative scores); and (d) High Reactivity group (high positive scores, high negative scores). The number of subjects in the Positive Valence, Negative Valence, Low Reactivity, and High Reactivity group, respectively, was 21, 21, 10, and 10 at 2 months and 16, 16, 15, and 15 at 6 months of age. That there are sizable numbers of subjects in all four groups suggests that emotional valence and reactivity level may be relatively separate dimensions of infant temperament.

It was of interest to examine the stability in the positive and negative valence scores and the consistency in the four-group temperament classification between 2 and 6 months of age. There was considerable cross-age stability in positive and negative valence ($r = .70$ and .53, respectively). Moreover, there was cross-age consistency in the four-group temperament classification ($p < .001$ by chi-square test). These findings suggest that emotional valence and reactivity level are dimensions of temperament that are characteristic of individual infants.

---

[1]Comparable results to those presented in this chapter were obtained when the positive and negative valence scores were calculated based on standardized scores of the separate IBQ scales.

Infant Stress Responsivity and Its Relation
to Infant Temperament

From birth on there are large individual differences in infants' response to stress (Worobey & Lewis, 1989). In our past work, we have used both adrenocortical and behavioral measures of stress responsivity (Lewis & Ramsay, 1995a, 1995b; Lewis & Thomas, 1990; Ramsay & Lewis, 1994). The absence of behavioral indications of stress does not necessarily mean that infants are not stressed (Lewis, Ramsay, & Kawakami, 1993). Our own and others' work indicates that the two types of measures are not strongly related to each other (Gunnar, 1986; Lewis & Thomas, 1990). Thus, along with other researchers (Boyce, Barr, & Zeltzer, 1992; Fox & Calkins, 1993), we believe that both behavioral and physiological measures are needed to adequately assess individual differences in infant stress responsivity (Lewis, 1992,1995).

Studies on infant cortisol response to the stress of routine inoculation have found that the more mature organization of the adrenocortical system is not present until approximately 6 months of age (Gunnar, Brodersen, Krueger, & Rigatuso, 1996; Lewis & Ramsay, 1995a, 1995b. Lewis & Ramsay, 1999a; Ramsay & Lewis, 1994). There is a decline in the magnitude of cortisol response (post- minus pre-stressor cortisol level) and cortisol level (pre- plus post-stressor cortisol level) during the 2- to 6-month period. Moreover, stable individual differences in cortisol response emerge during this period. In these studies, behavioral responses have included the rate of quieting following the perturbation. Consistent with the cortisol results, there is an age trend toward more rapid quieting during the 2- to 6-month period. A large literature indicates an age-related time course in the frequency of infant crying behavior (to include fussiness and colic). This time course involves a peak in the 2nd month followed by a decrease in the 3rd and 4th months with little change thereafter (Barr, 1989, 1990a, 1990b; Bell & Ainsworth, 1972; Emde, Gaensbauer, & Harmon, 1976; van den Boom & Hoeksma, 1994). Thus, there is a decrease in infant crying during the period when the more mature state of adrenocortical functioning emerges.

It is likely that individual behavioral and physiological measures of stress will show different relations to the two temperament dimensions of emotional valence and reactivity level. That a high behavioral response to stress is an indicator of a difficult temperament (involving the expression of predominately negative as opposed to positive emotions) suggests that behavioral measures of stress should be related only to emotional valence or to both emotional valence and reactivity level. That a given physiological response simply reflects degree of arousal suggests that it will be related only to reactivity level (Cacioppo, Klein, Berntson, & Hatfield, 1993; Fox & Calkins, 1993). Nonetheless, individual physiological responses probably differ in their sensitivity to differences in hedonic tone or emotional quality, and therefore, should differ in their relation to emotional valence as opposed to reactivity level. For example, infant heart rate does not simply reflect degree of arousal because heart rate increase versus decrease to a given stimulus has been found to reflect a defensive versus orienting response to the event (Graham & Clifton, 1966; Kagan & Lewis, 1965; Lewis, Kagan, Campbell, & Kalafat, 1966). Moreover, for a given physiological measure, basal and response-related levels of activity could well be differentially related to reactivity level and/or emotional valence. Basal and response measures of vagal tone, for example, have been found to be related to different aspects of infants' emotional expression and regulation (Porges, Doussard-Roosevelt, & Maiti, 1994).

Past work on infant adrenocortical functioning has not systematically examined the relations of basal cortisol level and cortisol response to both emotional valence and reactivity level. Gunnar and her colleagues (Gunnar, Larson, Herstgaard, Harris, & Brodersen, 1992; Gunnar, Mangelsdorf, Larson, & Hertsgaard, 1989; Gunnar, Porter, Wolf, Rigatuso, & Larson, 1995) found a relation between infants' cortisol response and various measures of their proneness to distress. Kagan and his colleagues (e.g., Kagan, Reznick, & Snidman, 1987; Kagan, Snidman, & Arcus, 1992) found that a high basal cortisol level was an indicator of behavioral inhibition in young children. It appears that little work has directly evaluated whether adrenocortical functioning is differentially related to emotional valence and reactivity level. Nonetheless, the results from these studies indicate the need to examine these relations separately for cortisol response and cortisol level.

We examined these relations in the same longitudinal sample whose temperament was assessed at 2 and 6 months of age. At each age, infants' reaction to the stress of inoculation was observed, and measures of cortisol response, cortisol level, and behavioral quieting were obtained. As in previous samples (e.g., Lewis & Ramsay, 1995a), there was an age-related decline in each stress response (as reported in Lewis & Ramsay, 1999a). However, it was also apparent that there were large individual differences in overall amount of stress responsivity across the two age groups. Thus, for each stress response, summary measures of the age-related decline in stress responsivity and the amount of stress responsivity across age were obtained. For each stress response, the difference between 2- and 6-month responses was used to index age-related decline in stress responsivity, and the average of the 2- and 6-month responses was used to index cross-age amount of stress responsivity.

The four-group temperament classification (Positive Valence, Negative Valence, Low Reactivity, High Reactivity) was used to examine the relation of the temperament dimensions of emotional valence and reactivity level to both the age decline in stress responsivity and the cross-age amount of stress responsivity. The use of these four groups allowed examination of differences in infant stress responsivity by emotional valence and reactivity level while keeping the two dimensions separate. Given the stability found in temperament between 2 and 6 months of age (discussed previously), relations between temperament and stress responsivity were examined using a four-group temperament grouping across the two age groups. Across age, the four groups were formed by averaging the 2- and 6-month positive and negative valence scores and dividing subjects at the median. The number of subjects in the Positive Valence, Negative Valence, Low Reactivity, and High Reactivity group was 18, 18, 13, and 13, respectively. Comparable results to those presented below were obtained when the separate 2- and 6-month temperament groupings were used.

Figure 2.1 (a,b,&c) shows age decline in stress responsivity and cross-age amount of stress responsivity for each stress response by temperament group. To simplify the presentation, the stress responses were standardized ($M = 50$, $SD = 10$). With respect to decline in stress responsivity (see left-hand side of Fig. 2.1), the High Reactivity group showed the smallest decline in responsivity, whereas the Low Reactivity group and/or Positive Valence group showed the largest decline in responsivity. With respect to amount of stress responsivity (see right-hand side of Figure 2.1), the Negative Valence and High Reactivity groups showed greater responsivity than the Positive Valence and Low Reactivity groups.

Figure 2.1(d) shows temperament group differences in overall stress responsivity across the three stress responses (that is, the average of the three stress responses). Examining temperament group differences in overall stress responsivity reflected the results of our data analysis that indicated that the temperament group differences in both the decline in stress responsivity and the amount of stress responsivity were comparable across the three responses.[2] Both the behavioral and the cortisol results indicate the need to consider both emotional valence and reactivity level in examining differences in infant temperament and their relation to infant stress responsivity.

---

[2]Two way (stress response [3], temperament group [4]) MANOVAs performed on the age decline data as well as on the cross-age amount data yielded significant main effects of temperament group ($p < .05$ and $.003$, respectively). The interaction was not significant in either MANOVA. Post hoc t-tests were used to examine differences between the four temperament groups in overall stress responsivity (see Fig. 2.1d). With respect to decline in stress responsivity, the Low Reactivity group showed a significantly larger age decline in responsivity than the High Reactivity group ($p < .02$). The greater decline in responsivity by the Low Reactivity group as opposed to the Negative Valence group approached conventional levels of significance ($p < .07$). With respect to amount of stress responsivity, both the Negative Valence and High Reactivity groups showed greater responsivity than both the Positive Valence and Low Reactivity groups ($p < .03$ or better). There was no significant difference in responsivity between the Positive Valence and Low Reactivity groups or between the Negative Valence and High Reactivity groups.

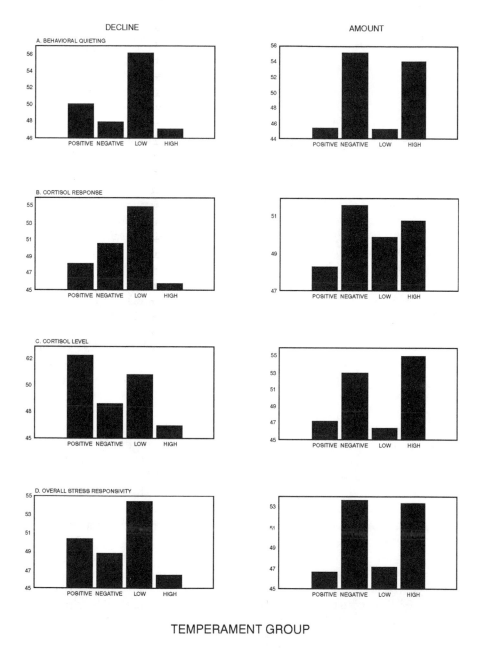

FIG. 2.1. Age decline in stress responsivity and cross-age amount of stress responsivity by temperament group.

Maternal Soothing and Its Relation to Infant Temperament and Stress Responsivity

Most views on infant temperament emphasize a strong role for constitutional and/or genetic factors in accounting for individual differences in emotionality at birth and cross-age stability of these differences throughout infancy. Despite this emphasis, these views typically do acknowledge some role for environmental factors, including the role of the caregiver, in influencing infant emotionality (e.g., van den Boom & Hoeksma, 1994; Wachs et al., 1993). Similarly, environmental and caregiver factors could impact on individual differences and age change in infants' behavioral and cortisol responses to stress. With respect to the potential impact of the caregiver, infants' behavioral response is directly observable, whereas manifestations of infants' physiological response may be only indirectly apparent. Thus, caregiver factors could well have a greater impact on infants' behavioral rather than physiological stress response (cf. Barr, 1989; Lewis, 1989; Lewis et al., 1993; Lewis & Michalson, 1983; Lewis & Saarni, 1985; Malatesta & Haviland, 1982; Suomi, 1991).

Of particular importance in terms of the role of the caregiver in infant temperament and stress responsivity is her response to her infant's distress. Surprisingly, there are relatively few studies that have examined maternal responsivity to infant distress in the early months of life (see Wachs et al., 1993, for relevant data in the 18- to 30-month age period). Bell and Ainsworth (1972) reported that the more contingently mothers responded to their infants' crying from early infancy the less the infants cried when they were 1 year old. Gewirtz and Boyd (1977), however, argued that there was little support for such a relation in Bell and Ainsworth's data. More recently, Barr (1989; Hunziker & Barr, 1986) found that although maternal soothing reduced the duration of infant cry bouts, it did not affect the frequency of the cry bouts. Hubbard and van IJzendoorn (1991) found no evidence that high maternal responsivity led to less infant crying; in fact, they found a relation between more frequent delay of maternal response and a reduced frequency of infant cry bouts over the first half-year of life. There is no evidence that maternal differences are involved in infant colic (Barr, 1989, 1990a, 1990b) or fussiness (Emde et al., 1976) in the first few months of life. Similarly, there is no evidence that maternal differences are involved in various aspects of infant crying behavior such as its increased frequency in the evening hours or its age-related time course (Barr, 1989, 1990a, 1990b). Nonetheless, the belief that maternal soothing in early infancy is crucial in affecting infant socioemotional functioning is widely held (e.g., Ainsworth, Blehar, Waters, & Wall, 1978; Eisenberg & Fabes, 1992; Fox, 1994; Gianino & Tronick, 1988; Kopp, 1989; Lamb, 1981; Schore, 1994; Sroufe, 1996; Tronick, 1989).

Infant crying may be related to a variety of physiological factors. For example, White, Donzella, Vraa, Armasti, Robison, and Barr (1997), in looking at possible physiological differences, found evidence for dysregulation in physiological rhythms in colicky infants including a flatter circadian rhythm in cortisol production. It is not apparent that the physiological differences could be attributed, to any great extent, to differences in maternal behavior including maternal responsivity to infant distress. In normative samples, maternal differences have not been reported by Gunnar et al. (1989, 1992, 1995) who found a relation between high cortisol response and proneness to distress at different ages in the first 13 months of life. Moreover, infant crying does seem to be related to differences in the endogenous opioid system, as indicated by studies on the differential calming efficacy of sucrose as opposed to other stimuli (Blass & Ciaramitaro, 1994). In contrast to the findings on the effects of maternal responsivity on infant crying, there is consistent evidence for the efficacy of sucrose in reducing crying in newborn and older infants (Barr et al., 1995; Blass, 1997; Blass & Smith, 1992).

A few studies have examined the impact of maternal behavior on differences in infant adrenocortical response to distress. At 3, 6, and 9 months, Spangler, Schieche, Ilg, Maier, and Ackermann (1994) found that maternal insensitivity during a mother–infant free play session was associated with a greater infant cortisol response over the session. Other studies have indicated a relation between quality of mother–infant attachment and infant cortisol response with insecurely attached 12- to 19-month-old infants showing a greater response (Hertsgaard, Gunnar, Erickson, & Nachmias, 1995; Nachmias, Gunnar, Mangelsdorf, Parritz, & Buss, 1996; Spangler & Grossmann, 1993). Whereas these findings might suggest that maternal behavior affects infant adrenocortical functioning, they might also indicate that infant characteristics that are related to differences in adrenocortical functioning affect maternal behavior. In any case, with the exception of our recent work (Lewis & Ramsay, 1999a, 1999b), past research has not examined the effect of maternal soothing per se on infant adrenocortical functioning in the early months of life.

Lewis & Ramsay (1999a, 1999b) examined the relation of maternal soothing to infant adrenocortical and behavioral stress responsivity. Using a variety of maternal soothing measures (including those described below for the present sample), there was no evidence that maternal soothing was efficacious in lowering infants' cortisol or behavioral stress response. The few findings for a relation between maternal soothing and infant stress responsivity involved relations between more maternal soothing and greater infant stress responsivity. We interpreted the relation between more maternal soothing and greater infant stress responsivity as indicating the effect of the infant on the mother rather than the influence of the mother on the infant. For the present sample, evidence in support of this view included relations between maternal soothing and infant quieting such that more maternal soothing at 4 months was associated with longer times to quiet at both 2 and 6 months of age.

To extend these findings, it was of interest to determine whether maternal soothing was related to infant emotional valence and/or reactivity level. For the present longitudinal sample when the infants were 4 months of age, mothers' soothing behavior was assessed both when their infants were inoculated and during more everyday episodes of distress (see Study 2 in Lewis & Ramsay, 1999a). The everyday distress episodes involved such nonphysically painful stressors as diaper change or dressing. For inoculation and the everyday distress episodes, the amount of specific proximal (e.g., hold, touch, rub) and distal (e.g., emotion expression, sounds, speech) behaviors that mothers used to sooth their infants was determined. To assess maternal soothing to everyday distress, mother–infant interactive behavior was observed during the entire 4-month well baby pediatric office visit. The everyday distress episodes occurred at different points during the visit when the mothers and infants had been left alone in the examining room by the pediatric staff. Mothers had been told that our interest in observing the office visit was to compare infants' stress response to the inoculation with their reactions to the well baby physical examination.

There was consistency of individual differences in maternal soothing across the episodes of everyday distress and across everyday distress and inoculation. Moreover, amount of maternal soothing behavior was related to other measures of maternal responsivity or sensitivity to infant distress. These other measures included the latency and variety of the peak response to inoculation, maternal empathic behavior following the inoculation, and global ratings of maternal interactive behavior during the entire well baby visit that preceded the inoculation (Lewis & Ramsay, 1999a, 1999b). The findings indicated that amount of maternal soothing across inoculation and everyday distress provided a sensitive index of maternal differences. The reliability of this soothing measure is indicated by these findings and previous results showing relations between more maternal soothing and greater infant stress responsivity.

Figure 2.2 shows amount of maternal soothing to inoculation, everyday distress, and both stressors combined by temperament group. The results indicate greater amounts of maternal soothing for the Negative Valence and High Reactivity groups than for the Positive Valence and Low Reactivity groups. Nonetheless, the differences in maternal soothing by temperament group were not significant. The trend for more maternal soothing in the Negative Valence and High Reactivity groups (see Fig. 2.2) is consistent with the view of the infant affecting the mother rather than the mother influencing the infant. Examination of proximal and distal maternal soothing behaviors to the two stressors (see Lewis & Ramsay, 1999a) also did not reveal any temperament group difference. Other maternal responsivity measures including the global ratings of maternal interactive behavior also did not differ by temperament group.

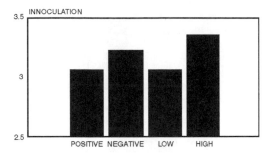

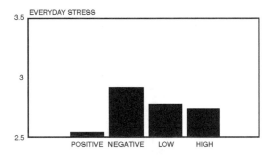

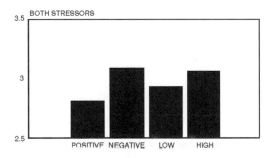

TEMPERAMENT GROUP

FIG. 2.2.   Maternal soothing to inoculation, everyday distress, and both stressors combined by temperament group.

Thus, although we found relations between infant temperament and stress responsivity, there was no evidence that maternal soothing played a role in infant temperament or stress responsivity. Nonetheless, it was of interest to confirm that the relations found between infant temperament and stress responsivity held after consideration of maternal soothing. To address this concern, we examined infant stress responsivity as a function of both

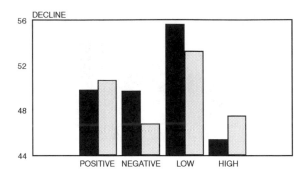

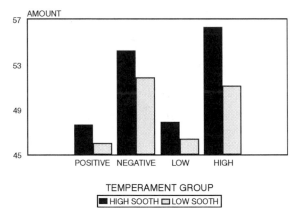

FIG. 2.3.   Age decline in stress responsivity and cross-age amount of stress responsivity by temperament group and maternal soothing.

temperament group and high versus low maternal soothing. High versus low maternal soothing groups were formed based on a median split in the amount of maternal soothing to inoculation and everyday distress combined. Figure 2.3 shows age decline in overall stress responsivity and cross-age amount of overall stress responsivity (as shown in Fig. 2.1d) by temperament group and by high versus low maternal soothing. Although both the decline in stress responsivity and the amount of stress responsivity differed significantly by temperament group, there was no significant effect of maternal soothing.[3]

---

[3]Two way (temperament group, maternal soothing) ANOVAs performed on age decline in and cross-age amount of overall stress responsivity yielded significant main effects of temperament group ($p = .052$ and $p < .008$, respectively). The main effect of maternal soothing and the maternal soothing by temperament group interaction were not significant in either ANOVA.

Our other measures of maternal responsivity, including maternal interactive behavior, also did not impact on the relations found between infant temperament and stress responsivity.

SUMMARY AND IMPLICATIONS OF FINDINGS

The temperament data on emotional behavior reveal that it is possible to describe four different types of children, at least as characterized by their mothers. This description allows for consideration of temperament along two dimensions, emotional valence (predominately negative or positive) and reactivity level (high or low). Without consideration of these two dimensions, it is possible to confound our descriptions of children. For example, if we looked only at each child's positive emotion score, we would include subjects who were high on Positive Valence and low on Negative Valence as well as subjects who were high on both Positive and Negative Valence.

There was evidence for a relation of infant temperament to infant behavioral and cortisol responses to stress that involved both emotional valence and reactivity level. In general, Low Reactivity was associated with a greater age-related decline in stress responsivity between 2 and 6 months of age than was High Reactivity, with both Positive Valence and Negative Valence being associated with intermediate age-related declines in stress. In addition, High Reactivity and Negative Valence were associated with greater stress responsivity across 2 and 6 months of age than were Low Reactivity and Positive Valence. These results confirm that the two dimensions of temperament are relatively independent, and they indicate that both dimensions are needed to adequately assess the relation of infant temperament to stress responsivity.

Our behavioral and cortisol stress measures tended to provide complementary evidence on the relations between infant temperament and stress responsivity. In other situations, behavioral and cortisol stress measures have been found to be not strongly related such that both were needed to adequately assess differences in stress responsivity (Lewis, 1992, 1995; Lewis et al., 1993). The relations between infant temperament and stress responsivity were more apparent for cortisol level than cortisol response. When using cortisol measures of infant temperament or stress responsivity, the present results underscore the need to obtain both basal and response measures of activity. For other physiological measures, there is evidence that both basal and response measures of activity are related differentially to various aspects of infant emotionality (cf. Fox & Calkins, 1993; Porges et al., 1994). At present, little is known about the pattern of relations of basal and stress-related adrenocortical functioning to different aspects of emotionality in infants (cf. Stansbury & Gunnar, 1994).

In our recent work, we have developed a variety of measures of maternal responsivity or sensitivity to infant distress (Lewis & Ramsay, 1999a, 1999b). We have found evidence for cross-age stability and cross-stressor consistency of individual differences in maternal soothing during the 2- to 6-month period. Nonetheless, we have not obtained any evidence that maternal soothing is efficacious in ameliorating infant temperament or lowering infant stress responsivity. Moreover, the relations reported here between infant temperament and stress responsivity were not affected by differences in maternal soothing. As reviewed above, previous work has not found any consistent evidence that maternal soothing is efficacious in reducing infant crying in the first 6 months of life (cf. Barr, 1990a, 1990b). The evidence for this lack of efficacy in maternal soothing stands in contrast to the prevailing view that maternal responsivity to infant distress is crucial in affecting infant socioemotional functioning (Ainsworth et al., 1978; Bell & Ainsworth, 1972; Gianino & Tronick, 1988; Sroufe, 1996; Tronick, 1989).

Role of Maternal Behavior in Infant Temperament and Stress Responsivity

Even though maternal soothing appears to be relatively unimportant, maternal behavior in nondistress situations may be important in affecting infant temperament and stress responsivity. Mothers not only sooth their infants when distressed, they also engage in positive interactions when their infants are not stressed. Providing positive environments may prevent distress from occurring and may lead to less infant distress when distress does occur. Thus, maternal behavior that prevents or buffers distress may be more important than maternal soothing in affecting infant temperament and stress responsivity (cf. Lewis & Ramsay, 1999a, 1999b). There is a variety of evidence in support of a prevention or buffering role of the mother. Maternal behavior in mother–infant play interactions is related to infant socioemotional and cognitive functioning (Bornstein & Tamis-LeMonda, 1997; Lewis & Goldberg, 1969; Watson, 1966, 1985). Positive experiences provided by mothers have been found to be associated with lowered adrenocortical functioning in infants (Hertsgaard, Gunnar, Larson, Brodersen, & Lehman, 1992; Larson, Gunnar, & Hertsgaard, 1991). Other infant cortisol research (Hertsgaard et al., 1995; Nachmias et al., 1996; Spangler & Grossmann, 1993; Spangler et al.,1994) suggests that a history of positive mother–infant interactions is associated with lowered infant adrenocortical activity.

Despite the lack of efficacy of maternal soothing behavior in reducing infant distress, mothers likely believe in the efficacy of their behavior. Regardless of their belief, infants' distress eventually ceases in the context of their mothers' administrations. With cognitive development, this association may become a representation by the child of a caring mother and of a self worthy of attention (Bretherton, 1990). Thus, an additional role for maternal caregiving involves children's growing mental representation of the mother as a source of support and comfort (Lewis & Ramsay, 1999a, 1999b).

In addition to maternal behavior, our present and previous results suggest that temperament may play a role in differences in infant stress responsivity.

Our results provide some indication that more maternal soothing is associated with a more difficult temperament (i.e., Negative Valence and/or High Reactivity) and greater behavioral and cortisol stress responsivity. This likely reflects the infant influencing the mother rather than the mother affecting the infant. As reviewed above, in contrast to the lack of evidence for the efficacy of maternal soothing in reducing infant distress, there is increasing evidence that physiological factors are involved in differences in crying in newborn and older infants (Barr et al., 1995; Blass, 1997; Blass & Ciaramitaro, 1994; White et al., 1997). Whatever role maternal behavior may play in infant temperament and stress responsivity, it would appear that maternal soothing alone is an insufficient explanation of differences in infant temperament and stress responsivity during the 2- to 6-month period.

REFERENCES

Ainsworth, M. D. S., Blehar, M. C., Waters, E., & Wall, S. (1978). *Patterns of attachment. A psychological study of the strange situation*. Hillsdale, NJ: Lawrence Erlbaum Associates.

Barr, R. G. (1989). Recasting a clinical enigma: The case of infant crying. In P. R. Zelazo & R. G. Barr (Eds.), *Challenges to developmental paradigms: Implications for theory, assessment, and treatment* (pp. 43–64). Hillsdale, NJ: Lawrence Erlbaum Associates.

Barr, R. G. (1990a). The colic enigma: Prolonged episodes of a normal disposition to cry. *Infant Mental Health Journal, 11,* 340–348.

Barr, R. G. (1990b). The normal crying curve: What do we really know? *Developmental Medicine and Child Neurology, 32,* 356–362.

Barr, R. G., Young, S. N., Wright, J. H., Cassidy, K.-L., Hendricks, L., Bedard, Y., Yaremko, J., Leduc, D., & Treherne, S. (1995). Sucrose analgesia and diphtheria-tetanus-pertussis immunizations at 2 and 4 months. *Developmental and Behavioral Pediatrics, 16,* 220–225.

Bates, J. E. (1980). The concept of difficult temperament. *Merrill-Palmer Quarterly, 26,* 299–319.

Bates, J. E. (1987). Temperament in infancy. In J. D. Osofsky (Ed.), *Handbook of infant development* (2nd ed., pp. 1101–1149). New York: Wiley.

Bell, S. M., & Ainsworth, M. D. S. (1972). Infant crying and maternal responsiveness. *Child Development, 43,* 1171–1190.

Blass, E. M. (1997). Infant formula quiets crying human newborns. *Developmental and Behavioral Pediatrics, 18,* 162–165.

Blass, E. M., & Ciaramitaro, V. (1994). A new look at some old mechanisms in human newborns: Taste and tactile determinants of state, affect, and action. *Monographs of the Society for Research in Child Development, 59* (Serial No. 239), 1–101.

Blass, E. M., & Smith, B. A. (1992). Differential effects of sucrose, fructose, glucose, and lactose on crying in 1- to 3-day-old human infants: Qualitative and quantitative considerations. *Developmental Psychology, 28,* 804–810.

Bornstein, M. H., & Tamis-LeMonda, C. S. (1997). Maternal responsiveness and infant mental abilities: Specific predictive relations. *Infant Behavior and Development, 20,* 283–296.

Boyce, W. T., Barr, R. G., & Zeltzer, L. K. (1992). Temperament and the psychobiology of childhood stress. *Pediatrics, 90,* 483–486.

Bretherton, I. (1990). Open communication and internal working models: Their role in the development of attachment relationships. In R. A. Thompson (Ed.), *Nebraska Symposium on Motivation: Vol. 36. Socioemotional development* (pp. 57–113). Lincoln: University of Nebraska Press.

Buss, A. H., & Plomin, R. (1984). *Temperament: Early developing personality traits.* Hillsdale, NJ: Lawrence Erlbaum Associates.

Cacioppo, J. T., Klein, D. J., Berntson, G. C., & Hatfield, E. (1993). The psychophysiology of emotion. In M. Lewis & J. M. Haviland (Eds.), *Handbook of emotions* (pp. 119–142). New York: Guilford Press.

Eisenberg, N., & Fabes, R. A. (Eds.). (1992). *Emotion and its regulation in early development. New Directions in Child Development* (No. 55). San Francisco: Jossey-Bass.

Emde, R. N., Gaensbauer, T. J., & Harmon, R. J. (1976). *Emotional expression in infancy. A biobehavioral study.* (Psychological Issues, Vol. X, No.1, Monograph 37). New York: International Universities Press.

Fox, N. A. (Ed.). (1994). The development of emotion regulation: Biological and behavioral considerations. *Monographs of the Society for Research in Child Development, 59* (Serial No. 240), 1–199.

Fox, N. A., & Calkins, S. D. (1993). Multiple-measure approaches to the study of infant emotion. In M. Lewis & J. M. Haviland (Eds.), *Handbook of emotions* (pp. 167–184). New York: Guilford Press.

Gewirtz, J. L., & Boyd, E. F. (1977). Does maternal responding imply reduced infant crying? A critique of the 1972 Bell and Ainsworth report. *Child Development, 48,* 1200–1207.

Gianino, A., & Tronick, E. Z. (1988). The mutual regulation model: The infant's self and interactive regulation and coping and defensive capacities. In T. M. Field, P. M. McCabe, & N. Schneiderman (Eds.), *Stress and coping across development* (pp. 47–68). Hillsdale, NJ: Lawrence Erlbaum Associates.

Goldsmith, H. H. (1986). *Toddler behavior assessment questionnaire.* Eugene, University of Oregon: Department of Psychology.

Goldsmith, H. H. (1996). Studying temperament via construction of the toddler behavior assessment questionnaire. *Child Development, 67,* 218–235.

Goldsmith, H. H., & Campos, J. J. (1986). Fundamental issues in the study of early temperament: The Denver twin temperament study. In M. E. Lamb, A. L. Brown, & B. Rogoff (Eds.), *Advances in developmental psychology* (Vol. 4, pp. 231–283). Hillsdale, NJ: Lawrence Erlbaum Associates.

Graham, F. K., & Clifton, R. K. (1966). Heart rate change as a component of the orienting response. *Psychological Bulletin, 65,* 305–320.

Gunnar, M. R. (1986). Human developmental psychoneuroendocrinology: A review of research on neuroendocrine responses to challenge and threat in infancy and childhood. In M. E. Lamb, A. L. Brown, & B. Rogoff (Eds.), *Advances in developmental psychology* (Vol. 4, pp. 51–103). Hillsdale, NJ: Lawrence Erlbaum Associates.

Gunnar, M. R., Brodersen, L., Krueger, K., & Rigatuso, J. (1996). Dampening of adrenocortical responses during infancy: Normative changes and individual differences. *Child Development, 67,* 877–889.

Gunnar, M. R., Larson, M. C., Hertsgaard, L., Harris, M. L., & Brodersen, L. (1992). The stressfulness of separation among 9-month-old infants: Effects of social context variables and infant temperament. *Child Development, 63,* 290–303.

Gunnar, M. R., Mangelsdorf, S., Larson, M., & Hertsgaard, L. (1989). Attachment, temperament, and adrenocortical activity in infancy: A study of psychoendocrine regulation. *Developmental Psychology, 25,* 355–363.

Gunnar, M. R., Porter, F. L., Wolf, C. M., Rigatuso, J., & Larson, M. C. (1995). Neonatal stress reactivity: Predictions to later emotional temperament. *Child Development, 66,* 1–13.

Hertsgaard, L., Gunnar, M., Erickson, M. F., & Nachmias, M. (1995). Adrenocortical responses to the strange situation with disorganized/disoriented attachment relationships. *Child Development, 66,* 1100–1106.

Hertsgaard, L., Gunnar, M., Larson, M., Brodersen, L., & Lehman, H. (1992). First time experiences: When they appear to be pleasant, do they activate the adrenocortical stress response? *Developmental Psychobiology, 25,* 319–333.

Hubbard, F. O. A., & van IJzendoorn, M. H. (1991). Maternal unresponsiveness and infant crying across the first 9 months: A naturalistic longitudinal study. *Infant Behavior and Development, 14,* 299–312.

Hunziker, U. A., & Barr, R. G. (1986). Increased carrying reduces infant crying: A randomized control trial. *Pediatrics, 77,* 641–648.

Kagan, J., & Lewis, M. (1965). Studies of attention in the human infant. *Merrill-Palmer Quarterly, 11,* 95–127.

Kagan, J., Reznick, J. S., & Snidman, N. (1987). The physiology and psychology of behavioral inhibition in children. *Child Development, 58,* 1459–1473.

Kagan, J., Snidman, N., & Arcus, D. M. (1992). Initial reactions to unfamiliarity. *Current Directions in Psychological Science, 1,* 171–174.

Kopp, C. (1989). Regulation of distress and negative emotions: A developmental perspective. *Developmental Psychology, 25,* 343–354.

Lamb, M. E. (1981). The development of social expectations in the first year of life. In M. E. Lamb & L. R. Sherrod (Eds.). *Infant social cognition* (pp. 155–175). Hillsdale, NJ: Lawrence Erlbaum Associates.

Larsen, R. J., & Diener, E. (1987). Affect intensity as an individual difference characteristic: A review. *Journal of Research in Personality, 21,* 1–39.

Larsen, R. J., & Ketelaar, T. (1991). Personality and susceptibility to positive and negative emotional states. *Journal of Personality and Social Psychology, 61,* 132–140.

Larson, M. C., Gunnar, M. R., & Hertsgaard, L. (1991). The effects of morning naps, car trips, and maternal separation on adrenocortical activity in human infants. *Child Development, 62,* 362–372.

Lewis, M. (1989). Culture and biology: The role of temperament. In P. R. Zelazo & R. G. Barr (Eds.), *Challenges to developmental paradigms: Implications for theory, assessment, and treatment* (pp. 203–223). Hillsdale, NJ: Lawrence Erlbaum Associates.

Lewis, M. (1992). Individual differences in response to stress. *Pediatrics, 90,* 487–490.

Lewis, M. (1995). Individual differences in response to stress. *25th roundtable on critical approaches to common pediatric problems: Children, families, and stress* (pp. 35–43). Columbus, OH: Ross Laboratories.

Lewis, M., & Goldberg, S. (1969). Perceptual-cognitive development in infancy: A generalized expectancy model as a function of the mother–infant interaction. *Merrill-Palmer Quarterly, 15,* 82–100.

Lewis, M., Kagan, J., Campbell, H., & Kalafat, J. (1966). The cardiac response as a correlate of attention in infants. *Child Development, 37,* 63–71.

Lewis, M., & Michalson, L. (1983). *Children's emotions and moods: Developmental theory and measurement.* New York: Plenum.

Lewis, M., & Ramsay, D. S. (1995a). Developmental change in infants' responses to stress. *Child Development, 66,* 657–670.

Lewis, M., & Ramsay, D. S. (1995b). Stability and change in cortisol and behavioral responses to stress during the first 18 months of life. *Developmental Psychobiology, 28,* 419–428.

Lewis, M., & Ramsay, D. S. (1999a). Effect of maternal soothing on infant stress response. *Child Development, 70,* 11–20.

Lewis, M., & Ramsay, D. S. (1999b). Environments and stress reduction. In M. Lewis & D. Ramsay (Eds.), *Stress and soothing* (pp. 171–192). Mahwah, NJ: Lawrence Erlbaum Associates.

Lewis, M., Ramsay, D. S., & Kawakami, K. (1993). Differences between Japanese infants and Caucasian American infants in behavioral and cortisol response to inoculation. *Child Development, 64,* 1722–1731.

Lewis, M., & Saarni, C. (1985). Culture and emotions. In M. Lewis & C. Saarni (Eds.), *The socialization of emotions* (pp. 1–17). New York: Plenum.

Lewis, M., & Thomas, D. (1990). Cortisol release in infants in response to inoculation. *Child Development, 61,* 50–59.

Malatesta, C. Z., & Haviland, J. (1982). Learning display rules: The socialization of emotion expression in infancy. *Child Development, 53,* 991–1003.

Nachmias, M., Gunnar, M., Mangelsdorf, S., Parritz, R. H., & Buss, K. (1996). Behavioral inhibition and stress reactivity: The moderating role of attachment security. *Child Development, 67,* 508–522.

Porges, S. W., Doussard-Roosevelt, J. A., & Maiti, A. J. (1994). Vagal tone and the physiological regulation of emotion. In N. A. Fox (Ed.), The development of emotion regulation: Biological and behavioral considerations. *Monographs of the Society for Research in Child Development* (Serial No. 240, Vol. 59), 167–186.

Ramsay, D. S., & Lewis, M. (1994). Developmental change in infant cortisol and behavioral response to inoculation. *Child Development, 65,* 1491–1502.

Rothbart, M. K. (1978). *Infant behavior questionnaire.* Eugene, University of Oregon: Department of Psychology.

Rothbart, M. K. (1986). Longitudinal observation of infant temperament. *Developmental Psychology, 22,* 356–365.

Rothbart, M. K., & Derryberry, D. (1981). Development of individual differences in temperament. In M. E. Lamb & A. L. Brown (Eds.), *Advances in developmental psychology* (Vol. 1, pp. 37–86). Hillsdale, NJ: Lawrence Erlbaum Associates.

Schore, A. N. (1994). *Affect regulation and the origin of the self: The neurobiology of emotional development.* Hillsdale, NJ: Lawrence Erlbaum Associates.

Spangler, G., & Grossmann, K. E. (1993). Behavioral organization in securely and insecurely attached infants. *Child Development, 64,* 1439–1450.

Spangler, G., Schieche, M., Ilg, U., Maier, U., & Ackermann, C. (1994). Maternal sensitivity as an external organizer for biobehavioral regulation in infancy. *Developmental Psychobiology, 27,* 425–437.

Sroufe, L. A. (1996). *Emotional development. The organization of emotional life in the early years.* New York: Cambridge University Press.

Stansbury, K., & Gunnar, M. R. (1994). Adrenocortical activity and emotion regulation. In N. A. Fox (Ed.), The development of emotion regulation: Biological and behavioral considerations. *Monographs of the Society for Research in Child Development* (Serial No. 240, Vol. 59), 108–134.

Suomi, S. (1991). Primate separation models of affective disorders. In J. Madden (Ed.), *Neurobiology of learning, emotion, and affect* (pp. 195–214). New York: Raven Press.

Thomas, A., & Chess, S. (1977). *Temperament and development.* New York: Brunner/ Mazel.

Thomas, A., Chess, S., & Birch, H. G. (1968). *Temperament and behavior disorders in children.* New York: New York University Press.

Tronick, E. (1989). Emotions and emotional communication in infants. *American Psychologist, 44,* 112–119.

van den Boom, D. C., & Hoeksma, J. B. (1994). The effect of infant irritability on mother–infant interaction: A growth-curve analysis. *Developmental Psychology, 30,* 581–590.

Wachs, T. D., Bishry, Z., Sobhy, A., McCabe, G., Galal, O., & Shaheen, F. (1993). Relation of rearing environment to adaptive behavior of Egyptian toddlers. *Child Development, 64,* 586–604.

Watson, D., & Tellegen, A. (1985). Toward a consensual structure of mood. *Psychological Bulletin, 98,* 219–235.

Watson, J. S. (1966). The development and generalization of contingency awareness in early infancy: Some hypotheses. *Merrill-Palmer Quarterly, 12,* 123–135.

Watson, J. S. (1985). Contingency perception in early social development. In T. M. Field & N. A. Fox (Eds.), *Social perception in infants* (pp. 157–176). Norwood, NJ: Ablex.

White, B. P., Donzella, B., Vraa, R., Armasti, M., Robison, K., & Barr, R. G. (1997, April). *Evidence of sleep differences and possible dysregulation of daily cortisol activity in infants with colic.* Poster session presented at the biennial meeting of the Society for Research in Child Development, Washington, DC.

Worobey, J. (1990). Behavioral assessment of the neonate. In J. Colombo & J. Fagen (Eds.), *Individual differences in Infancy: Reliability, stability, prediction* (pp. 137–161). Hillsdale, NJ: Lawrence Erlbaum Associates.

Worobey, J., & Blajda, V. M. (1989). Temperament ratings at 2 weeks, 2 months, and 1 year: Differential stability of activity and emotionality. *Developmental Psychology, 25,* 257–263.

Worobey J., & Lewis, M. (1989). Individual differences in the reactivity of young infants. *Developmental Psychology, 25,* 663–667.

3 Inhibited and Uninhibited Children: Biology in the Social Context

Doreen Arcus
University of Massachusetts Lowell

"Nature, Mr. Allnut, is what we were put in this world to rise above."
—Katherine Hepburn in *The African Queen*,
screenplay by James Agee and John Huston, 1951

My 8-year-old son was playing at a friend's house. After they had exhausted their repertoire of electronics, athletics, and royal rumbles with armloads of action figures, they decided to pretend that they were going on a double-date. The only problem seemed to be that they both liked the same girl at school. But it did not remain a problem for long. They simply decided to pretend that she had a twin.

Such an implicit acknowledgment of the contribution of biology to personality is a notion that is centuries old but one that has only recently acquired a substantial body of empirical support. For most of this century a confluence of social and political factors, including massive immigration to the United States, emergent social welfare policies, the genocide of World War II, and the moral imperative of the civil rights movement, made the suggestion that psychological variation might be related to biology or genes an uncomfortable one, and rendered temperament a largely unstudied phenomenon (see Kagan, 1994). Not until the landmark work of Thomas, Chess, & Birch (1968) and Thomas, Chess, Birch, Hertzig, & Korn (1963) did a substantial literature begin to emerge.

Although the specific definitions and methods of assessment may vary, there is general consensus that temperament refers to biologically based individual differences in emotions or motivations. In this chapter, observations of two types of children are discussed, who differ in their disposition toward inhibited or uninhibited reactions to conditions of novelty and uncertainty, without claim that the relations we observe would extend to other temperamental categories or conceptualizations.

BEHAVIORAL INHIBITION IN CHILDHOOD

More than a decade ago, Kagan and his colleagues identified two groups of children in the 2nd or 3rd year whose reactions to unfamiliar persons or events were observed to vary consistently across a variety of incentives. Inhibited children were hesitant to explore new environments and stayed close to their mothers. In contrast, uninhibited children explored eagerly, approaching the examiner and making overtures toward others frequently. Follow-up assessments through early adolescence revealed modest stability of those original behavioral profiles, though the outward signs changed with the developmental level of the child. Children who were originally inhibited were more frequently quiet, timid, and shy. Uninhibited children, on the other hand, were more likely to be outgoing, talkative, and spontaneous (Garcia-Coll, Kagan, & Reznick, 1984; Kagan, Reznick, & Snidman, 1987, 1988; Reznick et al., 1986).

From the beginning, these behavioral profiles were characterized in context, that is, in the presence of salient psychological incentives involving unpredictability and uncertainty. An inhibited profile may not be apparent in the 2-year-old child when his or her own mother enters a room, in contrast to what might be seen when a stranger or an adult covered in dark shroud enters that same room. The older child who is loquacious with friends or siblings at home may make few spontaneous comments with unfamiliar peers or in an unfamiliar setting.

Moreover, inhibited and uninhibited children cannot be reliably distinguished on the basis of their reactions to a single hallmark event. There is no litmus test. Instead, differences between the groups are better captured by aggregates of behavior across a variety of events and stimuli, for example, unfamiliar adults, unfamiliar peers, costumed adults, expectancy violations, mild cognitive stress, and intrusions such as applying a blood pressure cuff (Kagan, 1994; Reznick, Gibbons, Johnson, & McDonough, 1989).

These two temperamental groups are presumed to differ fundamentally in the physiological circuits that participate in response to novelty and regulation of approach–avoidance, that is, the structures of the limbic system and their projections to the sympathetic chain, skeletal muscles, and hypothalamic-pituitary-adrenal axis. The likelihood that these differences contribute to the emergence and maintenance of the behavioral differences between these two groups has modest support in the data.

Inhibited children display higher baseline and more accelerated heart rates, decreased heart rate variability, more pupillary dilatation, greater skeletal muscle tension of the vocal cords as indexed by restricted variation in pitch period, and modestly elevated levels of salivary cortisol and urinary norepinephrine compared to uninhibited children (Coster, 1986; Kagan, Reznick, & Snidman, 1987; Reznick et al., 1986). Inhibited children and their relatives are also more susceptible to allergies and more likely to have blue eyes than their uninhibited peers, suggesting the involvement of additional biological systems (Kagan, Snidman, Julia-Sellers, & Johnson, 1991; Rosenberg & Kagan, 1987). Finally, inhibited children show more right than left frontal activation in their resting EEG profile, a pattern typical of children's general response to stress (Davidson, 1994).

These associations, although modest, are notable because peripheral psychophysiological measures are noisy estimates of the complex, dynamic, and intricately balanced processes from which they originate, complicating the search for a direct relation between brain and behavior. As is the case with behavior, aggregate physiological indices may be more useful in distinguishing inhibited from uninhibited children than reliance on any single variable (Kagan, Reznick & Snidman, 1988).

In sum, the study of inhibited and uninhibited children first identified in the 2nd or 3rd year of life provides a rich corpus of data indicating that individual differences among children can be observed reliably across childhood, and are associated with physiological profiles that implicate fundamental differences in the central mediating mechanisms.

However, the modest effect sizes associated with many of these results suggested that whatever biological influences were operating, they were not deterministic. Environment appeared to influence the preservation of behavior as well. The task of uncovering temperament-environment interactions, however, was complicated. It would require that a temperament assessment occur much earlier in life than age 2 or 3 years, at an age when socialization influences, if not absent, at least had less opportunity to have taken effect. Further, the identification of inhibited and uninhibited temperaments in early infancy would have to rely on the discovery of antecedent profiles because young infants lack the cognitive maturity to evaluate the salience of novel stimuli.

Reactivity in Infancy: The Bias of Biology

Advances in the neurosciences, primarily based on animal work, suggested that the developmental path linking high reactivity in infancy to later inhibition might reflect underlying variation in arousal of the amygdala and its projections to sites that participate in motor and vocal control, especially the corpus striatum, central gray, cingulate, hypothalamus, and sympathetic nervous system (de Lanerolle & Lang, 1988; Hitchcock & Davis, 1986; Jurgens, 1982; Kelley, Domesick, & Nauta, 1982; Mishkin & Aggleton, 1981). In other words, it was plausible that the ease of evoking arousal—displayed in the young infant as motor activity and cry—might display in the older infant as avoidant reactions to novelty. This paradoxical link, a longitudinal inversion of intensity, although not a new observation in human infants, had not previously been considered an index of temperamental variation (Bell, Weller, & Waldrop,1971; Bronson, 1972; Yang & Halverson, 1976).

Kagan and Snidman (1991) followed one hundred 4-month-old infants into the 2nd year, and found that the ease and valence of arousal to stimuli at 4 months predicted later inhibited and uninhibited behavioral profiles. High levels of motor activity and fretting or crying to varied stimuli were characteristic of high reactive infants and associated with fearful and inhibited behavior at 14 and 21 months. Conversely, low reactive infants, those who showed low levels of motor activity, crying, and fretting at 4 months, were likely to be fearless and uninhibited at the later ages (Kagan, 1994).

Infant reactivity was also associated with multiple aspects of infant biology. Higher sleeping heart rates at 2 weeks and 2 months of age and greater sympathetic activity in the cardiac spectrum at 2 months, predicted high reactivity at 4 months (Snidman, Kagan, Riordan, & Shannon, 1995). Although high and low reactive infants did not differ at 9, 14, or 21 months in baseline heart rates or in the distribution of spectral power, more subtle heart rate patterns did distinguish the groups at later ages. For example, more high than low reactive infants had both minimal and maximal heart rate values across the 14 month assessment that fell in the highest quartile of each distribution, with the opposite profile for low reactives (Kagan, 1994).

Although it is not obvious that the two should be linked, infant reactivity is associated with anthropometric variation. Arcus and Kagan (1995a) found children who had been categorized as high reactive at 4 months to have larger facial width measurements across the bizygomatic arch (the cheekbones) than children who had been identified as low reactives at both 14 and 21 months. Children with the narrowest faces were significantly more fearful than children with the broadest faces at later ages. This aspect of craniofacial variation, like sympathetic activity and pigmentation, is a derivative of the embryological neural crest, suggesting that these heterotypic correlates of temperament may be linked through common developmental origins and influences.

Finally, infant reactivity is associated with cerebral asymmetries similar to those observed in older inhibited and uninhibited children and characteristic of the response of children to stressful events (Fox, Calkins, & Bell, 1994). High reactive infants show greater EEG activation in the right frontal areas, and low reactive infants show greater activity in the left areas during the first two years. Moreover, infants who demonstrate both high negative affect and high motor activity at 4 months, combined with right frontal EEG asymmetry at 9 months, are likely to demonstrate fear and wariness at 14 months (Calkins, Fox, & Marshall, 1996).

The EEG results are supported by patterns of temperature asymmetries. Because cerebral activation is associated with sympathetically mediated vasoconstriction, cooler skin temperatures occur on the same side as the greater EEG activation. In a follow-up assessment at 4½ years, high reactive infants who had been fearful in the 2nd year had significantly cooler left finger temperatures compared to low reactives who were not fearful at age 2 years (Arcus & Kagan, 1995b).

The identification of infant antecedents of inhibited and uninhibited behavior profiles has strengthened the argument that biology contributes to these temperament categories. However, the developmental pathway is not absolute. Not every high reactive infant becomes a fearful, inhibited child, nor does every low reactive infant become highly sociable and exuberant. These observations raise several possibilities. Genetically driven forces may emerge with later development, the environment may exert influence on the developmental trajectory of an initial biological bias, and there may be interactions of environmental influences and biological dispositions. None of these possibilities is mutually exclusive to any of the others.

The potential for modification of the initial temperamental bias is illustrated by the proportion of children whose behavior remains extreme over time (Arcus & Kagan, 1995b). As seen in Fig. 3.1, more than one third of the infants originally classified as high reactive were highly fearful at both 14 and 21 months whereas only 3% showed minimal fear at the two later ages. In contrast, more than one third of the low reactive infants were minimally fearful at the same two ages and only 4% showed high fear. This asymmetry was not apparent for the remaining children, among whom equal proportions showed either extremely high or low fear at both ages.

In other words, the odds of a high or low reactive infant displaying an extreme profile at age 1 and 2 years that was consistent with his or her original classification were about 7 times greater than the odds of those same children displaying extreme behavior inconsistent with the 4 month classification. For children not of either category, for whom these behavioral and temperamental profiles were not especially salient, there was no difference. This tendency extended to follow-up assessments at 4½ years when few extreme violations of the initial classification were observed (Kagan, Snidman, & Arcus, 1998).

CONTEXTUAL MODERATORS: INFLUENCES ON EXPRESSION

There are at least two kinds of contextual moderators of inhibited and uninhibited behavior. The first lies in the contexts that evoke these temperamental cat-

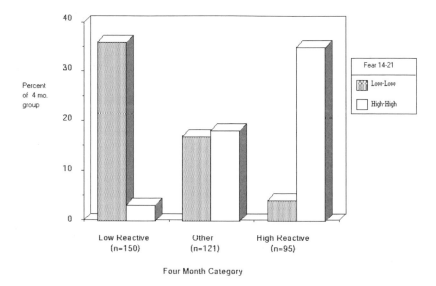

FIG. 3.1.   Proportion of children in 4 month temperament groups showing consistently high or low fear at both 14 and 21 month assessments.

egories, those marked by sufficient and sufficiently salient novelty or uncertainty. Such events are not typically present in the young child's daily home routine, except, for example, when visitors arrive. The need for specificity in the incentive situations may contribute to the poor correspondence between maternal report and laboratory assessments or direct observations of temperamentally motivated behavior (Arcus & McCartney, 1989; Goldsmith & Campos, 1990; Kagan, 1994; Seifer, Sameroff, Barrett, & Krafchuk, 1994).

Such contextual variants also require that laboratory assessments of individual differences in inhibited and uninhibited behavior sample broadly across a variety of kinds of events. The mean number of episodes that evoked fearful reactions across a sample of 14-month-old children was 2.6 ($SE = 0.10$) out of a total of 17 and, on average, less than one third of the children displayed fear to any particular incentive (Kagan, 1994). Procedures that rely on one or two types of events are probably less reliable predictors of behavior over time.

Observations in both home and school settings support the ecological validity of the categories of inhibited and uninhibited. In our longitudinal study of 98 infants in their homes using a sample evenly divided by reactivity, sex, and birth order, few but relevant differences between the temperament groups were noted. High reactive infants fretted and cried more often at 5 and

7 months than low reactives. Low reactive infants, on the other hand, accounted for the majority of infants who laughed most often at later visits from 9 to 13 months with a stranger present in the home; however, it is possible that this observation may be limited to home settings in which an intruder, such as our camera operator, is present (Arcus, Gardner, & Anderson, 1992; Arcus & Kagan, 1995b).

The presence or absence of siblings provided an interesting context for the interpretation of infant approach behavior in the home and the laboratory. Older siblings, who were often intrigued by the home visitor and were physically more adept at getting to her first compared to the younger infant, provided secondborns with more obstacles to overcome in order to approach the examiner in the home. Firstborn infants of both temperamental groups approached the examiner more than 3 times as often as secondborn infants in the homes, but it was secondborn infants who approached more in the 14 month laboratory, apparently unfettered by competition from their older siblings. Given the obstacle presented by the sibling, home approach appeared a more sensitive index of approach–avoidance for secondborns, among whom it predicted approach to test stimuli in the laboratory for high reactive infants.

In other words, the context of the laboratory assessment appeared to vary in accordance with the way the presence or absence of older siblings defined its contrast to the typical context of the home. Compared to the firstborns, who were accustomed to being able to approach individuals in their home without competition, secondborns may have experienced the undivided attention of examiners and the exclusive access to interesting laboratory stimuli as an opportunity not to be missed. Similar issues have arisen in the application of a variety of assessment techniques across populations. The maternal separations involved in the Strange Situation, for example, may be overwhelming in the context of typical Japanese childrearing in which such separations are rare occurrences, thus contributing to the overrepresentation of insecure attachment classifications among these children (Takahashi, 1990).

Two related studies have examined inhibited and uninhibited children in the school environment during their kindergarten year. In the first of these, children originally classified as inhibited or uninhibited in the 2nd year were observed in the fall and spring of their kindergarten year (Gersten, 1989). During the fall visits, inhibited children were quieter and more subdued in their classrooms and on the playground compared to uninhibited children. Later in the year, the differences between the groups diminished, though there was modest stability between the fall and spring aggregate indices of inhibition across both groups ($r = .42, p < .01$).

The focus of Gersten's work was to examine ways in which this important developmental context challenged inhibited children during a period of maximal uncertainty with new peers, teachers, and physical environs. Since then we have learned that uninhibited children may face their own set of challenges, not in the newness of the setting, but in the requirement for self-discipline, containment, and obedience to authority.

These issues were examined when Rimm-Kaufman (1996) followed children who were either high reactive infants who subsequently showed moderate or high levels of inhibition in the 2nd year, or low reactive infants who were subsequently uninhibited in the 2nd year, on multiple occasions early and later in their kindergarten year. Like the children in Gersten's (1986) study a decade before, high reactive, inhibited children talked and volunteered less, approached the examiner less frequently, and violated classroom rules less often than low reactive, uninhibited children. However, especially among boys, additional differences were noted as the school year progressed.

Two thirds of the low reactive, uninhibited boys evidenced aggressive behavior on at least one school visit. Five of these six boys displayed similar patterns in this behavior, following their aggressive overture with laughter. Conversely, physical aggression was observed in a single high reactive, inhibited boy. As the year progressed, children who had been low reactive infants were also more likely than high reactives to evoke reproach from the teacher and to talk out of turn—whispering during teacher-guided activities and yelling during unstructured times (Rimm-Kaufman, 1996).

These observations were consistent with the findings of a laboratory assessment at age 4½ years. Children who had been classified as high reactive at 4 months displayed infrequent spontaneous comments and smiling with the unfamiliar examiner. However, the children who had been low reactive, although chatty, were also less likely to be intimidated by the authority of the adult examiner. In one episode the children were asked to perform benign actions that would typically be prohibited by parents (e.g., "Pour the juice on the table"). In the most striking trial, the examiner opened a photo album containing pictures of herself, took out a large color photograph and, as she handed it to the child, said, "This is my favorite picture. Tear up my favorite picture." Many more low than high reactives either asked her why they should perform the action or simply refused to do it. Social dominance of the uninhibited child was also apparent. At the completion of a play session involving three unfamiliar same-sexed children, the examiner came into the large playroom with an attractive, remote control toy, placed it down and left it for the children. Low reactive, uninhibited children were most often the ones to secure initial possession of the toy. When they were not, they tended to persist in their efforts to obtain it (Arcus & Kagan, 1995b).

Dominance, although it may sometimes be expressed as leadership, is not always a prosocial phenomenon. Depending on the contextual demands for conformity and the existence of limited resources for which there is likely to be competition, the assertiveness of low reactive, uninhibited children may violate local norms or be viewed as aggression. We see evidence for this pattern as early as infancy. Our home visits revealed secondborn infants to be the targets of a substantial amount of intrusive and, occasionally, aggressive behavior from the older sibling. Although there were only three cases of younger infants fighting back and returning an aggressive overture, all three infants were low reactives. When interviewed, mothers of low reactives were more likely to report difficulties with discipline and compliance compared to mothers of high reactives. Perhaps the child who is not easily aroused by external stimulation has a higher threshold for parental admonitions as well.

CONTEXTUAL MODERATORS: INFLUENCES ON DEVELOPMENT

The second type of contextual moderator is one that influences the developmental path as temperament and experience interact to shape the degree to which the dispositional bias will be actualized. Such temperament-environment interactions have been studied more extensively in animals than they have been in humans, beginning with Scott and Fuller's (1965) comparison of the outcomes of similar rearing conditions with different breeds of dog. More recently, Jones, Mills, and Faure (1991) raised two lines of quail chicks under different conditions, the two lines differing in their proneness to freezing in the open field. Chicks that were prone to immobility and raised in an enriched environment with regular handling displayed less freezing than other members of their strain raised in more subdued environments with less handling. However, they were still more fearful than the strain of chicks who initially showed minimal immobility raised under either condition.

Interactions can result in biological as well as behavioral outcomes. When crabeater macaques that varied in the tendency to be affiliative were raised under more or less stressful conditions, only those in the stressful condition that were also temperamentally disposed to isolation showed compromised immune function (Cohen, Kaplan, Cunnick, Manuck, & Rabin, 1992).

The assumption of analogous interactions between temperament and environment in human children is not a new idea. The goodness of fit between an infant's temperament and the characteristics of his or her family has been acknowledged as a critical feature of early development (Thomas & Chess, 1977). Further, it has been hypothesized that children of varied temperaments experience similar environments differently (the organismic-specificity hypothesis) and that temperament and environment exert mutual influences on the infant's regulation of emotion from the earliest days of life (Rothbart, 1989; Wachs & Gandour, 1983).

Discovery of the infant antecedent profiles of later inhibited and uninhibited behavior permitted the exploration of experiential variation that might be associated with different outcomes for high and low reactive infants, beginning with an assessment of temperament when socialization influences—although never absent—were less cumulative than at later ages. By assessing reactivity at 4 months, following children and their mothers in the home from 5 to 13 months, and assessing inhibition in the laboratory at 14 months, we hoped to identify ways in which experience interacted with temperament to predict differential outcomes for high and low reactive infants over the 1st year. The sample was constrained with regard to factors that have been shown to vary with maternal practice in order to control for confounds; all infants were Caucasian, healthy, and born into middle- or upper-middle-class families (Arcus, Gardner & Anderson, 1992; Arcus & Kagan, 1995a).

Even in this relatively homogeneous sample, there was substantial variability in infant experience. During early visits we coded mothers' variation in their selective attention to infant distress (SAID). The distribution of maternal holding and kissing relative to infant state was defined as the ratio of (a) the difference between the likelihood of holding or kissing the infant when he or she was fretting and when not, to (b) the sum of the likelihoods of the same response under conditions of fretting and not fretting. Positive values indicated that the infant was more likely to be picked up or kissed when fretting or crying than when not distressed. Negative values indicated that the infant was less likely to be picked up when fretting or crying than when not. SAID scores at the 5 and 7 month visits were independent of the observed amount of infant fretting-crying ($r = .13$, n.s.). Maternal behavior during fret and cry at later visits from 9 to 13 months, however, was more easily influenced by the mobile and increasingly competent infant, resulting in a modest relation between SAID scores and the amount of fretting and crying ($r = .33, p < .01$).

Mothers also varied in their responses to infant transgressions after the onset of independent mobility when infants begin to explore in ways that could be messy, unhealthy, or dangerous to themselves, something, or someone else. Some mothers were likely to employ direct limit setting strategies (taking objects, removing the infant, blocking access, or delivering a command), whereas others were less direct and intervened infrequently or indirectly. Maternal limit setting as observed during the later visits from 9 to 13 months was independent of the total time of infants spent in transgression ($r = .03$, n.s.).

Among mothers of firstborns, 75% displayed consistency in maternal style from early to later visits (high SAID-low limit setting or low SAID-high limit setting). This style seemed to reflect a fundamental, though not intransigent, commitment to one or another child rearing philosophy as summarized in Fig. 3.2.

The behavior of mothers of secondborn infants seemed less clearly tied to the infant, perhaps more a function of these mothers' attempts to juggle the needs of two children. Compared to mothers of firstborns, mothers of secondborns spent about half the time in setting limits with their infants, and maternal behavior did not vary by reactivity group or by sex of the infant.

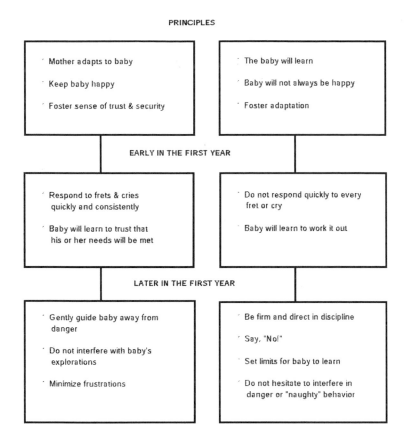

PRINCIPLES

Mother adapts to baby	The baby will learn
Keep baby happy	Baby will not always be happy
Foster sense of trust & security	Foster adaptation

EARLY IN THE FIRST YEAR

Respond to frets & cries quickly and consistently	Do not respond quickly to every fret or cry
Baby will learn to trust that his or her needs will be met	Baby will learn to work it out

LATER IN THE FIRST YEAR

Gently guide baby away from danger	Be firm and direct in discipline
Do not interfere with baby's explorations	Say, "No!"
Minimize frustrations	Set limits for baby to learn
	Do not hesitate to interfere in danger or "naughty" behavior

FIG. 3.2.   Schematic illustration of maternal styles over the first year.

Variation in maternal behavior in the home was associated with variation in 14 month inhibited behavior in the laboratory within temperament category and ordinal position. Firstborn, high reactive infants whose mothers displayed high SAID scores at 5 to 7 months and low limit setting at 9 to 13 months were more fearful than the infants whose mothers displayed the opposite profile. In other words, mothers who consistently protected their infants from minor stresses by permitting their infants to engage in transgressions without reproach or interference and by selectively attending to the frets and cries of their young infants, holding their child proportionately more often during crying than during periods of neutral or positive affect, appear to have made it more, rather than less, difficult for the firstborn, high reactive child to control the initial urge to retreat from strangers and unfamiliar events. Equally accepting mothers who did not differentially attend to fretting and crying and who set firm limits for their children, making mundane age appropriate demands for cleanliness or conformity, appeared to have helped their high reactive firstborns overcome their fearfulness.

As seen in Fig. 3.3, the contribution of maternal limit setting held for children of both ordinal positions. High reactive infants, both first and secondborn, whose mothers were firm and direct in their discipline, were significantly less inhibited at 14 months than high reactive infants whose mothers placed few or indirect limits on their transgression behaviors in the home.

The mechanism mediating the association of high maternal limit setting to low inhibition among high reactive infants may be related to the enhancement of regulatory abilities. Direct limit setting may promote regulation of the tendency to react to uncertainty with inhibition and distress for high reactive infants by providing them with experience in dealing with minor stresses in the comfort and security of their home.

To illustrate, imagine that an 11-month-old infant has crawled over to an inactive fireplace and begun to play with one of the dirty, sooty tools. The mother who sets direct limits may whisk the object away from the child and say, "No!" at the same time. Alternatively, she may whisk the child away from the fireplace. In either case, the child's activity has been interrupted abruptly, creating momentary frustration with which the child must cope. Soon he or she moves on to another activity, with or without prompting from mother, and the situation has been resolved.

Another child's mother, who is low in limit setting, will be much less direct. She may stoop down to the child's level, hold out her hand, and ask, "Do you want to give that to me?" She might also offer another object in exchange. This mother allows her child to decide when to surrender the object, and does not frustrate his or her agenda. It is important to note that she is neither ignoring the child nor disregarding safety. The activity is terminated without imposing direction on the child's behavior. This child does not experience frustration, but also does not experience its resolution.

It is evident that children of this age understand and can anticipate their mother's interventions when those interventions are clear and direct. Our videotapes captured several examples of children pausing to glance furtively over their shoulder while crawling toward a forbidden object, presumably to check, "Is the coast clear?" Therefore, when confronted with the challenges of an unfamiliar laboratory setting, children may be able to call upon those experiences. Our first child may have coping strategies with which to respond, but our second child, not having been afforded the opportunity to develop such strategies, may become distressed or turn to mother to manage the situation.

Independent investigations have yielded similar findings. Boys who displayed high negativity as infants were found to be less inhibited at age 3 years when their mothers were more intrusive and fathers less sensitive, with fa-

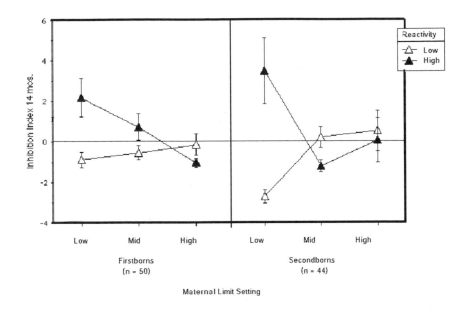

FIG. 3.3.   Level of inhibition at 14 months for children whose mothers demonstrated low (lowest quartile), moderate (midrange), or high (highest quartile) levels of limit setting behavior in the homes from 9 to 13 months by temperament group and birth order.

ther's behavior somewhat more predictive than mother's behavior, of 3 year inhibition (Park, Belsky, Putnam, & Crnic, 1997). Children with a fearful temperament and mothers whose behavior was judged to be overly solicitous were among the most inhibited children in a group of toddlers, with compromised security of the mother–child relationship suggested as a possible mediating mechanism (Rubin, Hastings, Stewart, & Henderson, 1997; Rubin, Stewart, & Coplan, 1995). In a series of longitudinal studies, the interaction of maternal control and child temperament has repeatedly been observed to influence the development of conscience and internal self control (Kochanska, 1995, 1997). Finally, Bates, Petit, Dodge, and Ridge (1998) replicated the observation that interactions of temperament and parental control predicted externalizing behavior across two independent samples.

Whereas these observations collectively suggest a moderating influence of maternal socialization behavior on the emergence of social and emotional behavior in accordance with the child's temperament, there are several caveats to be considered. First, variation in maternal discipline has been observed within a restricted range; there were no instances of abuse or neglect observed in our home visits. Therefore, our results must not be extrapolated linearly to ranges of disciplinary behavior—harsh discipline or abusive practices—that may be qualitatively different and may have different outcomes.

Terr (1990), for example, compared the fears held by children who had been victims of trauma with fears of a group of control children, and found qualitative differences. Although the numbers of children who were reported to be fearful of mundane items or events were similar in each group (except for fear of the dark), the traumatized children's fears were intense and terrifying. Just as we should be careful not to confuse terror with trepidation, we should also be careful about what we place on a limit setting continuum and what should be considered categorically different. Until the data suggest otherwise, we would be wise to err on the side of caution.

Second, although we found maternal behavior to account for a significant proportion of the variation in 14 month behavior for high reactive infants, additional variance was accounted for by examining the role of the siblings in the case of secondborns. Observed sibling intrusiveness—boisterous, annoying behavior—was associated with decreased infant inhibition at 14 months beyond the contributions of maternal limit setting. One might imagine a secondborn child experiencing the expectancy violations of the 14 month assessment, and, accustomed to an older sibling's intrusive and unpredictable behavior, thinking to herself, "This is nothing. You should see my big sister."

Hence, we are reminded that we seldom sample the salient sources of influence in any child's life exhaustively. Mothers, fathers, siblings, and daycare providers are the most frequently examined individuals, yet are only a limited selection of the members in the infant's ecological niche who contribute to the sum of the child's experiences.

A third caution lies in the cultural specificity of these data. Super and Harkness (1999) remind us that, "all developmental correlations found in a single cultural setting may be the result of a much larger matrix of practices and meanings that is characteristic only of that society.... [and] risk mistaking the structure of the environment for the structure of development" (p. 295). The relations we report may not hold for children or families in which the values for child rearing or stresses of daily life are different. Consider that parental preference for authoritarian discipline methods is associated with poor school performance in the United States, but better performance in Japan, presumably because the central role of interdependence in Japanese childrearing provides a different meaning for the same behavior in the two cultures (Hess & Azuma, 1990). Similarly, Chao (1994) has argued that the restrictive, controlling childrearing strategies of Chinese mothers do not yield the negative academic outcomes associated with such parenting in samples from the United States because these practices occur in the context of a cultural prescription defining concerned, caring parenting by restriction and control. In fact, it is entirely possible that temperaments in different ethnic or cultural groups may vary, not only for the beliefs that shape the development of children, but for the temperaments themselves that prevail in those groups (Kagan et al., 1994).

FUTURE DIRECTIONS

In sum, there is abundant evidence that the distinction between inhibited and uninhibited children first identified as high and low reactive infants is, at least in part, driven by biology. However, there is a growing body of literature indicating that this biological bias acts in the context of the environment, and observational studies have suggested specific ways in which aspects of the child's experience may interact with the initial temperamental bias to influence the development of social behavior.

There is much to be done. Continued exploration of the nature of the temperamental categories demands more sophisticated psychophysiological and genetic studies, along with a deep appreciation of the limits of those measures and the complexity of the organism. Similarly, continued exploration of the mechanisms of the experiential modification of temperamental bias requires us to go beyond traditional approaches designed to apportion the variance but not to explicate the complex interplay of child and environment. Toward this end, there is no substitute for observationally based, longitudinal studies on carefully specified populations.

Among those specified populations, more inclusive studies need to focus beyond white, healthy, middle-class samples. Temperamental differences no doubt contribute to differences in children's experiences of chronic and punctate stressors, such as the experience of harsh parental discipline, parental unemployment, death in the family, and perhaps even racism or poverty. Traditional risk-resiliency conceptualizations of temperaments as continuous dimensions are challenged by the observation that contextual demands may present one type of challenge to inhibited children and another type to their uninhibited peers. Clearly, further study is needed.

Examining temperamentally inhibited and uninhibited children out of context is a futile effort. Whether in a laboratory or naturalistic observation, the specificity of multiple contextual factors—setting, social demands, psychological relevance, type of participants, as well as age, gender, ordinal position, and history of the child—gives meaning to the data. Only by attending to and specifying those contextual features will that meaning become clear and capable of being built upon.

REFERENCES

Agee, J., & Huston, J. (Screenwriters). (1951). *The African Queen* [Film adapted from the novel by C. S. Forester]. Hollywood, CA: Twentieth Century Fox.

Arcus, D., Gardner, S., & Anderson, C. (1992, May). Infant reactivity, maternal style, and the development of inhibited and uninhibited behavioral profiles. Paper presented at the International Conference for Infant Studies, Miami.

Arcus, D., & Kagan, J. (1995a). Temperament and craniofacial variation in the first two years. *Child Development, 66,* 1529–1540.

Arcus, D., & Kagan, J. (1995b, March). Temperamental contributions to social behavior. Paper presented at the biennial meeting of the Society for Research in Child Development, Indianapolis.

Arcus, D., & McCartney, K. (1989). When baby makes four: Family influences on the stability of behavioral inhibition. In J. S. Reznick (Ed.), *Perspectives in behavioral inhibition* (pp. 197–218). Chicago: University of Chicago Press.

Bates, J., Petit, G., Dodge, K., & Ridge, B. (1998). Interaction of temperamental resistance to control and restrictive parenting in the development of externalizing behavior. *Developmental Psychology, 34,* 982–995.

Bell, R. Q., Weller, G., & Waldrop, M. F. (1971). Newborn and preschooler: Organization of behavior and relations between periods. *Monographs of the Society for Research in Child Development, 36* (1 and 2, Serial No. 142).

Bronson, G. (1972). Infants' reactions to unfamiliar persons and novel objects. *Monographs of the Society for Research in Child Development, 37* (Serial No. 148).

Calkins, S., Fox, N., & Marshall, T. R. (1996). Behavioral and physiological antecedants of inhibited and uninhibited behavior. *Child Development, 67,* 523–540.

Chao, R. K. (1994). Beyond parental control and authoritarian parenting style: Understanding Chinese parenting through the cultural notion of training. *Child Development, 65,* 1111–1119.

Cohen, S., Kaplan, J. R., Cunnick, J. E., Manuck, S. P., & Rabin, B. S. (1992). Chronic social stress, affiliation, and cellular immune response in nonhuman primates. *Psychological Science, 3,* 301–304.

Coster, W. (1986). *Aspects of voice and conversation in behaviorally inhibited and uninhibited children.* Unpublished doctoral dissertation, Harvard University.

Davidson, R. J. (1994). Temperament, affective style, and frontal lobe asymmetry. In G. P. Dawson & K. P. Fischer (Eds.), *Human behavior in the developing brain* (pp. 518–536). New York: Guilford Press.

de Lanerolle, N. C., & Lang, F. F. (1988). Functional neural pathways for vocalization in the domestic cat. In J. D. Newman (Ed.), *The physiological control of mammalian vocalization* (pp. 21–42). New York: Plenum.

Fox, N. A., Calkins, S. D., & Bell, M. A. (1994). Neural plasticity and development in the first two years of life. *Developmental Psychopathology, 23,* 233–240.

Garcia-Coll, C., Kagan, J., & Reznick, J. S. (1984). Behavioral inhibition in young children. *Child Development, 55,* 1005–1019.

Gersten, M. (1986). *The contribution of temperament to behavior in natural contexts.* Unpublished doctoral dissertation, Harvard University, Graduate School of Education.

Gersten, M. (1989). Behavioral inhibition in the classroom. In J. S. Reznick (Ed.), *Perspectives in behavioral inhibition.* (pp. 71–92). Chicago: University of Chicago Press.

Goldsmith, H. H., & Campos, J. J. (1990). The structure of temperamental fear and pleasure in infants. *Child Development, 61,* 1944–1964.

Hess, R. D., & Azuma, H. (1990). Cultural support for schooling: Contrasts between Japan and the United States. *Educational Researcher, 20,* 265–288.

Hitchcock, J., & Davis, M. (1986). Lesions of the amygdala, but not of the cerebellum or red nucleus, block conditioned fear as measured with the potentiated startle paradigm. *Behavioral Neuroscience, 100,* 11–22.

Jones, R. B., Mills, A. D., & Faure, J. M. (1991). Genetic and experiential manipulation of fear related behavior in Japanese quail chicks (Cortumix cotomix japonica). *Journal of Comparative Psychology, 105,* 15–24.

Jurgens, U. (1982). Amygdala vocalization pathways in the squirrel monkey. *Brain Research, 241,* 189–196.

Kagan, J. (1994). *Galen's prophecy.* New York: Basic.

Kagan, J., Arcus, D., Snidman, N., Wang, Y. F., Hendler, J., & Greene, S. (1994). Ease of arousal in infants: A cross-national comparison. *Developmental Psychology, 30,* 342–345.

Kagan, J., Reznick, J. S., & Snidman, N. (1987). The physiology and psychology of behavioral inhibition. *Child Development, 58,* 1459–1473.

Kagan, J., Reznick, J. S., & Snidman, N. (1988). Biological bases of childhood shyness. *Science, 240,* 167–171.

Kagan, J., & Snidman, N. (1991). Infant predictors of inhibited and uninhibited behavioral profiles. *Psychological Science, 2,* 40–44.

Kagan, J., Snidman, N., & Arcus, D. (1998). Childhood derivatives of infant reactivity. *Child Development, 69,* 1483–1493.

Kagan, J., Snidman, N., Julia-Sellers, M., Johnson, M. O. (1991). Temperament and allergic symptoms. *Psychosomatic Medicine, 53,* 332–340.

Kelley, A. E., Domesick, V. B., & Nauta, W. J. H. (1982). The amygdalostriatal projection in the rat: An anatomical study by anterograde and retrograde tracing techniques. *Neuroscience, 7,* 615–630.

Kochanska, G. (1995). Children's temperament, mothers' discipline, and security of attachment: Multiple pathways to emerging internalization. *Child Development, 66,* 597–615.

Kochanska, G. (1997). Multiple pathways to conscience for children with different temperaments: From toddlerhood to age 5. *Developmental Psychology, 33,* 228–240.

Mishkin, M., & Aggleton, J. (1981). Multiple functional contributions of the amygdala in the monkey. In Y. Ben-Ari (Ed.), *The Amygdaloid Complex, INSERM Symposium 20* (pp. 409–420). New York: Elsevier/North Holland.

Park, S. Y., Belsky, J., Putnam, S., & Crnic, K. (1997). Infant emotionality, parenting, and 3-year inhibition: Exploring stability and lawful discontinuity in a male sample. *Developmental Psychology, 33,* 218–227.

Reznick, J. S., Gibbons, J., Johnson, M. O., & McDonough, P. (1989). Behavioral inhibition in a normative sample. In J. S. Reznick (Ed.), *Perspectives on behavioral inhibition* (pp. 25–49). Chicago: University of Chicago Press.

Reznick, J. S., Kagan, J., Snidman, N., Gersten, M., Baak, K. & Rosenberg, A. (1986). Inhibited and uninhibited children: A follow-up study. *Child Development, 57,* 660–680.

Rimm-Kaufman, S. E. (1996). *Infant predictors of kindergarten behavior: The contribution of inhibited and uninhibited temperament types.* Unpublished doctoral dissertation, Harvard University, Cambridge, MA.

Rosenberg, A., & Kagan, J. (1987). Iris pigmentation and behavioral inhibition. *Developmental Psychobiology, 20,* 377–392.

Rothbart, M. K. (1989). Temperament and development. In G. A. Kohnstamm, J. E. Bates, & M. K. Rothbart (Eds.), *Temperament in Childhood* (pp. 59–76). Chichester: Wiley.

Rubin, K. H., Hastings, P. D., Stewart, S. L., & Henderson, H. A. (1997). The consistency and concomitants of inhibition: Some of the children, all of the time. *Child Development, 68,* 467–483

Rubin, K. H., Stewart, S. L., & Coplan, R. J. (1995). Social withdrawal in childhood: Conceptual and empirical perspectives. *Advances in Clinical Child Psychology, 17,* 157–196.

Scott, J. P., & Fuller, S. (1965). *Genetics and social behavior of the dog.* Chicago: University of Chicago Press.

Seifer, R., Sameroff, A., Barrett, L. C., & Krafchuk, E. (1994). Infant temperament measured by multiple observations and mother report. *Child Development, 65,* 1478–1490.

Snidman, N., Kagan, J., Riordan, L., & Shannon, D. (1995). Cardiac function and behavioral reactivity in infancy. *Psychophysiology, 31,* 199–207.

Super, C. M., & Harkness, S. (1999). The environment as culture in developmental research. In T. D. Wachs & S. L. Friedman (Eds.), *Measuring environment across the lifespan* (pp. 279–326). Washington, DC: American Psychological Association.

Takahashi, K. (1990). Are the key assumptions of the strange situation procedure universal? A view from Japanese research. *Human Development, 33,* 23–30.

Terr, L. (1990). *Too scared to cry.* New York: Basic.

Thomas, A., & Chess, S. (1977). *Temperament and Development.* New York: Bruner/ Mazel.

Thomas, A., Chess, S., & Birch, H. G. (1968). *Temperament and behavior disorders in children.* New York: New York University Press.

Thomas, A., Chess, S., Birch, H. G., Hertzig, M. E., & Korn, S. (1963). *Behavioral individuality in early childhood.* New York: New York University Press

Wachs, T. D., & Gandour, M. J. (1983). Temperament, environment, and six-month cognitive-intellectual development: A test of the organismic specificity hypothesis. *International Journal of Behavioral Development, 6,* 135–152.

Yang, R. K., & Halverson, C. F. (1976). A study of the inversion of intensity between newborn and preschool-age behavior. *Child Development, 47,* 350–359.

4 Temperamental Change, Parenting, and the Family Context

Charles F. Halverson
University of Georgia

James E. Deal
North Dakota State University

The focus of much temperament research has been on the description of individual differences at various points of time in infancy and childhood (e.g., see Goldsmith et al., 1987). When longitudinal data on temperament have been analyzed, the focus has been primarily on stability of measurement and secondarily on the links between early assessments of temperament and later measures of psychosocial functioning. Very few studies have examined whether and how temperament measures may change over childhood (see Matheny, 1984; Maziade, Cote, Bernier, Boutin, & Thivierge, 1989 for exceptions to this generalization). Very little is known about specific contextual factors that might influence temperamental change. Previous research suggests that long-standing environmental influences may be influential in changing temperamental dimensions, and that changes can also be directed by genes (i.e., maturation, see, for example, Matheny & Dolan, 1975). Basic data on change, however, are sparse. In this chapter we examine individual and group patterns of change in temperament for children who were aged 4 years at the beginning of our study and 7 years at the end. We then examine how individual change scores for one selected dimension of temperament (Persistence) are affected by variables reflecting parenting, marriage, and family contexts, and examine how change in Persistence is also moderated over time by changes in other temperament dimensions.

GROWTH MODELS IN DEVELOPMENTAL RESEARCH

Whereas it may seem axiomatic that the study of development should involve the study of processes of change over time, much of the work is concentrated on measures of children at single points in time or, at best correlates of measures across a few time periods. All too infrequent is an examination of some growth function of a phenomenon and its correlates (Willett, 1988; Wohwill, 1973). Three problems have inhibited such work in the past, two general problems and one specific to temperament research. The two general problems have been: (a) the difficulty in studying developmental phenomena over enough occasions required for estimation of growth functions, and (b) the lack of clarity about data analytic procedures needed to quantify growth in a systematic way. The third problem for temperament research is the theoretical notion that temperament should be stable (or it is not temperament). This assumption has led to an almost exclusive focus on stability (and much of interest has been found; see, e.g., Maziade et al., 1986 for a typical review). In recent years, however, people have become more aware that stability (same rank order over time) is conceptually independent of change over time (changes in mean level). There is no a priori reason that temperament dimensions cannot be examined for both stability and change. Further, researchers have come to appreciate that individual change cannot be captured by measures of mean change for a group.

THE ANALYSIS OF CHANGE

Our focus in this chapter is the examination of how change in temperament can itself be viewed as an individual difference measure, and how such measures of change can be linked to other developmental phenomena. Here we only briefly describe some of the approaches designed to quantify change over time.

Mostly used in past studies of change has been the analysis of variance (ANOVA). Typically, some version of repeated measures ANOVA is employed to assess equality of mean levels of a construct measured at two or more different time points. (We illustrate this approach with our data in a later section.) The ANOVA approach can, however, only test a general hypothesis about mean changes over time—individual patterns of change are obscured by this approach (see Burchinal & Appelbaum, 1991; Willett, 1988).

Fortunately, we now have more direct approaches that can be used to examine individual patterns of change across multiple time periods; generically they go by such names as individual growth modeling, latent growth curve modeling, hierarchical linear modeling (HLM) or random regression (see many references, e.g., Bryk & Raudenbush, 1987; Raudenbush, 1995; Willett, 1988; Willett & Sayer, 1994). For our chapter here we can briefly outline the approach: The same temperament measure is employed for each child at multiple intervals, for example, 4 or 5 yearly assessments (in our case, the Temperament Assessment Battery, TAB; Martin, 1994). For each child in our study, we performed an ordinary least squares regression where the vector of the temperament measure was the criterion and the vector for time (year or age) was the predictor. Two parameters were obtained for each child from this procedure: the slope and intercept (as in any regression model: $y = b_0 + b_1x_1$). This slope (b_1) quantifies the modeled rate of change across the yearly time points of the study. The intercept (b_0) is the modeled mean across the observations (beyond the scope of our presentation here is a discussion of the requirement to center the data so that time 0 is at the midpoint of first and last assessment). In this chapter we focus on the slope of the temperament scores that can describe increasing (positive slope) or decreasing (negative slope) scores for individuals as well as the magnitude of change (larger slopes indicate more change in the direction indicated).

In this chapter, two important features of our within-child regression procedure are noted. First, in our model we examined only the linear change parameter. More complex models can be devised that include polynomials with quadratic or cubic terms to examine more complex change curves (or even nonlinear models using exponential functions, if an examination of individual curves merits such models). For the initial investigation we chose the simplest linear change model as the most parsimonious model. The second point to note is that this modeling procedure is tolerant of missing data and minor variations in time of assessment. Because each regression is for an individual child, obviously there is no requirement that all children change the same way. There are rule-of-thumb lower boundaries for the reliable assessment of change. Willett (1988) recommends at least four time points to estimate relatively stable linear parameters. In this preliminary study we limited our sample to the 88 children with 4 years of complete data.

In summary, we examined individual changes in temperament as well as group change. We also focused on how family contextual variables may have influenced individual change in combination with within-individual changes in other temperament dimensions. We predicted that change in Persistence over time would be linked to Mothers' parenting and marriage variables and to changes in other temperament dimensions.

Method

Participants

In this chapter we focus on 88 children (45 boys and 43 girls) and their mothers who had complete data for the first four years of an ongoing longitudinal study. Target children averaged 4 years of age at the beginning of the study (range 3.5 to 4.5) and 7 years in the 4th year of the study. Families were recruited from preschools, day-care centers, and radio and newspaper announcements, and were paid for their participation. The sample was predominantly white and middle-class. All families were intact, with fathers employed full-time and mothers equally divided among full-time employment, part-time employment, and full-time homemaking. Families came into the laboratory each year and completed several videotaped interaction tasks involving family members. Mothers and fathers also completed questionnaires on the child, the family, and their parenting practices.

Measures

The assessment of temperament was done each year with the Temperament Assessment Battery (TAB), a 48-item questionnaire that measures five preschool dimensions with excellent psychometric properties. Table 4.1 summarizes the TAB dimensions.

Although we analyzed the change measures for all the TAB dimensions, for simplicity in presentation we focus on the predictors of change in one dimension—Persistence. We chose this dimension as a likely candidate for parental efforts aimed at increasing Persistence, because it is likely that they view Persistence as a basic skill for academic readiness and because in other research we are currently conducting we find TAB Persistence to be closely linked to our new measures of openness-intellect in 6- to 8-year-old children (Halverson & Havill, 1998). The items in the Persistence factor are summarized in Table 4.2

Family Measures.   We chose four measures that represented parenting, marriage, family functioning, and individual parent adjustment. We included

TABLE 4.1   Temperament Assessment Battery (TAB)

Parent Scoring

1. Negative Emotionality (alpha = .82)

   11 items depicting angry, moody, and difficult behavior at the high end of scale to easygoing, easy-to-manage behavior at the low end.

2. Social Inhibition (alpha = .86)

   10 items depicting shy, withdrawn behavior at the high end to relaxed, at-ease social behavior at the low end.

3. Activity Level (alpha = .79)

   9 items, high to low.

4. Adaptability (alpha = .68)

   8 items reflecting rapid, easy adjustment to new situations.

5. Persistence (alpha = .77)

   5 items (see next table)

TABLE 4.2   **Persistence Factor: TAB**

Item	
2:	When my child starts a project such as a model, puzzle, painting, he/she works at it for a long time.
20:	When learning a new physical skill (such as hopping, skating, bike riding), my child will spend long periods of time practicing.
27:	When a toy or game is difficult, my child will turn quickly to another activity (reverse scored).
32:	My child tends to give up when faced with a puzzle or a block structure which is difficult (reverse scored).
43:	My child seems highly motivated to learn new skills even if they are difficult for him/her.

Note. Average item-total correlation = .53. Average item intercorrelation = .40 (n = 887).

one summary measure that we devised to measure family risk. To keep the presentation simple, we focus here only on mother data (although we have father and observational data as well). The variables we used to measure family context are summarized in Table 4.3.

We chose to use year 1 measures only and consider them as predictors of change. (Other models are possible; e.g., using these measures as outcomes or creating change scores for them and linking family change with child change; but this is much beyond the space in the current chapter.

Results

First, we examine the group stabilities for these scales. We note that the stabilities are generally quite good. Figure 4.1 summarizes stability coefficients for parental ratings of the TAB scales over 1 , 2 , and 3 year periods. For three of the scales we obtained a straightforward simplex structure with stabilities declining in an orderly way as the retest interval extends from 1 to 3 years. For the Adaptability of Persistence scales, stability at the group level was fairly high for 2- and 3-year intervals. Figure 4.2 describes group stability as a function of age. For four of the five scales we obtained fairly dramatic 1-year differences between younger (4 to 5 years) and older children (7 to 8 years). In every case except for the Inhibition dimensions, the correlations were significantly higher for older children by z test (shown by asterisks on the figure).

Second, we present the typical change score analysis done with repeated measures ANOVA, based on our largest N for each year (includes siblings and many children with some missing data).

TABLE 4.3   Family Context Measures

Variable	Description
1. Good Parent Score:	Score based on cluster of positive parenting attributes identified by correlations of parent Q-sort of Block's (1980) childrearing practices report (CRPR) and expert consensus of good parenting practices (Q-sort correlations).
2. Marital Functioning:	Combination score based on the scoring of the Relationship Inventory (RI, Wampler & Powell, 1982) and the Dyadic Adjustment Scale (DAS, Sharpley & Cross, 1982, Spanier, 1976). Summed were Regard and Empathy scales for the RI and total scores for the DAS (alpha = .92).
3. Family Context:	Family functioning was measured by the sum of the adaptability and cohesion subscales from FACES II (Olsen, McCubbin, Larsen, Muxen, & Wilson, 1982) and the sum of 3 cohesion scales from the Family Environment Scale (FES, Moos & Moos, 1986; alpha = .85).
4. Parent Individual Adjustment:	We used the Global Severity Index of the Symptom Checklist 90 (SCL-90, Derogatis, 1977; alpha = .80).
5. Family Risk Index	A composite measure of family risk for husband and wife was obtained by summing extreme scores (no risk, some risk) across 10 areas of family functioning: Family self-report measures (FACES and FES), family observation measure (Georgia Family Q-sort), parenting self-report (Block), parenting observation measure, work satisfaction, parent individual adjustment, agreement (husband–wife agreement on FACES, FES, DAS, and RI), and parent education. For each of the 10 areas, a score in the lowest 25% was considered "risk" and assigned a risk score of 1, and a score in the highest 75% was assigned a risk score of 0. Thus risk scores could range from 1 to 10. The mean risk score for wives was 2.8 (SD = 2.0) in year 1. The range was 0 to 8 for wives. Wife and husband risk scores correlated .62 in year 1.

In each of these figures we see that the group data show considerable change with time. For Social Inhibition (see Fig. 4.3), there were orderly and linear decrements by age for both Fathers $F_{(3,264)} = 7.5, p < .001$, mean slope = $-.24$, and Mothers $F_{(3,252)} = 7.01, p, < .001$, mean slope = $-.24$. In each figure, significances for yearly comparisons are indicated by asterisks between years compared.

For Negative Emotionality (see Fig. 4.4), children rated by both parents showed an orderly decline [Fathers $F_{(3,249)} = 10.62, p < .001$, mean slope = $-.29$; Mothers $F_{(3,267)} = 12.60, p < .001$, mean slope = $-.36$]. Figure 4.5 summarizes the group change function for Activity Level. For both parents; Activity declined considerably, Fathers $F_{(3,255)} = 24.4, p < .001$, mean slope = $-.43$, Mothers $F_{(3,255)} = 8.99, p < .001$, mean slope = $-.27$). Figure 4.6 summarizes

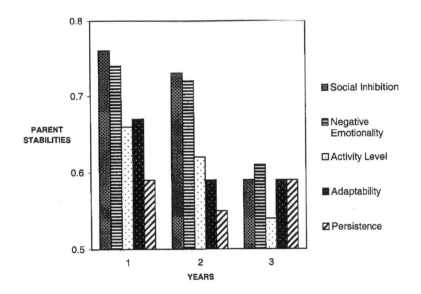

FIG. 4.1. Stabilities of parents' ratings of children's Social Inhibition, Negative Emotionality, Activity Level, Adaptability, and Persistence from 1 to 3 years' duration.

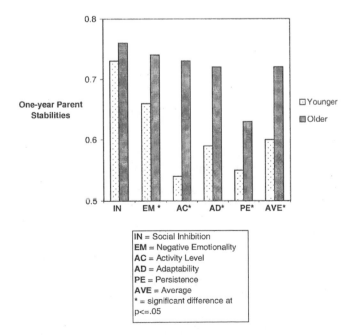

FIG. 4.2. One-year stabilities in temperament ratings for older and younger temperament groups.

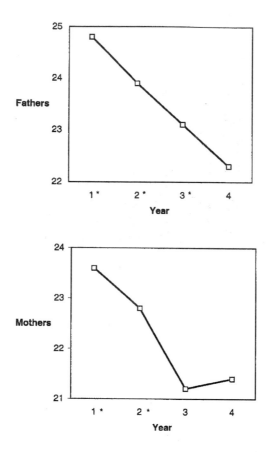

FIG. 4.3.   Mean-level changes in Social Inhibition over four waves.

the modest increases in Adaptability over 4 years for Fathers $F_{(3,255)} = 7.35, p <$ .001, mean slope $= +$ .22 and Mothers $F_{(3,255)} = 2.48, p < .06$, mean slope $= +$ .13). Finally in Fig. 4.7, we can see that ratings of Persistence increased for Fathers $F_{(3,211)} = 5.21, p < .001$, mean slope $= +$ .25) whereas ratings for Mothers indicated no group change in Persistence $F_{(3,261)} = 1.15$, ns, mean slope $= +$ .11. Obviously, we learn much about the general form of change for our longitudinal sample from the above mean analyses, but learn nothing about individual change or what might be associated with it. We want to emphasize here the logical and methodological independence of measures of individual change and group change. They are separate and one cannot be derived from the other, giving rise to the possibility that much new interesting and important information can be derived from the analysis of individual change scores.

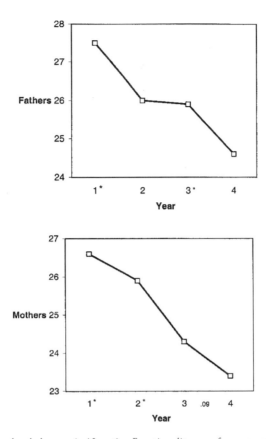

FIG. 4.4. Mean-level changes in Negative Emotionality over four waves.

INDIVIDUAL ANALYSIS OF CHANGE

First, we present the intercorrelations of the change scores for each of the temperament dimensions for mothers.

For illustrative purposes, we chose to demonstrate the analysis of change using mothers' ratings across four waves of our longitudinal data on temperament. We also demonstrate changes in teacher ratings although we don't analyze them further in this chapter. Moreover, we decided to simplify our analysis for this chapter by focusing on correlates of change in Persistence ratings over the four waves. First, As Table 4.4 indicates, changes in Persistence are linked in important ways to changes in other temperament dimensions: As Activity Level decreases, Persistence increases; as Adaptability increases, Persistence increases as well; and increases in Negative Emotionality are linked to

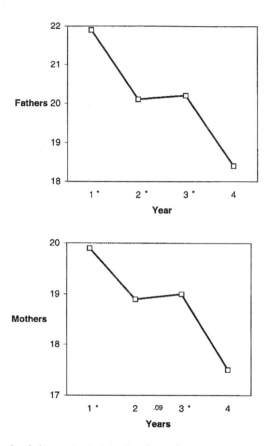

FIG. 4.5. Mean-level changes in Activity Level over four waves.

decreases in rated Persistence. Changes in teacher-rated Persistence show similar links to changes in rated Inhibition and Negative Emotionality. As both Inhibition and Emotionality increase, Task Persistence decreases. These data are interesting because different teachers provided data on temperament at each wave. Further, for Mothers' Persistence change scores, there were significant links to the change scores on Persistence for Fathers $r_{(88)} = .32$, $p < .05$ and Teachers $r_{(88)} = .26$, $p < .05$. These correlations lend support to the validity of our Persistence changes scores. Each source, mothers, fathers and teachers were assessing changes in Persistence in the same way. Next, we present the correlations of our family context variables with our selected change score, Persistence. First, to illustrate the variability in change, we present two figures of individual curves: for the total sample and, for illustrative purposes, a sample of 29 cases who did not change much over the 4 years.

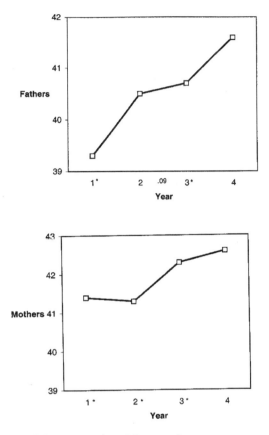

FIG. 4.6.   Mean-level changes in Adaptability over four waves.

Clearly, there is much variability in Persistence over time, both within and between children. For Fig. 4.8, the mean slope is .11, $SD = .08$, with slopes ranging from – .17 to + .22. There are increases (positive slopes) as well as decreases (negative slopes) and children who don't change much over the 4 years (shown in Fig. 4.9, the mean slope is – .01, $SD = .02$, with slopes ranging from – .04 to + .03). Because the Persistence scale could theoretically vary from 5 to 25, one can see that these changes over time are relatively small. Even though change was quite restricted, we obtained evidence that such change was reliable and orderly. As discussed earlier, the individual slopes can be used to assess the correlates of individual change. For our purposes we use family context variables at wave 1 to predict changes in temperamental Persistence over 4 years. These data are summarized in Table 4.5

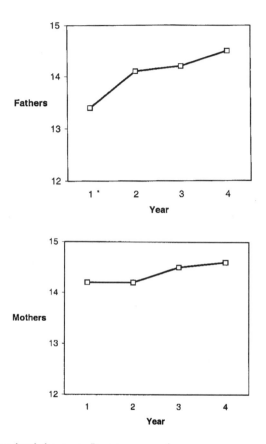

FIG. 4.7.   Mean-level changes in Persistence over four waves.

The correlations show clear and consistent links for maternal ratings of family context to individual change in Persistence over time. All of our family context dimensions were significantly linked to change in Persistence. Our measures of good parenting, positive marital and family functioning coupled with good parental psychological adjustment, all predicted increases in Persistence over time whereas our composite family risk score was related to a decreasing level of Persistence over time.

Combining Family and Temperament Change Data to Predict Changes in Persistence Over 4 Years

In this analysis we show how change in Persistence is related to both family context variables and changes in temperament over time. Basically we first en-

TABLE 4.4 Intercorrelations of Individual Change Scores Over 4 Years

Mothers	1	2	3	4	5
1. Activity change	–				
2. Adaptability change	– .40*	–			
3. Inhibition change	.03	– .01	–		
4. Negative Emotionality change	.02	– .30*	.22*	–	
5. Persistence change	– .34*	.37*	.01	– .22*	–
Teachers					
1. Inhibition change	–				
2. Negative Emotionality change	.14	–			
3. Task Persistence change	– .38*	– .40*			

Note. *p < .05

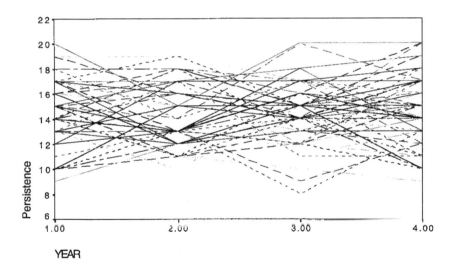

Fig. 4.8. Individual growth curves for Persistence over four waves.

tered the family change scores as a block and then entered the temperament change scores as a block, and assessed in a hierarchical analysis the separate contributions of both types of data: *within child* and *family context*. See Table 4.6.

The analysis was quite informative and powerful, accounting for 36% of the reliable change in Persistence over 4 years. Both *family context*—positive

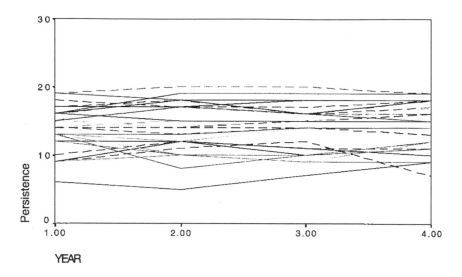

Fig. 4.9.   Individual growth curves for Persistence for children who changed little.

TABLE 4.5   Zero-Order Correlations of Changes in Persistence With Family Context Variables (Year 1)

	Persistence Slope
1. Good Parent	.35*
2. Marital Functioning	.35*
3. Family Functioning	.45*
4. Parent Adjustment	.28*
5. Risk Score	−.40*

Note. *$p < .05$

characterizations of family functioning in year 1 by mother, and changes in other temperament dimensions predicted change over time.

DISCUSSION

We have demonstrated in this chapter the necessity of assessing temperament change at the individual level. Because we used individual change scores we were able to demonstrate important predictors of individual change at both

TABLE 4.6   Multiple Regression Combining Temperament Change and Family Context to Predict Persistence

BLOCK 1	Family Variables	
Multiple R	.39	
R-square	.15	
$F(5, 71) =$	2.52, $p = .04$	
	Significant Beta's	Beta
	Family Functioning	.26
	Parenting	.22
BLOCK 2	**Adding Within Child Change**	
Multiple R	.60	
R-square	.36	
$F(9, 67) =$	4.12, $p = .0003$	
	Significant Beta's	Beta
	Family Functioning	.35
	Activity Slope	$-.30$
	Adaptability Slope	.23

the temperament and family level that would have been impossible and, therefore, overlooked with traditional group summaries of stability or change. Note that this is true, whether we use mean-level analysis or stability coefficients as is traditionally done. We agree completely with Rogosa (1995) that very limited information about change can be derived from the analyses of correlation or covariance matrices. In fact, the analysis of such matrices cannot support any strong inferences about individual stability or change. Many personality and temperament theorists have limited their analyses to group data similar to what was presented at the beginning of this chapter, and then go on to conclude that individual personality or temperament is stable (see for example, Costa & McCrae, 1992, 1994 for the typical treatment of group data with conclusions about stability at the individual level). The message is, however, you simply can't get from one to the other with only group data.

When individual estimates of change are available, we see stability at the group level and considerable change at the individual level over 4 years. Further, such individual change was predicted by changes in other temperament dimensions as well as by family context. We discovered a considerable amount of change in all the temperament dimensions that were assessed, and the findings of changes in one temperament dimension being linked to changes in other dimensions opens up the possibility of exploring how the changing structure of temperament is individually organized over time. For our young children, Activity, Inhibition, and Negative Emotionality declined over time whereas Adaptability and Persistence increased. Our analysis of Persistence change showed that increases in Adaptability and decreases in Activity were significantly linked to increases in Persistence over time for individual children. Some of this change may be genetic or maturational whereas other changes may be driven by contextual variables. We can't say much about the changes in internal structure of temperament over time except to say that such temperamental change is an important and independent predictor of changes in Persistence over time.

Family context also adds to the prediction of change in Persistence, especially our composite of family functioning and parenting competence. These domains of family context, along with changes in other temperament dimensions, account for a remarkable 36% of the individual change in Persistence. Such change is not noise or random fluctuations but appears instead to be directly tied to family context and temperamental change.

This chapter was intended to be illustrative of the utility of temperament change scores. Many other analyses could have been done but would have made this chapter too lengthy and complex. For this chapter, our analysis was limited to examining linear change. This was, for our purposes, probably a good strategy, because inspection of individual curves shows them to be mostly linear. There are analysis strategies that examine other nonlinear models of change, however, that could be applied to the data. Also, we predicted main effects only, that is, positive changes in Persistence. Because of our relatively small sample size, we could not analyze contextual predictors for groups characterized by decreases, increases, or no change. There may be different contextual predictors of these subgroups—a potentially powerful way to look at change when sample size allows it. We did not analyze by gender of child although one needs, with larger samples, to see if change is linked to the same or different variables in boys and girls. The issue of gender differences in change needs careful examination. For this chapter, we did not attempt to examine change in aggregate variables (e.g., aggregated across mother, father, teacher, observations, etc.). We found some convergence in change scores calculated separately, but have not, as yet, examined whether aggregation improves precision. There are also analyses that could be done linking change scores in family context variables with change scores in temperament. Such analyses would come close to a transactional perspective. For example, possible increases in positive family functioning could be linked to increases in positive temperamental traits and/or decreases in negative ones. Such analyses are important but beyond the scope of this chapter.

If investigators take the measurement of change in temperament or personality seriously (as we believe they should), the issue of intervals between data waves becomes important to consider in designing longitudinal studies (see Wohlwill, 1973 for a lucid description of those issues and recently, Cohen, 1991 and Collins & Graham, 1991). We have too often been fairly thoughtless in choice of intervals. A careful analysis of the phenomena we wish to characterize may suggest short intervals in some cases and longer ones in others. What is apparent is that a "one interval fits all" strategy may be wasteful or actually miss many important change phenomena.

When we began these analyses, we were skeptical about the possibility of finding any change in questionnaire data. We suspected all parents, teachers, and raters do some implicit "age correcting" as they rate items. Change might be better measured with less reactive measures. Even with this caveat, we found small, but reasonable and fairly robust measures of change. It is possible the items in the TAB are sufficiently behavioral and specific to allow the measure of true change with questionnaire items.

In summary, we have demonstrated in this chapter the feasibility and necessity for analyzing children's temperament ratings for individual level change. With these change scores we found important and reasonable predictors of increases in Persistence at both the temperament and family context level. Temperament changes are responsive to family-level measurement and we should continue to examine carefully the links between contextual variables, stability, and change characterized at the individual level. We have the methods. Let us begin.

ACKNOWLEDGMENTS

This research was supported by NIMH Grant 39899 to the first author.

REFERENCES

Block, J. (1980). *The childrearing practices Report* (CRPR): *A Q-set of Q items for description of parental socialization attitudes and values*. Berkeley: University of California, Institute of Human Development.

Bryk, A. S., & Raudenbush, S. W. (1987). Application of hierarchical linear models to assessing change. *Psychological Bulletin, 101,* 147–158.

Burchinal, M., & Applebaum, M. I. (1991). Estimating individual developmental functions: Methods and their assumptions. *Child Development, 62,* 23–43.

Cohen, P. (1991). A source of bias in longitudinal investigations of change. In L. M. Collins & J. L. Horn (Eds.), *Best methods for the analysis of change* (pp. 18–25). Washington, DC: American Psychological Association.

Collins, L. M., & Graham, J. W. (1991). Comments on a source of bias in longitudinal investigations of change. In L. M. Collins & J. L. Horn (Eds.), *Best methods for the analysis of change* (pp. 26–30). Washington, DC: American Psychological Association.

Costa, P. T., & McCrae, R. R. (1992). Trait psychology comes of age. In T. B. Sonderegger (Ed.), *Nebraska Symposium on Motivation: Psychology and aging, 39* (pp. 169–204). Lincoln: University of Nebraska Press.

Costa, P. T., & McCrae, R. R. (1994). Set like plaster? Evidence for the stability of adult personality. In T. Heatherton & J. Weinberger (Eds.), *Can personality change?* (pp. 21–40). Washington, DC: American Psychological Association.

Derogatis, L. R. (1977). *The SCL-90 manual I: Scoring administration and procedures for the SCL-90.* Baltimore, MD: Johns Hopkins University Press.

Goldsmith, H. H., Buss, A. H., Plomin, R., Rothbart, M. K., Thomas, A., Chess, S., Hinde, R. A., & McCall, R. B. (1987). Roundtable: What is temperament? Four approaches. *Child Development, 58,* 505–529.

Halverson, C. F., & Havill, V. (1998). *The development of the inventory of child individual differences.* Unpublished manuscript, University of Georgia.

Martin, R. P. (1994). *The temperament assessment battery.* Athens, GA: Developmental Metrics.

Matheny, A. P. (1984). Toddler temperament: Stability across settings and over ages. *Child Development,* 1200–1211.

Matheny, A. P., & Dolan, A. B. (1975). Persons, situations, and time: A genetic view of behavioral change in children. *Journal of Personality and Social Psychology, 32,* 1106–1110.

Maziade, M., Caperaa, P., Laplante, B., & Boudreault, M. (1986). Value of difficult temperament among 7-year-olds in the general population for predicting psychiatric diagnosis at age 12. *Annual Progress in Child Psychiatry and Child Development,* 397–403.

Maziade, M., Cote, R., Bernier, H., Boutin, H., & Thivierge, J. (1989). Significance of extreme temperament in infancy for clinical status in preschool years: II. Patterns of temperament change and implications for the appearance of disorders. *British Journal of Psychiatry, 154,* 544–551.

Moos, R. H., & Moos, B. S. (1986). *Family environment scale manual* (2nd ed.). Palo Alto, CA: Consulting Psychologists Press.

Olsen, D., McCubbin, H., Larsen, A., Muxen, M., & Wilson, M. (1982). *Family inventories.* St. Paul, MN: Family Social Science.

Raudenbush, S. W. (1995). Hierarchical linear models to study the effects of context on development. In J. M. Gottman (Ed.), *The analysis of change* (pp. 165–202). Mahwah, NJ: Lawrence Erlbaum Associates.

Rogosa, D. (1995). Myths and methods: Myths about longitudinal research plus supplemental questions. In J. M. Gottman (Ed.), *The analysis of change* (pp. 3–66). Mahwah, NJ: Lawrence Erlbaum Associates.

Sharpley, C., & Cross, D. (1982). A psychometric evaluation of the Spanier dyadic adjustment scale. *Journal of Marriage and the Family, 44,* 739–742.

Spanier, G. B. (1976). Measuring dyadic adjustment. *Journal of Marriage and the Family, 38,* 15–28.

Wampler, K. S., & Powell, G. (1982). The Barrett-Lennard relationship inventory as a measure of marital satisfaction. *Family Relations, 31,* 139–145.

Willett, J. B. (1988). Questions and answers in the measurement of change. In E. Z. Rothkopf (Ed.), *Review of research in education* (vol. 15, pp. 345–422). Washington, DC: American Educational Research Association.

Willett, J. B., & Sayer, A. G. (1994). Using covariance structure analysis to detect correlates and predictors of individual change over time. *Psychological Bulletin, 116,* 363–381.

Wohlwill, J. F. (1973). *The study of behavioral development.* New York: Academic Press.

5 Temperament and Context: Correlates of Home Environment With Temperament Continuity and Change, Newborn to 30 Months

Adam P. Matheny, Jr.
Kay Phillips
Department of Pediatrics
School of Medicine
University of Louisville, KY

Even though theoretical statements regarding infant temperament dwell on individual differences, the contributions of environmental contexts should not be regarded as an irrelevant issue. Items for temperament questionnaires are almost always worded with social and physical environments explicitly stated as settings within which a temperament characteristic is to be rated. Moreover, social contexts such as family or school are explicit locales for the application of a variety of questionnaires. Laboratory-based observations also have specific situational contexts that may produce situational effects even though individual differences of temperament will presumably become salient across situations (Phillips & Matheny, 1997). Although we consider that temperament characteristics have the attributes of traits because the characteristics are somewhat stable across contexts and time (Matheny, Wilson, & Nuss, 1984), the search for context-free temperament may lead to the neglect of identifying aspects of temperament associated with or dependent on contexts.

Research on the associations between contexts and temperament has shown that both broad and specific (usually social) measures of context are associated with temperament for different ages of infancy, for changes in temperament, and for the functional concept of goodness of fit. Broad measures, such as socioeconomic status (SES), race, and ethnicity have been related to differences among group means for temperament characteristics, patterns among temperament characteristics, and, by inference, differences in childrearing practices and cultural expectations (e.g., Fullard, Simeonsson, & Huntington, 1989; Super & Harkness, 1986). The largest body of literature concerns the relations between infant temperament and the social environment, including parents, siblings, and unfamiliar persons (e.g., Kohnstamm, Bates, & Rothbart, 1989). As discussed by Rothbart (1989), temperament characteristics such as sociability, behavioral inhibition, and approach–withdrawal may be particularly germane to the child's social interactions. Nevertheless, all temperament characteristics may play a role in a transactional social process by which child temperament may influence, as well as be influenced by, the social behavior of others. The degree to which this social equation is in or out of balance is central to the concept of goodness of fit (Thomas & Chess, 1977).

PHYSICAL ENVIRONMENT AND TEMPERAMENT

Although it may be self-evident that a child's temperament plays out on a stage populated with other actors who have their own roles, the physical environment of the stage—props and all—contributes to the total effect. Wachs (1979, 1989; Wachs, Francis, & McQuiston, 1979) has developed a framework for isolating those specific features (the microenvironment) of the physical (and social) environment that may contribute to infant development. This framework was suggested by a broad hypothesis, the environmental specificity hypothesis (Hunt, 1979; Wachs & Gruen, 1982) that narrowed environmental considerations to specific relations between specific features of the environment and specific features of child development.

In general, the relevance of the social environment to temperament has received considerably more attention than that paid to contextual measures. However, contextual measures are potentially less subject to the immediate influences of persons, especially the child. Although measures such as socioeconomic status, culture, and ethnicity are insensitive to immediate social influences, these serve as proxy measures that suggest, but do not demonstrate, specific environmental contexts associated with temperament. Wachs (1988) proposed that specific measures of household features such as number of siblings, rooms-to-persons ratio, and household noise may represent contextual variables less influenced by infant temperament. To document this proposal, Wachs showed that several directly observed features of 12-month-old infants' households were associated with maternal ratings of toddler temperament obtained from the Toddler Temperament Scale (TTS; Fullard, McDevitt, & Carey, 1984). Significant correlations between household features and toddler temperament ranged from 0.18 to 0.26, and showed, for example, that toddlers living in homes where there were more siblings were rated as less approachable, less adaptable, and more intense. In addition, a lower rooms-to-persons ratio (i.e., a more crowded household) was related to toddlers' being rated as less approachable, less adaptable, and having a more negative mood. Wachs further suggested that there could be a direct relation between crowding and less desirable temperamental qualities.

Matheny, Wilson, & Thoben (1987) investigated relations between features of the physical environment and characteristics of toddler temperament. They obtained factor scores for clusters of items rated during direct observation of the households of research participants. These household factor scores, as well as factor scores representing measures of toddler temperament and mother temperament/personality, were examined for their contribution to the prediction of toddler temperament measures by the TTS at 12, 18, and 24 months. Hierarchical regression analyses indicated that at 18 and 24 months, a Noise-confusion factor, represented by items developed by Wachs (1979), was associated with a Temperament factor after the effects of toddler and mother characteristics had been accounted for. The Temperament factor, representing the tractability of a toddler, was composed of ratings of adaptability, mood, intensity, activity, and approach–withdrawal. At 18 and 24 months, toddlers rated as less tractable lived in households rated as noisier and more disorganized (partial rs of – .30 and – .23, respectively).

These two studies (Matheny et al., 1987; Wachs, 1988), in combination, suggest that three aspects of the home environment (number of siblings, rooms-to-persons ratio, and noise-confusion) are correlates of characteristics of infant temperament. Moreover, there may be sex differences for these associations between infants' household environments and infants' temperament in view of the fact that variations of these same aspects of the household have been associated with individual differences among boys' development of cognition and temperament (Wachs, 1992). One methodological problem for studies relating context to infant temperament is that the ratings of infant temperament were made by the infants' mothers. Therefore, there is a potential confound of maternal characteristics with her contributions to infant temperament ratings and her organization or management of the household. This potential confound can be alleviated, of course, when temperament ratings are obtained from trained observers and infants are observed within contexts other than the home.

One set of contextual measures potentially less influenced by the mother (or infant) can be obtained within laboratory settings which, although designed for infants in general, are not arranged or immediately modified according to the requirements of individual parents and their infants. As one possible setting, the laboratory-based ratings of infant behaviors taking place during standardized activities within a playroom at the Louisville Twin Study are neither dependent on mothers' ratings nor largely subject to mothers' organization of the environment (Matheny, 1991b). Within this playroom setting, previous research has shown that ratings of Emotional Tone or emotionality is a core feature of infant temperament and is linked with emotionality as rated within other laboratory-based contexts (e.g., Bayley testing) as well as ratings from questionnaires completed by infants' parents (Matheny, Wilson, & Nuss, 1984).

Another limitation of the studies of Matheny et al. (1987) and Wachs (1988) was the relatively limited age span (12 to 24 months) of the toddlers' assessments. Clearly, the hypothesis regarding environmental specificity is implicitly developmental; specific features of the environment may be related to specific features of the child at one age and not another. Therefore, further elaboration of the hypothesis leads to consideration of wider spans of time and longitudinal changes within the wider spans.

A LONGITUDINAL PERSPECTIVE: AN EXPLORATORY STUDY

As a means for examining specific aspects of the infant's physical environment that potentially correlate with infant temperament for several ages and that are not dependent on parental reports of temperament, we elected to focus on Emotional Tone (emotionality). Emotionality rated in a playroom setting was the dependent temperament measure. The playroom setting incorporated a wide range of ecologically valid activities for infants/toddlers, provided a prolonged time period for sampling infant behaviors, and was potentially less influenced by the presence of the mother who was absent during prolonged periods of playroom activities. The independent measures of primary interest included two measures of the home environment: rooms-to-persons ratio and noise-confusion. Ratings of Emotional Tone obtained during assessment of physical stature and Bayley testing were also included as predictors because these two contexts could potentially evoke emotional states that could carry over to emotionality assessed in the playroom at the same research center on the same day. Finally, two measures obtained within the playroom were added as independent variables because the two measures (Social Orientation to the Staff and Attentiveness) could help to establish if interactions among measures of the infant's physical environment and measures of infant temperament not directly rated for emotionality would contribute to the prediction of emotionality. For example, Wachs (1988) found that 12-month-old infants from homes with a higher rooms-to-persons ratio were more sociable and more adaptable, as well as more positive in mood. Also, one might expect that noise-confusion would be associated with infant attentiveness. In view of the fact that playroom ratings of infants' emotionality, sociability to staff, and attentiveness have been found to be intercorrelated (Matheny, Wilson, & Nuss, 1984), it is also likely that the prediction of playroom emotionality will be improved by including for analyses the interactions between rooms-to-persons ratio and sociability to staff, and the interactions between noise-confusion and attentiveness.

Although this longitudinal study was exploratory in nature, previous studies led to two tentative predictions: First, infants from households with lower rooms-to-persons ratio and with greater noise-confusion will be more emotionally negative; second, the relation between the infants' home environmental measures and emotionality will be especially manifest for boys. Two additional tentative predictions were afforded by the project being longitudinal: First, infants who become more emotionally negative from one age to the next will be from households with lower rooms-to-persons ratio and with greater noise-confusion; second, the relation between the infants' home environmental measures and change of emotionality from one age to the next will be especially manifest for boys.

Longitudinal Sample and Assessments

The sample of infants was drawn from the population of MZ (monozygotic) and DZ (dizygotic) twins followed longitudinally by the Louisville Twin Study. Because both twins within a pair share the same home environment, there is a lack of independence for half of the sample's measures of home environments. Therefore, only one twin from each pair of MZ and DZ twins was selected so that each household was represented by but one infant. Additional constraints on selecting the longitudinal sample were the following: Infants were assessed as neonates during the lying-in-period in the hospital after delivery; infants had complete laboratory-based assessments at 6, 12, 18, 24, and 30 months; and infants' mothers had completed a questionnaire developed to measure household noise, hubbub, and disorganization. The final sample consisted of 58 girls and 60 boys. The families were represented by mothers with education ranging from 10 to 20 years ($M = 13.9$, $SD = 2.5$). Socioeconomic status, measured by the Duncan Index (Reiss, 1961) for the head of household ranged from unskilled laborers to professionals such as attorneys, and had a mean of 52 ($SD = 28.2$). This mean is within a 10-point range representing a wide variety of skilled crafts, office workers, sales clerks, and salaried managers of small businesses. Differences between either the socioeconomic status or maternal education for the girls' and boys' families were not significant for means and variances.

Neonatal Assessments

The detailed procedures for the neonatal assessment have been described elsewhere (Riese, 1983). Neonates were seen between the 1st and 4th day of life unless medical complications occurred. If there were complications then the neonate was seen shortly before discharge from hospital. The assessment sequence took place during an entire metabolic cycle of about 3 hours representing an interval from one feeding to the next. A series of ratings on 5-point scales were composited to yield measures of six categories of behavior.

1. Irritability—sum of ratings of irritability that occurred spontaneously and from all stimulation;

2. Resistance to soothing—sum of ratings of soothability after stimulation or spontaneous irritability;

3. Reactivity—sum of ratings of orienting to visual and auditory stimuli;

4. Activity awake—sum of ratings of large and small body movements;

5. Activity asleep—same as 4 but during sleep;

6. Reinforcement value—a single summary rating of the effect of the neonate's behavior on the attitude of the examiner to the neonate.

The interrater reliabilities for these six categories ranged from 0.79 to 0.99. Differences between boys' and girls' neonatal ratings were not significant for means and variances.

Laboratory Assessment

The standardized procedures, including the sequence of videotaped play activities, the toys used, and rating scales may be found in Matheny (1991b). The measures obtained during a laboratory visit consisted of the following: ratings during a brief warm-up period, after which mother left both twins alone with staff member; subsequent ratings during a solo episode with the staff engaged with each twin while the co-twin, accompanied by the mother, was taken for Bayley testing; ratings of infant behavior during Bayley testing obtained by the Infant Behavior Record (IBR; Bayley, 1969); and ratings of infant behavior during assessments of physical stature, which required infants to be somewhat restrained while head circumference, weight, and recumbent length were being measured. The primary ratings from the playroom activities were a sum of ratings for a series of twenty 2-minute periods spanning the entire playroom activities. The aggregate scores represented Emotional Tone, Activity Level, Attentiveness, and Social Orientation to Staff. To these four scores were added Emotional Tone rated during physical measures, and Emotional Tone rated during Bayley testing. Thus, at each age the laboratory assessment was represented by six scores, all of which have figured prominently in laboratory assessments of temperament. Interrater reliabilities for these measures have varied somewhat by age but most reliability coefficients have been in the range from 0.70 to 0.95. Differences between boys' and girls' means and variances for all of the laboratory measures were not significant except that at 12 months, the boys' mean for Emotional Tone-Playroom was significantly higher than the girls' mean (boys: $M = 5.00$; girls: $M = 4.68$).

Rooms-to-Persons Ratio.   The number of persons living within a household was obtained from parents during interviews. The number of rooms within a household was obtained from visits made to the household or from interviews. The rooms-to-persons ratio was obtained by dividing the number of rooms by the number of persons within a household. The ratios obtained for households of boys and girls were not significantly different for means and variances.

CHAOS Questionnaire.   The initial research establishing the importance of household noise and confusion to infant temperament was based on ratings made during visits to infants' households (Matheny, Wilson, & Thoben, 1987; Wachs, 1988). Given the time and costs to be allocated to home visits for a large number of families, construction of a low-cost method to measure physical features of the household was initiated. Our approach was to create a short questionnaire that obtained parental perceptions of the household characteristics of noise, confusion, clutter, hubbub, and disorganization. The final version of the questionnaire, the Confusion, Hubbub, and Order Scale or CHAOS, included 15 items to be endorsed by a true–false response format that yielded a single score. Examples of items are the following: (Item 1) There is very little commotion in our home; (Item 2) We can usually find things when we need them; (Item 10) Our home is a good place to relax; and (Item 14) The atmosphere in our home is calm. The true or false responses were scored so that a higher score represented more chaotic, disorganized, and noisy home settings. A more complete description of CHAOS was provided by Matheny, Wachs, Ludwig, and Phillips (1995) who showed that CHAOS scores had moderate-level correlations with specific aspects of homes directly assessed during visits by trained raters. For example, CHAOS scores correlated with number of siblings ($r = 0.55$), noise ratings ($r = 0.31$), noise level measured by a sound pressure meter ($r = 0.34$), and rooms-to-persons ratio ($r = -0.33$). CHAOS scores used for this study were obtained from questionnaires provided when infants were, on average, about 12 months old. A subsample of mothers who completed two CHAOS questionnaires with a 12-month interval between the initial and subsequent questionnaires provided a test-retest stability correlation of 0.74. Coefficient alpha for CHAOS was 0.79. The CHAOS scores obtained for boys' homes and girls' homes were not significantly different for either means or variances.

Analyses

Two large sets of analyses were conducted. The first sought for the predictors of emotionality at each age. The second sought for the predictors of change for emotionality from one age to the next.

Emotionality at Each Age.

Emotional Tone as represented by the playroom ratings was the single predicted variable at each age. The methodological approach was to introduce antecedent measures of infant temperament and household-context measures as potentially independent predictors contributing to the multiple regression analyses. Because the sample of infants was followed longitudinally, the multiple regression analyses were applied as a series of "platforms" so that Emotional Tone-Playroom at any age, 6 months and older, was forced into the regression as the initial variable for predicting Emotional Tone-Playroom at the following age. This analytic approach was based on a rationale that the developmental history of emotionality at any age was at least partially founded on the antecedent predictors that converged on Emotional Tone-Playroom at the nearest preceding age. For example, if all six measures of the neonate were significantly entered in the multiple regression analyses and thereby became multiple predictors of Emotional Tone-Playroom at 6 months, Emotional Tone-Playroom at 6 months became a proxy for these six measures and was forced to enter first into the multiple regression analyses for predicting Emotional Tone-Playroom at 12 months. After Emotional Tone-Playroom at one age was forced to be entered first into the multiple regression analysis predicting Emotional Tone-Playroom at the next age, all other independent measures were entered with no preset order of entry. Entry of these measures continued until no additional measure was found to make a significant ($p < .05$) contribution to the set of multiple predictors.

Forcing the entry of Emotional Tone-Playroom also had the virtue of removing the common variance shared by all other measures with Emotional Tone-Playroom. In effect, the common variance largely represented the temperament trait of emotionality. Once this was removed, the residualized scores for other measures had no overlap with the temperament trait of emotionality as measured in the context of the playroom. As the analyses show, this standard procedure for forced entry of Emotional Tone-Playroom was not necessary for most ages because Emotional-Tone Playroom would have been entered first into the regression anyway.

Emotionality Change for Adjacent Ages.   The second large set of analyses determined, by multiple regression analysis, the contributions of physical context measures and temperament measures to change in Emotional Tone rated in the playroom from one age to the next. There were four analyses—6 to 12 months, 12 to 18 months, 18 to 24 months, and 24 to 30 months—performed for girls and four analyses of the same type performed for boys. For these analyses, Emotional Tone in the playroom at one age also was forced to enter first into the multiple regression analysis for predicting change in Emotional Tone-Playroom from this age to the next age.

Results

Emotionality at Each Age

Table 5.1 shows the results from the multiple regression analyses for predicting Emotional Tone-Playroom at 6, 9, 12, 18, 24, and 30 months. An overview of the predictors for all of the ages indicates that the longitudinal pattern was not similar for girls and boys; therefore, the results are described separately.

Girls.   None of the measures of the neonate, home environment, and girl's temperament at 6 or 12 months were significant predictors of Emotional Tone in the playroom at 6 or 12 months. At 18 months, girls' Emotional Tone in the playroom at 12 months and two sociability measures— Orientation to the Staff at 6 and 12 months—were entered as significant predictors. Girls who were more emotionally positive at 12 months and were more socially oriented to staff members at 6 and 12 months were more emotionally positive at 18 months.

At 18 months, Emotional Tone-Playroom at 12 months followed by Orientation to Staff at 6 months and then 12 months provided a multiple *R* of .61 with Emotional Tone-Playroom at 18 months. Two of the measures had positive partial correlations, a girl infant who was more emotionally positive in the playroom at 12 months and was more socially oriented to staff members at 6 months was more emotionally positive in the playroom at 18 months.

Emotional Tone-Playroom at 24 months was the first instance for which physical context measures significantly contributed to the multiple set of predictors. The Rooms-to-Persons ratio and the CHAOS measure were entered as predictors but the sign of partial correlation was opposite from what would be expected intuitively. The results showed that girls who were more emotionally positive in the playroom at 24 months were more likely to be from homes that were more crowded and tumultuous.

Finally, at 30 months, in addition to the forced predictor of Emotional Tone-Playroom at 24 months, Emotional Tone during physical measures at 6

TABLE 5.1 Multiple Regression Analyses for Prediction of Emotional Tone-Playroom at 6, 12, 18, 24, and 30 Months

AGE	GIRLS			BOYS		
	Predictor	Part. r	Mult. R	Predictor	Part. r	Mult. R
6 months	None			CHAOS	-.46	.46
				Neo. Irrit.	.28	.52
12 months	Emot.Tone-Play (6 months)	.02	.02 F	Emot.Tone-Play (6 months)	.15	.15 F
				Neo. Irrit.	-.42	.44
18 months	Emot.Tone-Play (12 months)	.42	.42 F	Emot.Tone-Play (12 months)	.23	.23 F
	Orient. Staff (6 months)	.41	.56	CHAOS	-.34	.41
	Orient. Staff (12 months)	-.29	.61	Orient. Staff (12 months)	.28	.48
				Emot.Tone-Phys. Meas. (12 months)	.28	.54
24 months	Emot.Tone-Play (18 months)	.57	.57 F	Emot.Tone-Play (18 months)	.67	.67 F
	Ratio: Rm/Per.	-.30	.62	Emot.Tone-IBR (18 months)	.43	.74
	CHAOS	.29	.66	Attentive (12 months)	.27	.76
	Orient. Staff (12 months)	-.26	.69			
30 months	Emot.Tone-Phys. Meas. (6 months)	.38	.38 F	Emot.Tone-Play (24 months)	.70	.70 F
	Emot.Tone-Phys. Meas. (6 months)	.35	.50	Orient. Staff (18 months)	.47	.77
	Orient. Staff (6 months)	-.27	.55			

Note. F denotes a predictor forced to enter the multiple regression analysis. partial $r \geq .26$, significant $p \leq .05$.

months and Orientation to Staff at 6 months were entered as significant predictors. The evidence that Orientation to Staff at 6 months is negatively correlated with Emotional Tone-Playroom at 30 months is perplexing. It could
be an anomalous finding except that a similar association was found for the
negative correlations between Orientation to Staff at 12 months with Emotional Tone-Playroom at 18 and 24 months, respectively.

All analyses were examined for potential interactions among predictors at
every age. None were found.

Boys.   Boys' Emotional Tone in the playroom at 6 months was predicted by two measures: CHAOS, and Irritability rated from the neonatal assessment. Boys were more emotionally positive at 6 months when they lived
in a less tumultuous home, and when they were more irritable as neonates. It
should be noted that Riese (1983) has suggested that more irritable neonates
may be more mature or more likely to evoke interactions with parents.

At 12 months, Irritability of the neonate made a significant contribution
to the multiple regression after Emotional Tone-Playroom at 6 months had
been forced as an entry; however, at this age, the more irritable boy neonate
was less emotionally positive. This developmental "inversion" may represent
variations of boys' maturation in terms of "catch-up" for subpopulations of
boys. It should be noted that Emotional Tone-Playroom at 6 months was not
a significant predictor.

Emotional Tone-Playroom at 12 months was also not a significant predictor of Emotional Tone-Playroom at 18 months, but after its forced entry,
CHAOS, Orientation to the Staff at 12 months, and Emotional Tone during
physical measures at 12 months made significant contributions as predictors.
In general, boys who were more emotionally positive in the playroom at 18
months were from less tumultuous homes, and were more emotionally positive during assessments of physical stature at 12 months.

Emotional Tone-Playroom at 18 months accounted for the greater proportion of the variance of Emotion Tone-Playroom at 24 months. After its forced
entry, Emotional Tone rated during mental testing at 18 months and Attentiveness in the playroom at 12 months contributed significantly to the multiple regression. Boys who were more emotionally positive at 18 months in the
playroom and during mental testing, and who were more attentive in the
playroom at 12 months, were more emotionally positive in the playroom at
24 months.

The greatest proportion of the variance of Emotional Tone-Playroom at 30
months was accounted for by the same measure at 24 months. Additional contributions were made by Orientation to Staff at 24 months and Attentiveness
in the playroom at 6 months. Boys at 24 months who were more emotionally
positive and more socially oriented to the staff, and who were more attentive in
the playroom at 6 months were more emotionally positive in the playroom at
30 months. No significant interactions were found at any age.

Emotionality Change

Table 5.2 shows the results from the multiple regression analyses for predicting change in Emotional Tone-Playroom at the following adjacent ages: 6 to 12 months, 12 to 18 months, 18 to 24 months, and 24 to 30 months. Again, analyses were made separately for girls and boys. As noted for previous analyses, no significant interactions were detected.

Girls.   The entry of Emotional Tone-Playroom at 6 months was the only contributor to girls' change in the measure from 6 to 12 months. The negative correlation between Emotional Tone-Playroom at 6 months and the change from 6 to 12 months was expected for this and following intervals (for girls and boys) because if there is a change, the lowest ratings at 6 months were more likely to increase at the next age and the highest ratings at 6 months were more likely to decrease.

From 12 to 18 months, measures of Orientation to Staff at 6 months and 12 months contributed positively and negatively respectively, to the prediction of change. Girls who were more socially oriented to the staff at 6 months were likely to become more emotionally positive in the playroom from 12 to 18 months. Girls who were more socially oriented to the staff at 12 months were likely to show the reverse.

For the interval from 18 to 24 months, two measures of physical context—Rooms-to-Persons ratio, and CHAOS—provided significant predictors of change, but the predictive correlations were positive. Girls who lived in more crowded and more tumultuous homes were likely to become more emotionally positive in the playroom from 18 to 24 months. An additional contribution was made by the measure Orientation to Staff at 12 months in that girls who were less oriented to the staff at 12 months became more emotionally positive in the playroom from 18 to 24 months.

During the final interval from 24 to 30 months, girls who had been rated as more emotionally positive during physical measures at 6 months and less socially oriented to the staff at 6 months were more likely to become more emotionally positive in the playroom from 24 to 30 months.

Boys.   For change in Emotional Tone-Playroom from 6 to 12 months, boys who had been rated as more irritable as neonates and who were from more tumultuous homes were likely to become more emotionally negative.

During the interval from 12 to 18 months, four measures in addition to Emotional Tone-Playroom significantly contributed to the multiple regression. Boys who became more emotionally positive in the playroom were more attentive in the playroom at 6 months, were from less crowded homes, were more oriented to the staff, and were more emotionally positive during physical measures at 12 months.

TABLE 5.2 Multiple Regression Analyses for Prediction of Change in Emotional Tone-Playroom for 6–12, 12–18, 18–24, and 24–30 Months

AGE	GIRLS			BOYS		
	Predictor	Part. r	Mult. R	Predictor	Part. r	Mult. R
6 to 12 months	Emot.Tone-Play (6 months)	-.51	.51 F	Emot.Tone-Play (6 months)	-.40	-.40 F
				Neo. Irrit.	-.42	.56
				CHAOS	-.27	.60
12 to 18 months	Emot.Tone-Play (12 months)	-.48	.48 F	Emot.Tone-Play (12 months)	-.58	.58 F
	Orient. Staff (6 months)	.41	.59	Attentive (6 months)	-.35	.64
	Orient. Staff (12 months)	-.29	.64	Ratio: Rm,Per.	.33	.69
				Orient. Staff (12 months)	.31	.73
				Emot.Tore-Phys. Meas. (12 months)	.31	.76
18 to 24 months	Emot.Tone-Play (18 months)	-.18	.18 F	Emot.Tone-Play (18 months)	-.44	.44 F
	Ratio Rm/Per.	-.30	.53	Emot.Tone-IBR (18 months)	.43	.58
	CHAOS	.29	.58	Attentive (12 months)	.27	.62
	Orient. Staff (12 months)	-.26	.62			
24 to 30 months	Emot.Tone-Play (12 months)	-.58	.58 F	Emot.Tone-Play (24 months)	-.21	.21 F
30 months	Emot.Tone-Phys. Meas. (6 months)	.35	.65	Orient. Staff (24 months)	.47	.50
	Orient. Staff (6 months)	-.27	.68	Attentive (5 months)	.31	.57

Note. F denotes a predictor forced to enter the multiple regression analysis. partial r ≥ .26, significant $p \leq .05$.

Increase in positive emotionality in the playroom from 18 to 24 months was related to more positive emotionality during mental testing at 18 months and more attentiveness in the playroom at 12 months.

Finally, the increase in positive emotionality in the playroom from 24 to 30 months was predicted by only one measure, and this measure was obtained during the neonatal period. Boys who became more emotionally positive from 24 to 30 months were more active when awake—as measured by the sum of ratings of neonatal activity throughout the neonate's period of wakefulness.

General Conclusions

During the first 18 months of infancy, measures pertaining to the home environment were associated with boys', but not girls', emotionality and changes in emotionality. In general, boys who were from households depicted as more disorganized, noisier, or more crowded were more likely to be rated as more emotionally negative, or were more likely to become more emotionally negative when ratings of emotionality changed from one age to the next. For girls, the 1st year of infancy provided no associations between measures of the home environment and ratings of emotionality or changes in ratings of emotionality. During the 2nd year of infancy, ratings of girls' emotionality and change in ratings of emotionality were associated with measures of the home environment, but the associations were opposite from what had been found for boys at younger ages. Girls from households depicted as more disorganized, noisier, or more crowded were more emotionally positive or became more emotionally positive.

It is not evident from these associations whether the one instance at which the household measures were obtained truly reflected the household context throughout the first 30 months of these children's development. The abatement of associations between measures of household and ratings of boys' emotionality past 18 months may have represented changes for at least some of the boys' households: placement of boy toddlers in day care, the employment of sitters, or assistance from relatives. None of these potentially ameliorative changes would be reflected by a single assessment obtained at about 12 months. The limitations of a one-time measure of chaotic conditions in the household does not account, however, for the finding that girls tended to be more emotionally positive for household conditions seemingly perverse for boys. The perversities of home, even if punctuated, appear to have quite different links with boys' and girls' emotionality.

MULTIDIMENSIONAL CONCEPTIONS AND IMPLICATIONS

Through an overview of theory and research, and an empirical exploratory study, this chapter has addressed two aspects of temperament in context: the potential associations between aspect of the physical environment and temperament in early childhood, and the possibility that these associations may not be equivalent for girls and boys. The most promising aspect is the further demonstration that a few conceptually distinct physical features of the home environment contribute to the prediction of infant and toddler temperament-emotionality. These physical features pertain to noisy, disorganized, and crowded conditions within the household. This aspect cannot be considered as divorced from human behavior, but as Wachs (1989) has suggested and demonstrated empirically, measures of the physical environment and measures of the social environment are not direct surrogates for each other.

The second aspect of temperament in context addressed by this chapter is that of sex differences as revealed by the provocative implication that the physical environment's contribution to temperament is different for girls and boys. On intuitive grounds, one might expect that more chaotic conditions of infants' homes would be associated with more negative emotionality regardless of the sex of the infants. This expectation was confirmed for boys at 6 and 18 months. Contrary to this expectation, the partial correlation between CHAOS and Emotional Tone for girls was positive in sign at 24 months. That is, girls from more tumultuous homes were likely to be more emotionally positive. Moreover, contrary to what one might also expect, girls who were from more crowded homes were likely to be more emotionally positive at 24 months.

The contrasting results by sex are not peculiar compared to the results from the multiple regression analyses. An examination of the original bivariate correlation matrices for girls and boys showed that girls' tumultuous home conditions were positively, but not always significantly, correlated with Emotional Tone-Playroom at all five ages (mean $r = 0.25$, range from 0.15 to 0.38). In contrast, corresponding correlations for boys were negative in sign (mean $r = -0.20$, range from -0.14 to -0.36).

Somewhat similar sex differences were found for the bivariate correlations between Rooms-to-Persons ratio and Emotional Tone-Playroom for the five ages (girls: mean $r = 0.10$, range from -0.28 to 0.23; boys: mean $r = 0.27$, range from 0.18 to 0.39). Thus, there was a trend for boys to be more emotionally positive when they were from homes with more rooms for the number of inhabitants. Conversely, the trend was for the girls to be more emotionally positive when they were from homes that were more crowded.

Wachs (1988) did not detail the specific mechanism(s) that could link crowding with, among other child characteristics, negative emotionality. He did suggest, however, that crowding may lead to overarousal. A similar link may be proposed between chaotic conditions and negative emotionality. For boys, at least, either tumult or crowding or the combination of the two, could lead to higher levels of arousal as manifested by negative mood. One could hypothesize that similar conditions would be associated with higher levels of activity and peculiarities of attention (either hyperalertia or hypoalertia).

Wachs (1988) also showed that higher levels of noise in the home were associated with higher levels of activity. No link was found between noise and attention, however. An examination of the correlations of the present study indicates that tumultuous home conditions were negatively related to laboratory ratings of boys' attentiveness at 6 months (− 0.30) and 30 months (− 0.25). Activity Level in the playroom provided no apparent sex differences for associations with measures of households.

Conceptual Links

The correlates between home conditions and emotionality that contrast boys and girls can be most broadly viewed as another instance of the ubiquitous phenomenon that males are more susceptible than females to the effects of environments (Gray & Buffrey, 1971; Hutt, 1972; Tanner, 1970; Zaslow & Hayes, 1986). From this perspective, boys may be more easily stressed by a wide variety of adverse environments. Whether expressed in terms of adaptability or resiliency, the vulnerability of boys relative to girls is revealed by a host of afflictions of childhood. For example, Matheny (1991a) alluded to the breadth of these sex differences when he examined the characteristics associated with unintentional injuries of girls and boys from opposite-sex pairs of twins. He found that boys' injuries were associated with home noise-confusion and a less structured household. No such associations were found for their twin sisters living in the same homes. Although this perspective is rooted in the biology of sex differences, it does not exclude the psychosocial conditions that may lead to gender-related differences in the treatment of girls and boys. The debate about the sources of sex differences, the magnitude of differences, and how differences might best be demonstrated (e.g., by means, variances, or patterns of correlations) remains to be resolved (e.g., Hoffman, 1991; Maccoby & Jacklin, 1974; Ounsted & Taylor, 1972).

More specific perspectives bridge across several lines of research where attention is directed to a relatively direct link between the physical or material environment and sex differences for a child's emotional behavior. These lines include sex differences for correlates of stimulus complexity and control, crowding, family stress, and self-regulation.

With regard to stimulus complexities and control, infant boys have been found to have less positive affect within households where inanimate stimuli were more complex ($r = -0.26$). For infant girls, more complex inanimate stimuli were associated ($r = 0.52$) with higher ratings of infant girls' positive affect (Yarrow, Rubenstein, & Pedersen, 1975). The association between complex or novel stimuli and infant affect also seems to depend on the degree to which an infant can control the stimuli. Gunnar-Vongnechten (1978) found that 12-month-old boy and girl infants differed in their strong negative emotional reactions to a toy whose actions could or could not be controlled by the infants. For boys having no control over the toy, the preponderant reaction was fussing and crying. This reaction contrasted sharply with the more positive reactions of the boys who could control the toy. For girls, not being given control of the toy was associated with neither a significant degree of negative affect nor a significant degree of positive affect. Gunnar-Vongnechten (1978) did not account for the sex difference; she did suggest, however, that control over events may help infants to reduce fear by increasing the event's predictability, and by allowing infants to modulate or maintain arousal levels within manageable bounds.

Crowding and family discord are also conditions over which children have no control. Boys, in contrast with girls, have been found to have greater discomfort and larger increases in stress-related arousal to crowding (Aiello, Nicosia, & Thompson, 1979; Evans, Lepore, Shejwal, & Palsane, 1998). Boys are also more vulnerable than girls to psychopathology arising from the effects of family discord and disruptions (Earls, 1987).

Some formulations of temperament posit a key construct, self-regulation, that entails processes for governing or modulating physiological, motoric, and affective arousal (e.g., Rothbart, 1989; Strelau, 1983). These processes include self-soothing behaviors, deployment of attention, approach or withdrawal, and vocalizations, among others. Evidence of sex differences during infancy for any or all of these processes has been fragmentary and often attributed to parents' differential treatment of girls and boys. Nevertheless, if boys are stressed (i.e., aroused) more easily by environmental conditions, boys could also differ from girls in the ease by which they self-regulate. In this regard, a recent study (Weinberg, Tronick, Cohn, & Olson, 1999) employed a face-to-face, still-face paradigm to elicit emotionality and self-regulation from 6-month-old infants. During the still-face condition, boys were more likely than girls to fuss, to cry, to show anger, to entreat being picked up, and to move as if to escape. Boys were also more likely to call on coordinated interactions from their mothers as a means to help them maintain self-regulation. In part, the results were interpreted as showing that boys, relative to girls, were less capable of self-regulation and were more likely to signal needs to mothers by means of both negative and positive emotional displays.

By joining just these three lines of research, we suggest that household noise, disorganization, general hubbub, and crowding are conditions of more complex and less controllable (at least by infants) stimulation. This stimulation is more stressful and provokes more arousal for boys with more reactive—that is, irritable or labile—temperament. In turn, some boys are less capable of, or have a more limited repertoire for, self-regulatory modulations of this stress-related arousal. Thus, emotionality as rated in a laboratory setting is detecting boys' individual differences, some of which represent a more reactive temperament characteristic arising with an ongoing set of arousing household conditions.

Further Research

This exploratory study has concentrated on the associations between infant girls' and boys' household environments and emotionality. Characteristics of the parents who organize and reorganize these environments, who participate in ongoing interactions with their children, and who are also subject to stresses within home environments were not a focus of study. Obviously, a more complete explication must take into account the personality (or temperament) of parents, how parents allocate their time and energy to the physical and social environment of the household, how the temperament of the infant affects parents or the general household, and how an organized or disorganized household affects parents. Regarding the last, Wachs (1993) has demonstrated that chaotic household conditions negatively influence parental behaviors that would facilitate child development. Following Wachs (1993), we speculate that more chaotic household conditions would be associated with higher stress among parents, less cohesive actions among all members of the family, and fewer opportunities for parents to foster infants' (and especially boys') self-regulation.

The multidimensional associations among characteristics of parents, environments, and children also remain incomplete when we fail to consider the genetic contribution to links among persons and environments (Plomin, DeFries, & Loehlin, 1977). For example, to the extent that emotionality is influenced genetically, one might expect that emotional instability of parents to be linked with negative emotionality of children along with concomitant indicators of household disharmony, tumult, and disorganization. In this sense, households reveal, rather than elicit, the interplay of genetically related characteristics of their inhabitants' entwined lives.

We recognize that our extrapolations from this exploratory study are limited as a consequence of having but one single assessment of households. Despite the fact that scores from the CHAOS measure have a 12-month stability coefficient of 0.74, a single assessment during a 30-month period is likely to miss some of the evolving changes of the ordinary and extraordinary quotidian events within households. For future research, this limitation can be offset by assessing infants' and toddlers' households more frequently, especially during the months when young infants are known to alter parents' allocation of energy, time, and sleep.

For the development of more complete measurement and analytic models incorporating multidimensional conceptions, larger samples are obviously needed to permit the inclusion of measures of parents and measures for more than one infant per household. To this end, measures of parents, household contexts, and infants from a larger sample of families with twins are being collected.

ACKNOWLEDGMENTS

This research was supported in part by U.S. Public Health Service research grants HD21395 and HD22637, as well as financial assistance from the John D. and Catherine T. MacArthur Foundation, and the University of Louisville. The authors are grateful to the families of the Louisville Twin Study for their generous cooperation and devotion, and to Marjorie Hinkle, Carol Hurst, Barbara Moss, Sharon Nuss, Deborah Rice, Marilyn L. Riese, Kendall Sears, Maureen Slaton, and Laura Teets for their professional contributions to the longitudinal research program. We also thank Theordore Wachs for suggestions that improved the clarity of this chapter.

REFERENCES

Aiello, J. R., Nicosia, G., & Thompson, D. E. (1979). Physiological, social, and behavioral consequences of crowding on children and adolescents. *Child Development, 50,* 195–202.

Bayley, N. (1969). *Bayley scales of infant development.* New York: Psychological Corp.

Earls, F. (1987). Sex differences in psychiatric disorders: Origins and developmental influences. *Psychiatric Developments, 1,* 1–23.

Evans, G. W., Lepore, S. J., Shejwal, B. R., & Palsane, M. N. (1998). Chronic residential crowding and children's well-being: An ecological perspective. *Child Development, 69,* 1514–1523.

Fullard, W., McDevitt, S. C., & Carey, W. B. (1984). Assessing temperament in 1- to 3-year-old children. *Journal of Pediatric Psychology, 9,* 205–217.

Fullard, W., Simeonsson, R. J., & Huntington, G. S. (1989). Sociocultural factors and temperament. In G. A. Kohnstamm, J. E. Bates, & M. K. Rothbart (Eds.), *Temperament in childhood* (pp.523–536). New York: Wiley.

Gray, J. A., & Buffrey, A. W. H. (1971). Sex differences in emotional cognitive behavior in mammals including man: Adaptive and neural bases. *Acta Psychologica, 35,* 89–111.

Gunnar-Vongnechten, M. R. (1978). Changing a frightening toy into a pleasant toy by allowing the infant to control its action. *Developmental Psychology, 14,* 157–162.

Hoffman, L. W. (1991). The influence of the family environment on personality: Accounting for sibling differences. *Psychological Bulletin, 110,* 187–203.

Hunt, J. McV. (1979). Psychological development: Early experience. *Annual Review of Psychology, 30,* 103–143.

Hutt, C. (1972). Sexual dimorphism: Its significance in human development. In F. J. Monks, W. W. Hartup, & J. DeWit (Eds.), *Determinants of behavioral development,* (pp. 169–196). New York: Academic Press.

Kohnstamm, G. A., Bates, J. E., & Rothbart, M. K.(Eds.). (1989). *Temperament in childhood.* New York: Wiley.

Maccoby, E. E., & Jacklin, C. (1974). *The psychology of sex differences.* Stanford, CA: Stanford University Press.

Matheny, A. P., Jr. (1991a). Children's unintentional injuries and gender: Differentiation by environmental and psychosocial aspects. *Children's Environmental Quarterly, 8,* 51–61.

Matheny, A. P., Jr. (1991b). Play assessment of infant temperament. In C. E. Schaefer, K. Gitlin, & A. Sandgrund (Eds.), *Play diagnosis and assessment* (pp. 39–63). New York: Wiley.

Matheny, A. P., Jr., Wachs, T. D., Ludwig, J. L., & Phillips, K. (1995). Bringing order out of chaos: Psychometric characteristics of the Confusion Hubbub and Order Scale. *Journal of Applied Developmental Psychology, 16,* 429–444.

Matheny, A. P., Jr., Wilson, R. S., & Nuss, S. M. (1984). Toddler temperament: Stability over ages and across settings. *Child Development, 55,* 1200–1211.

Matheny, A. P., Jr., Wilson, R. S., & Thoben, A. (1987). Home and mother: Relations with infant temperament. *Developmental Psychology, 23,* 323–331.

Ounsted, C., & Taylor, D. C. (Eds.). (1972). *Gender differences: Their ontogeny and significance.* London: Churchill.

Phillips, K. & Matheny, A. P., Jr. (1997). Evidence for genetic influence on both cross-situation and situation-specific components of behavior. *Journal of Personality and Social Psychology, 73,* 129–138.

Plomin, R., DeFries, J., & Loehlin, J. (1977). Genotype environment interaction and correlation in the analysis of human development. *Psychological Bulletin, 84,* 309–322.

Reiss, A. J., Jr. (1961). *Occupations and social status.* New York: Free Press of Glencoe.

Riese, M. L. (1983). Assessment of behavioral patterns in neonates. *Infant Behavior and Development, 6,* 241–246.

Rothbart, M. K. (1989). Temperament and development. In G. A. Kohnstamm, J. E. Bates, & M. K. Rothbart (Eds.), *Temperament in childhood* (pp. 187–247). New York: Wiley.

Strelau, J. (1983). *Temperament, personality, activity.* London: Academic Press.

Super, C. M., & Harkness, S. (1986). Temperament, development, and culture. In R. Plomin & J. Dunn (Eds.), *The study of temperament: Changes, continuities, and challenges* (pp. 131–149). Hillsdale, NJ: Lawrence Erlbaum Associates.

Tanner, J. M. (1970). Physical growth. In P. H. Mussen (Ed.), *Carmichael's manual of child psychology.* (3rd ed., pp. 77–156). New York: Wiley.

Thomas, A., & Chess, S. (1977). *Temperament and development.* New York: Brunner/Mazel.

Wachs, T. D. (1979). Proximal experience and early cognitive-intellectual development: The physical environment. *Merrill-Palmer Quarterly, 25,* 3–41.

Wachs, T. D. (1988). Relevance of physical environment influences for toddler temperament. *Infant Behavior and Development, 11,* 431–445.

Wachs, T. D. (1989). The nature of the physical microenvironment: An expanded classification system. *Merrill-Palmer Quarterly, 35,* 399–402.

Wachs, T. D. (1992). *The nature of nurture.* Newbury Park, CA: Sage.

Wachs, T. D. (1993). Nature of relations between the physical and social microenvironment of the 2-year-old child. *Early Development and Parenting, 2,* 81–87.

Wachs, T. D., Francis, J., & McQuiston, S. (1979). Psychological dimensions of the infant's physical environment. *Infant Behavior and Development, 2,* 155–161.

Wachs, T. D., & Gruen, G. (1982). *Early experience and human development*. New York: Plenum.

Weinberg, M. K., Tronick, E. Z., Cohn, J. F., & Olson, K. L. (1999). Gender differences in emotional expressivity and self-regulation during early infancy. *Developmental Psychology, 35,* 175–188.

Yarrow, L. J., Rubenstein, J. L., & Pedersen, F. A. (1975). *Infant and environment*. New York: Wiley.

Zaslow, M. J., & Hayes, C. D. (1986). Sex differences in children's responses to psychosocial stress: Toward a cross-context analysis. In M. E. Lamb, A. L. Bronn, & B. Rogoff (Eds.), *Advances in developmental psychology* (Vol. 4, pp. 285–337), Hillsdale, NJ: Lawrence Erlbaum Associates.

6 Temperament and Socioemotional Adjustment to Kindergarten: A Multi-Informant Perspective

H. Hill Goldsmith
Nazan Aksan
Marilyn Essex
Nancy A. Smider
Deborah Lowe Vandell
University of Wisconsin—Madison

The field has yet to arrive at a consensus on how to think about temperament and context. One notion is "temperament across contexts," a phrase implying that temperament should be constant in varying situations. At another extreme is the phrase, "temperament in context," which might imply that temperament cannot be defined without specification of context. In the absence of established designs/paradigms to examine temperament and context interrelations, issues such as these hinge crucially on how the concepts of temperament and context are defined. However, before we turn to our definitions of temperament and context, let us briefly examine some recent findings.

From one perspective, temperament and context interrelations refer to temperament by environment interactions. As recently noted by Bates, Pettit, Dodge, and Ridge (1998), however, there are few such replicated interactions. Bates et al. (1998) did replicate an interaction between infant-toddler restrictive parenting control strategies and resistant temperament on externalizing tendencies at school age. Kochanska (1991, 1995) also showed that nonpower assertive parenting strategies for inhibited toddlers and attachment security for bold children are associated with positive socialization outcomes. In relation to cognitive outcomes, active children tend not to be adversely affected by understimulating preschool environments relative to children low in activity level. Similarly, noisy learning environments tend to adversely affect children with a difficult temperamental profile relative to children without such profiles (Wachs, 1992).

Findings like these inform an examination of temperament and context interrelations in several different ways. First, the findings pertinent to social adjustment highlight relationship-specific dimensions of the home environment, such as parenting styles or attachment security. Second, findings pertinent to cognitive/learning outcomes highlight dimensions of the preschool/school environment that are either specific, such as noise levels, or more global in nature, such as level of stimulation. Third, in all of these cases environment refers to molar contexts such as home or school.

In this chapter, we also adopt a molar view of context as everyday settings such as home versus school. We examine temperament assessed twice in the preschool period as a predictor of emotional problems and quality of peer relations in a later context, kindergarten. Our findings will demonstrate a remarkably consistent role for temperament in predicting social maturity before the transition to kindergarten, and an indirect role for temperament in influencing the adjustment to kindergarten through its direct effects on prior social maturity. As an alternative to temperament by environment interactions, we use a multi-informant perspective to examine the role of prior temperament on kindergarten adjustment.

At the outset, we need to clarify the meanings we impute to the concepts of temperament and context. The construct of temperament is more limited than, developmentally prior to, and a core element of, adult personality. Despite variability in definitions of temperament, the construct generally refers to individual differences in emotionality and activity level (Goldsmith et al., 1983) and in how the expression of emotion is regulated (Rothbart & Bates, 1998). When highly differentiated sets of emotional dimensions in early childhood are measured, derived factor structures often parallel the three major dimensions of adult personality instruments: positive affectivity, negative affectivity, and control (Ahadi & Rothbart, 1994; Watson, Clark, & Harkness, 1994). Despite such parallels between childhood temperament and adult personality, temperament research has stronger links with emotion theory.

From a functionalist perspective, emotions are partially defined in terms of perceptions or appraisals of the microcontext. For example, perceptions or appraisals of contexts as goal blocking lead to anger whereas appraisals of loss lead to sadness (Campos, Barrett, Lamb, Goldsmith, & Stenberg, 1983). In examining the links between microcontexts and temperament within an emotion theory framework, let us first accept an oversimplified definition of temperamental anger proneness as individual differences in the readiness to express the emotion of anger, given exposure to goal-blocking situations (Goldsmith, 1994). With temperamental anger proneness defined in this way, the manifestation of temperament will be associated with the frequency of encountering goal-blocking situations. Goal-blocking situations are more likely to occur in some molar contexts than in others. Moreover, a temperamentally anger prone individual would probably appraise a broader range of contexts as goal blocking. If it were conceivable for no perceptions of goal blocking to occur, temperamental anger proneness would never be expressed. Over the time span of a child's development, the frequency and nature of emotion-relevant contexts encountered could be expected to affect the development of temperament, as notions of gene-environment covariation imply (Plomin, DeFries, & Loehlin, 1977; Scarr & McCartney, 1983). Thus, the appraised contexts associated with emotional reactions are also associated with temperament, and the nuances of these associations have been investigated empirically in infants (Goldsmith & Campos, 1990; Kochanska, 1998). These links between appraisals and resulting emotional reactions in particular situations are the source of theoretical connection between temperament and microcontexts.

Context, however, can also be construed in a more molar sense as everyday settings such as home, school, or work. From an emotion theory perspective, the "everyday setting" notion of context is not independent of the functionalist, appraisal-dependent notion of microcontexts. Each everyday setting comprises a particular constellation of emotion-related microcontexts to be appraised by participants. For example, the school setting typically makes higher demands on attention, interest, and behavioral control than the home context. Unlike interactions at home, social interactions at school take place in a group setting involving same aged peers and teachers.

The view of molar contexts in terms of their demand characteristics poses several difficulties in the design of correlational studies that attempt to examine temperament and molar context interrelations. Consider home versus school contexts. We can index structural characteristics of the home context with variables such as number of siblings, and school characteristics with variables such as class size. However, class size and similar variables are rather distal from processes that actually affect children's appraisal of microcontexts and thus their emotional experience. Perhaps a larger class size might be correlated with more novel (and stressful to a shy child) social encounters. However, these more crucial variables such as frequency of stressful social encounters are not easy to measure.

Another difficulty for this line of research is that other social actors who occupy molar contexts (e.g., kindergarten) become part and parcel of those contexts. For example, a parental versus a teaching role brings a different set of social expectations as well as responsibilities that impinge on children's environments, and their appraisals of those environments. Thus, informants' perceptions of a child's behavior are not independent of the social roles they occupy. The same is true for trained observers' judgments of a child's behavior in that their roles are those of the "scientist." In other words, observers/informants are not independent of the context and events that take place in that context (Herbert, 1985).

According to Achenbach, McConaughy, and Howell (1987), perceptions of informants who are embedded in molar contexts as essential actors, such as parents at home and teachers at school, are what largely defines molar contexts. Their meta-analysis of externalizing and internalizing ratings done by teachers and parents found low to moderate convergence. However, there was moderate to high convergence between mothers' and fathers' ratings of these behaviors. Achenbach et al. (1987) argued that the divergence between teachers and mothers is both a function of differences in context, home versus school, and a function of different observer perspectives, such as parental and teacher roles. Hinshaw, Han, Erhardt, and Huber (1992) have extended these findings to younger children's internalizing and externalizing tendencies rated by parents, teachers, and observers.

In this chapter, we examine the prediction of adjustment-related outcomes following transition to kindergarten from earlier temperament ratings using a multi-informant perspective. We define molar context in terms of the socially significant informants and the roles they occupied. Table 6.1 summarizes the design and assessments of the study. When children were 3.5 and 4.5 years of age, mothers, fathers, and familiar nonparental adult caregivers rated both children's temperamental characteristics and social maturity. At 4.5 years, unfamiliar adult observers also provided ratings after a home visit. Following children's transition to kindergarten a year later, we asked parents and kindergarten teachers to rate the quality of children's peer relations (peer acceptance, rejection, and isolation) as well as emotion and behavior problems (internalizing and externalizing tendencies). Multiple informants allowed us to examine cross-informant or cross-context consistency as defined by the social actors that occupy those contexts. We would expect cross-context correspondence to be attenuated if the macro contexts of home and school share few microcontextual features. For example, following Achenbach et al. (1987), we would expect maternal and paternal ratings to be more similar than parents' and teachers' ratings of internalizing tendencies.

The transition to kindergarten is a significant life event that may have long-standing implications for later functioning and outcomes (Alexander, Entwisle, & Horsey, 1997). Kindergarten is often the first context where many children are exposed to a structured learning environment. Although kindergarten programs vary, most prepare children for reading and rudimen-

TABLE 6.1   Description of Design and Assessments

Dimension/Instruments	Scales/Composites	Raters
Temperament at 3.5 and 4.5 years		
Children's Behavior Questionnaire (CBQ)	Activity, Approach, Anger, Sadness, Shyness, Inhibitory Control, Attention Focusing	M
Preschool Behavior Questionnaire (PBQ)	Hostility-Aggressiveness	M, F, FA
	Anxious/ Fearfulness	M, F, FA
	Distractibility	M, F, FA
Positive Affect Negative Affect Scales (PANAS)	Positive Affectivity	M, F, FA
	Negative Affectivity	M, F, FA
Observational Rating scales (at 4.5 years only)	Approach-related Negative Affect	O
	Withdrawal-related Negative Affect	O
	Control	O
	Positive Affect	O
Social Maturity Ratings at 3.5 & 4.5 years		
Adaptive Social Behavior Inventory (ASBI)	Compliance	M, F, FA
	Disruptiveness	M, F, FA
	Emotional Expressiveness	M, F, FA
Kindergarten outcomes		
(1) Behavior/ Emotion problems (HBQ)	Internalization	M, F, T
	Externalization	M, F, T
(2) Peer relationships (CABI)	Perceptiveness	M, F, T
	Acceptance	M, F, T
	Rejection	M, F, T
	Isolation	M, F, T
	Victimization	M, F, T

Note. M = mothers, F = fathers, FA = familiar adult (not teacher), T = teacher, and O = observers who spent two hours in the home.

tary mathematics. Kindergarten also typically represents an early exposure to group activity and projects, but without an atmosphere of grade-based performance comparisons. During this transition, peer networks expand and peer relationships deepen. The kindergarten experience for children from disadvantaged homes is associated with better achievement in the first grade, and first-grade achievement itself is a predictor of outcomes into the high school years. According to Alexander et al. (1997) and Entwisle and Alexander (1998), it is unclear how kindergarten prepares children for the social demands of formal schooling. However, their review suggests that maturity in personal characteristics predicts better achievement and social adjustment. Although the successful negotiation of kindergarten experiences appears to have long-lasting effects in domains such as school achievement to peer relations, the predictors of a successful transition to kindergarten are poorly understood. Based on previous research, we used measures of compliance and disruptiveness as indicators of social maturity and readiness for school prior to the kindergarten transition (Entwisle & Alexander, 1998).

Having multiple informants on both predictor and outcome measures allows us to draw inferences about the cross-situational consistency of temperament predictors and social behaviors both before and after the transition to kindergarten. For example, maternal and paternal ratings provided information on children's characteristics in the home context both before and after the transition period. Ratings from familiar adult caregivers before the transition to kindergarten provided information on characteristics from the nonparental perspective. Teacher ratings of peer relations and emotional problems following the transition to kindergarten supplied information on child characteristics during the second (spring) semester after the initial exposure to kindergarten in the fall semester.

We examined within- and cross-informant (context) predictability in outcome measures both before and after the transition into kindergarten. For example, we examined within- and cross-informant (context) predictability of behavioral ratings of compliance, disruptiveness, and socially appropriate emotional expressiveness at 4.5 years (before the transition to kindergarten) from temperament measures obtained contemporaneously as well as 1 year earlier. We also examined within- and cross-informant predictability of peer relations and emotional or social problems obtained following the transition to kindergarten from the earlier temperament and social behavior ratings. In these analyses, our temperament measures reflected broad individual difference characteristics such as positive affectivity, negative affectivity, and behavioral regulation.

In addition, we examined structural characteristics of children's experience at kindergarten, such as average hours per week spent at kindergarten and class size, as potential qualifiers of cross-context predictability. In addition to these associations involving structural characteristics, we examined whether the presence of friends in the same class upon initial entry to kindergarten in the fall semester might influence adjustment of shy children, relative to other shy children who did not have friends at that potentially stressful time. Presumably, the presence of friends on entry would make the novel kindergarten environment less intimidating for shy children. To examine these associations, we used maternal ratings of shyness at 4.5 years on the Children's Behavior Questionnaire (CBQ) and teacher ratings of outcome measures.

METHOD

Sample

In examining the interrelations of temperamental characteristics across the transition to kindergarten, we used a longitudinal sample of 570 families who had initially been recruited to study the effects of maternity leave on child development and related outcomes. Families initially resided in either the Milwaukee or Madison, Wisconsin areas (Hyde, Klein, Essex, & Clark, 1995). Recruiting occurred during pregnancy for the target child, and only mothers who were cohabiting with a partner and older than 18 years of age were included in the study. Of the initial 570 families, 488 at 3.5 years, and 451 at 4.5 years remained in the study, with about equal percentages of girls and boys at both time points. Only the 240 children who began the transition into kindergarten during the fall of 1997 were included in the analyses reported in this chapter, with the exception of some analyses using only data prior to the kindergarten transition (where the entire sample was used). The sample characteristics are provided in Table 6.2.

Predictors

Table 6.1 shows a list of questionnaires, and corresponding scales completed by several raters including parents and nonparental caregivers on two occasions (3.5 and 4.5 years), and by observers who visited the home on one occasion (age 4.5 years), before the transition into kindergarten, and once by teachers and parents following the transition into kindergarten. As Table 6.1 shows, four instruments tapped children's temperamental characteristics: observer ratings of temperament; the Positive Affect Negative Affect Scales (PANAS; Watson, Clark, & Tellegen, 1998); the Preschool Behavior Questionnaire (PBQ; Behar & Stringfield, 1974); and the Children's Behavior Questionnaire (CBQ; Ahadi & Rothbart, 1994; Ahadi, Rothbart & Ye, 1993). Whereas the PBQ and the PANAS were administered in their full version in this study, only 8 of the 16 scales from the full version of the CBQ were administered in somewhat abbreviated form (10 items for each of the eight

TABLE 6.2   Demographic Characteristics of the Sample

Ethnicity	Parental Education	Combined Family Income (1990–1991)
93% Caucasian	2–4% less than high school	2.3% < $15,000
2.4% African-American	15–18% high school only	7.4% = $15–25,000
1.8% Hispanic	19–20% some college	15% = $25–35,000
2.0% Indian-Alaskan	27–25% college degree	32.3% = $35–50,000
0.7% Asian	19–21% postcollege	24.2% = $50–65,000
		9.5% = $65–80,000
		7.5% > $80,000

scales). The eight scales were selected, with the assistance of Dr. Rothbart, for multidimensional representation of negative and positive affectivity and the modulatory components of individual differences. Sadness, Anger, Fearfulness, and Shyness scales were selected as components of negative affectivity; Activity Level and Approach scales were selected as components of hedonically positive anticipation or positive affectivity; and Inhibitory Control and Attentional Focusing scales represented behavioral modulatory components of temperament. Together, the observer ratings, PANAS, PBQ, and CBQ sample a broad set of both general and specific behaviors, pertaining to emotional and attentional characteristics of preschool-aged children.

The PANAS, PBQ, and CBQ questions share minimal item content overlap. The CBQ scales emphasize emotional reactions in specific situations, whereas the PBQ emphasizes more extreme behaviors indicative of anxious-fearfulness, aggressiveness, and distractibility in more globally described situations. For example, whereas several PBQ hostility-aggressiveness items make reference to bullying, kicking, hitting, blaming other children, telling lies, and inconsiderate behavior directed at others, CBQ Anger scale items concern expressions of anger and frustration in situations that involve specific incidences of goal blocking as well as irritation with inability to complete tasks or irritability when tired. On the other hand, the PANAS scales comprise emotion adjectives that are not embedded in any particular context, global or specific.

Observational ratings of children's temperamental characteristics were made at 4.5 years during a home visit. The ratings are the average of scores given by a child tester and a camera operator as they observed child characteristics in several standardized situations involving both social interactions with mother, sibling, and a series of emotion eliciting games. The majority of these rating scales were adapted from the Bayley Scales of Infant Development (Bayley, 1993). Additional rating scales tapping the degree of shyness, impulsivity, and proneness to anger and sadness were generated to sample a larger domain of emotional behavior relevant to temperament. For the purposes of the questions addressed here, we selected 14 scales relevant to temperament, and on the basis of correlations between these 14 scales we formed composites. These correlations suggested pooling "enthusiasm toward tasks," "extent of exploratory behavior," "extent of social engagement with the testers," "hyperactivity," and "anticipatory positive affect" as dimensions of extroversion (the Positive Affectivity composite). Ratings of "proneness to sadness," "shyness," and "object related fearfulness" were averaged as dimensions of withdrawal-related negative affectivity; and "proneness to anger" and "frustration with inability to complete tasks" were averaged as dimensions of Negative Affectivity associated with approach tendencies. Finally, "initial interest with task stimuli," "attention to tasks," "persistence in task completion," and "impulsivity" were combined as dimensions of Attentional or Regulatory components of temperament. The reliabilities for these items ranged from .84 to .92.

The scales from the Adaptive Social Behavior Inventory (Hogan, Scott, & Bauer, 1992) were used as indicators of social maturity prior to kindergarten. For example, the emotional expressiveness scale taps socially appropriate emotional expressiveness that includes some empathy, pride, and shyness content. The compliance scale taps compliance with social conventions and requests; and the disruptiveness scale measures the degree of inappropriate attention seeking behaviors, including temper tantrums. The latter two scales have been implicated in the development of internalized behavior (Kochanska & Aksan, 1995) as well as externalizing tendencies (Patterson, 1982).

Derivation of Temperament Composites.   Given the broad sampling of temperamental characteristics in this study, we carried out an exploratory factor analyses of maternal PANAS, PBQ, and CBQ ratings as a guide to forming temperament composites. Principal components extraction with varimax rotation yielded a three factor structure. The three factors could be interpreted as Positive Affectivity, Negative Affectivity, and Attentional/Regulatory components of temperament at both 3.5 and 4.5 years of age. The Positive Affectivity factor loaded the CBQ Approach (i.e., anticipatory positive affectivity) and the PANAS Positive Affect scales. The Negative Affectivity factor showed highest loadings for CBQ Anger, CBQ Sadness, CBQ Fear, CBQ Shyness, PBQ Anxious/Fearfulness and the PANAS Negative Affect scales. Finally, the Low Control factor loaded the following scales: CBQ Activity Level (positively), CBQ Attention Focusing (negatively), CBQ Inhibitory Control (negatively), PBQ Distractibility (positively) and PBQ Hostility/Aggressiveness (positively). With the exception of the PBQ Hostility/Aggressiveness factor, the pattern of primary factor loadings was consistent over the year between testing occasions. We formed unit weighted composites to represent the three factors. Because we did not have CBQ ratings from fathers and familiar adult caregivers, we used their PBQ and PANAS ratings to form Negative Affectivity, Positive Affectivity, and Control composites. In other words, for fathers and familiar adult caregivers the Negative Affectivity composite was an average of PBQ Hostility/Aggressiveness, PBQ Anxious/Fearfulness, and PANAS Negative Affect scales. The Positive Affectivity composite was simply the PANAS Positive Affect scale, and the Control composite was simply the PBQ Distractibility scale. To examine the extent of consistency among different reporters, we also formed maternal composites paralleling the father and familiar adult caregiver composites.

Outcomes.   As shown in Table 6.1, adjustment to kindergarten in the spring semester following entry in fall was measured in two domains: emotional and behavioral problems, and the quality of peer relations. The MacArthur Health and Behavior Questionnaire (HBQ; MacArthur Research Network on Psychopathology and Development, 1998), which is an expanded version of the Ontario Child Health Study questionnaire (Offord, Boyle, & Racine, 1989), assesses internalizing and externalizing tendencies. The Internalizing Tendencies scale consists of overanxiousness, inhibition, and depression subscales whereas the Externalizing Tendencies scale consists of conduct, oppositional defiance, and attention deficit hyperactivity disorder subscales. The quality of peer relations was measured by portions of the Child Adaptive Behavior Inventory (CABI) relevant to dimensions of peer relations, and the scales listed in Table 6.1 are based on factor analyses of the items relevant to peer relations (Cowan, Cowan, Heming, & Miller, 1995).

Results

We first inspected the intercorrelations among parental and caregiver ratings of temperamental characteristics as measured by the PANAS, PBQ, CBQ, and the social behavior ratings on the ASBI at 3.5 and 4.5 years of age. In addition, we examined intercorrelations among the outcome measures (listed above) collected after the transition to kindergarten, as rated by mothers, fathers, and teachers. Following the examination of these intercorrelations, we present a series of stepwise regressions examining the extent of cross-informant consistency in the predictability of peer relations and emotional problems from earlier parental and familiar adult caregivers' ratings on temperament and social behavior.

Correlational Evidence for Differential Cross-Situational Consistency Among Predictors and Outcomes.   Table 6.3 presents the intercorrelations among both predictor and outcome measures obtained from different informants at home and at school prior to and following the

TABLE 6.3 **Correlations Among Raters for Predictors at 3.5 and 4.5 Years and Outcome Measures Obtained Following the Transition into Kindergarten**

	Mother–Father	Mother–Familiar Adult	Father–Familiar Adult
Predictors			
PANAS: Positive Affect at 3.5 yrsa	.25	.18	.03
PANAS: Negative Affect at 3.5 yrs	.27	.14	.13
PANAS: Positive Affect at 4.5 yrsb	.24	.11	.15
PANAS: Negative Affect at 4.5 yrs	.25	.11	.13
PBQ: Hostile-Aggressive at 3.5 yrsc	.39	.26	.21
PBQ: Anxious-Fearful at 3.5 yrs	.34	.17	.17
PBQ: Distractible at 3.5 yrs	.37	.26	.25
PBQ: Hostile-Aggressive at 4.5 yrsd	.25	.24	.15
PBQ: Anxious-Fearfulness at 4.5 yrs	.20	.21	.21
PBQ: Distractible at 4.5 yrs	.37	.36	.22
ASBI: Expressive at 3.5 yrse	.35	.21	.16
ASBI: Compliant at 3.5 yrs	.44	.26	.28
ASBI: Disruptive at 3.5 yrs	.31	.15	.15
ASBI: Expressive at 4.5 yrsf	.43	.29	.27
ASBI: Compliant at 4.5 yrs	.38	.26	.22
ASBI: Disruptive at 4.5 yrs	.29	.20	.18
Outcome measures			
HBQ: Internalizing symptomsg	.30	.09	.08
HBQ: Externalizing symptoms	.44	.23	.31
CABI: Perceptiveh	.25	.22	.21
CABI: Acceptance	.07	.05	.17
CABI: Rejection	.21	.18	.07
CABI: Isolation	.32	.31	.22

Note. Correlations above .10 are significant at $p < .05$ (2-tailed). [a]$n = 440$; [b]$n = 398$; [c]$n = 398$; [d]$n = 347$; [e]$n = 419$; [f]$n = 377$; [g]$n = 221$, [h]$n = 221$.

transition to kindergarten. These correlations measure the consistency of both child temperament and social maturity as observed by parents and familiar adult caregivers at home prior to kindergarten transition, and consistency in internalizing, externalizing, and peer relation dimensions, as observed by parents at home and teachers at school following the transition to kindergarten. An examination of Table 6.3 reveals five patterns. First, in agreement with previous research, mothers and fathers agreed with each other more strongly than either agreed with adults in nonparental roles. Second, maternal ratings were more similar to familiar adult caregiver and teacher ratings than were paternal ratings to these nonparental informants. In a substantial number of cases, fathers agreed with the two nonparental raters less than mothers did. This could be a function of differences in reporter gender because the great majority of kindergarten teachers and familiar adult caregivers were female. Third, the magnitude of the correlations ranged from low to moderate, with the highest correlation being .44. Fourth, there appeared to be a higher degree of agreement for some instruments relative to others. For example, the degree of agreement for the PANAS and the CABI scales among different raters was lower compared with the PBQ, ASBI and the CABI ratings. This could reflect differential reliability between instruments as well as other differences of a psychometric nature. For example, comparing ratings pertaining to the temperament domain, PANAS scale intercorrelations suggested more cross-situational variability relative to the PBQ scales. As noted earlier, whereas the PBQ items make reference to specific behavioral responses in globally specified situations, the PANAS is a collection of adjectives without any contextual or situational specificity. Thus, different informants can evaluate the same adjective in different situations and contexts. Fifth, the degree of cross-situational consistency differed from dimension to dimension. Comparing ratings of children's social behaviors (such as compliance, disruptiveness, and socially appropriate emotional expressiveness on the ASBI) with peer ratings on the CABI, we found more similarity for the ASBI than the CABI. Furthermore, for some dimensions such as peer acceptance we observed no evidence of similarity across informants. Similarly, whereas externalizing tendencies measured by the HBQ showed a moderate degree of parent by "other adult" consistency, internalizing tendencies yielded no such consistency, replicating previous findings of Achenbach et al. (1987) and Hinshaw et al. (1992). Thus, some dimensions of behavior showed greater cross-situational consistency than others.

These findings confirm and extend previous findings regarding cross-informant consistency in ratings. The agreement between parents on externalizing and internalizing tendencies as measured by the HBQ was lower than that reported by Hinshaw et al. (1992) with preschoolers and also lower than the meta-analytic findings of Achenbach et al. (1987). This could be a function of differences in instruments or the relatively greater power of meta-analytic studies although our sample size of 240 was relatively large. Our findings also extend our understanding of the extent of cross-situational consistency in characteristics other than emotion and behavior problems to include temperamental characteristics, quality of peer relations, and social behavior.

Outcome Predictions.   We examined the degree of within- and cross-informant agreement in the prediction of three sets of outcomes measures. Specifically, we first examined the degree of within and cross-informant agreement in the prediction of socially appropriate emotional expressiveness, compliance, and disruptiveness as measured by the ASBI at 4.5 years of age using temperament composites at 4.5 and 3.5 years of age. As mentioned earlier, the ASBI scales can be conceptualized as an index of social maturity or readiness for schooling before the kindergarten transition. We then considered the degree of within- and cross-informant agreement in the prediction of HBQ internalizing and externalizing tendencies, as well as the CABI peer ratings (i.e., perceptiveness, acceptance, rejection, isolation, and victimization), using both the temperament and the ASBI ratings obtained at 3.5 and 4.5 years.

Temperament as a Cross-Situationally Consistent Predictor of Social Maturity Prior to Kindergarten.   Table 6.4 presents the results of a series of stepwise regressions, varying the source of both dependent and predictor variables, where the dependent measures are socially appropriate emotional expressiveness, compliance, and disruptiveness scales of the ASBI obtained at 4.5 years of age, and the predictors are the three temperament composites. The order of entry for these stepwise regressions was as follows: The three temperament composites from 4.5 years were entered as a block at the first step, and the equivalent composites from 3.5 years were entered as a block at the second step. In all of these regressions, a stepwise selection algorithm was employed within each block with a criterion of $p = .05$ for entry and $p = .10$ for removal.

Table 6.4 reveals several findings that are organized by the three social maturity outcome variables. For the outcome of "socially appropriate emotional expressiveness" (shortened to "expressiveness" in some of the tables), Temperamental Positive Affect was a remarkably consistent, significant predictor in 12 of 12 instances (4 informants for temperamental positive affect at 4.5 years by 3 informants for socially appropriate emotional expressiveness). This consistency is emphasized in Table 6.4 by the bold font. A second, strong but perhaps unremarkable finding was that when the informant was the same for temperament and social maturity, the percentage of variance accounted for was quite high, 20%, 26%, and 33% for mother, father, and familiar adult report, respectively. Third, Table 6.4 shows 10 other predictors that

TABLE 6.4 Predicting Three Components of Social Maturity at 4.5 Years From Temperament at 3.5 and 4.5 Years

	Temperamental Predictors							
	by Mother		by Father		by Familiar Adult		by Home Observer	
	(-/+) Predictors	R²	(-/+) Predictors	R²	(-/+) Predictors	R²	(-/+) Predictors	R²
Social Maturity Variables:								
Socially Appropriate Emotional Expressiveness								
by Mother at 4.5 yrs	(+) **Positive Affect**	.20	(+) **Positive Affect**	.06	(+) **Positive Affect**	.02	(+) **Positive Affect**	.08
	(-) Negative Affect	.03	(-) Control	.02	(-) Control	.01	(-) Anxious/Shyness	.02
	(-) Control	.01						
by Father at 4.5 yrs	(+) **Positive Affect**	.05	(+) **Positive Affect**	.26	(+) **Positive Affect**	.04	(+) **Positive Affect**	.02
	(-) Negative Affect	.02	(-) Negative Affect	.05				
at 3.5 yrs	None		(+) Positive Affect	.02	None	.02	Not Applicable	
by Familiar Adult at 4.5 yrs	(+) **Positive Affect**	.01	(+) **Positive Affect**	.03	(+) **Positive Affect**	.33	(+) **Positive Affect**	.03
					(-) Negative Affect	.11		
					(-) Control	.02		

Compliance

by Mother	(−) Negative Affect .27	(+) **Control** .07	(+) **Control** .06	(−) Anger/Frustration .01
at 4.5 yrs	(+) **Control** .03; (+) Positive Affect .01	(−) Negative Affect .01		
at 3.5 years	(+) **Control** .01; (+) Positive Affect .01	(−) Negative Affect .06	None	Not Applicable
by Father	(−) Negative Affect .06			
at 4.5 yrs		(+) **Control** .22; (−) Negative Affect .04; (+) Positive Affect .02	(+) **Control** .05; (−) Negative Affect .02	(+) Control .03
at 3.5 yrs	None	(+) **Control** .01; None	None	Not Applicable
by Familiar Adult	(+) **Control** .03	(+) **Control** .04	(−) Negative Affect .47	(−) Positive Affect .03
at 4.5 yrs		(+) **Control**; (+) Positive Affect	(+) **Control** .08; (+) Positive Affect .01	(+) **Control** .04

Disruptiveness

by Mother	(+) **Negative Affect** .36	(−) Control .05; (+) **Negative Affect** .02	(−) Control .04	(+) **Anger/Frustration** .02
at 4.5 yrs		(−) **Control** .01		
at 3.5 yrs	None	(+) **Negative Affect** .02	None	Not Applicable

continued on next page

Disruptive-ness	by Mother		by Father		by Familiar Adult		by Home Observer	
	(−/+) Predictors	R^2	(−/+) Predictors	R^2	(−/+) Predictors	R^2	(−/+) Predictors	R^2
	(continued)							
by Father	(+) Negative Affect	.04	(+) Negative Affect	.23	(+) Negative Affect	.03	None	.03
at 4.5 yrs	(+) Positive Affect	.03						
at 3.5 yrs	None		(+) Negative Affect	.01	(−) Control	.02	Not Applicable	.02
by Familiar Adult	(+) Negative Affect	.01	None	.01	(+) Negative Affect	.47	(+) Positive Affect	.04
at 4.5 yrs					(−) Control	.03	(−) Control	.02
at 3.5 years	(−) Control	.02	None	.02	None		Not Applicable	

Note. (+/−) refers to the sign of Beta.
In all of these regressions, on entry at each step, the dimensions were significant at p < .001; and the overall regressions were significant at p < .05.at 3.5 yrs(+) Negative Affect.01(−) Control.04 None Not Applicable.

accounted for independent variance in socially appropriate emotional expressiveness; however, these other temperament predictors were inconsistent or only partially consistent across informants/contexts. These other predictors were always in the expected direction, with lower negative affect and lower control associated with less socially appropriate emotional expressiveness.

For the outcome of "compliance," Temperamental Control was the most consistent predictor; control was a significant independent predictor in 10 of the 12 cases at age 4.5 years. For compliance, Temperamental Negative Affect was also a significant independent predictor in 7 of the 12 cases at age 4.5 years, but this effect was particularly strong only when the same informant rated both compliance and negative affect. For the outcome of "disruptiveness," Temperamental Negative Affectivity was typically a strong predictor, and it was largely consistent across informants in the different contexts.

Taken together, these findings show a remarkable degree of cross-situational consistency in temperamental characteristics that predict social maturity before the transition to kindergarten. Children who were rated as higher in positive affectivity by parents or other familiar adults at home showed more socially appropriate emotional expressiveness. Similarly, children who were rated as high in control (i.e., the behavioral regulatory components of temperament such as attention) were rated as more compliant both in their interactions with family members at home and by other familiar adults. On the other hand, temperamental negative affectivity, including aggressiveness and fearfulness, very consistently predicted disruptive behavior both at home and outside the home. Thus, despite moderately high negative intercorrelations between compliance and disruptiveness, these dimensions of social maturity were differentially and consistently associated with temperamental characteristics across contexts.

A Consistent Indirect Role for Temperament in Predicting Adjustment to Kindergarten.

We next examined the consistency with which temperamental characteristics predicted adjustment to kindergarten. Among measures of adjustment to kindergarten were emotional and behavioral problems such as internalizing and externalizing tendencies assessed by the HBQ (Offord et al., 1989) as well as the quality of peer relations as assessed by the CABI (Cowan et al., 1995). The prediction across the transition period involves both a qualitative shift in context from one-on-one interactions with adults to group activity with adult supervision and the passage of 1.5 years, on average, from the 4.5 year assessment. Given the findings from previous research that suggest that social maturity might be the only predictor of positive adjustment in kindergarten and first-grade transitions, we controlled for the effects of prior social maturity at 3.5 and 4.5 years, before examining the predictive power of temperament (Alexander et al., 1997). This is obviously a very conservative test of the role of temperament. Furthermore, because the correlations between structural characteristics qualifying children's kindergarten experiences, specifically, average hours spent at kindergarten, class size, and whether children had friends in the same class on initial attendance were not significantly associated with any of the outcome measures either in peer ratings or emotion/behavior problems, we did not include these structural variables in the predictions of outcome measures from earlier temperament and social maturity ratings. However, we carried out additional analyses, to be presented later, using more differentiated maternal ratings of the CBQ dimensions to examine teacher outcome ratings along with some of these structural variables.

Table 6.5 presents the results of a series of stepwise regressions, varying the source of both dependent and predictor variables, where the dependent measures are the maternal, paternal, and teacher peer relations ratings following the transition into kindergarten, and the predictors are the ASBI scales and temperament composites obtained from mothers, fathers, and familiar adult caregivers at 4.5 and 3.5 years. The order of entry for these regressions was as follows: the ASBI scales at 4.5 and 3.5 years of age were each entered in the first and second blocks, respectively, followed by the three temperament composites at 4.5 and 3.5 years of age entered in the third and fourth blocks, respectively. Within each block a stepwise selection algorithm was used with a criterion of $p = .05$ for entry and $p = .10$ for removal. Thus, these stepwise regressions first control for the degree of social maturity obtained prior to kindergarten transition before examining any additional contribution of temperamental differences.[1]

Table 6.5 shows that the strongest and most consistent predictors of peer relations dimensions were socially appropriate emotional expressiveness, compliance, and disruptiveness ratings of the ASBI rather than temperament composites. In other words, maturity in social interactions with parents and with adults in nonparental roles prior to kindergarten predicted all five positive and negative dimensions of peer relations following the transition to kindergarten. The degree of cross-informant consistency in the prediction of peer dimensions was not as high as for the predictions presented in Table 6.4, yet it was considerable. For example, children rated as compliant (printed in bold font) by mothers, fathers, or familiar adult caregivers tended to be rated later as perceptive by mothers, fathers, and teachers. However, perceptiveness was the only peer dimension that showed such consistency. Other dimensions of peer relations—acceptance, rejection, isolation, or victimization—were not consistently predicted by dimensions that general-

---

[1]Conceptually, the order of entry in these regressions presents the social maturity ratings from the ASBI as possible mediators of the relations between kindergarten outcome and temperament measures. Although we followed the logic of mediation tests proposed by Baron & Kenny (1986), we did not actually carry out a formal test for mediation given that we chose a stepwise selection algorithm in these regressions.

TABLE 6.5 Predicting Peer Relations Following the Transition into Kindergarten From Social Behaviors and Temperament at 4.5 and 3.5 Years

	Temperamental and social predictors					
	by Mother		by Father		by Familiar Adult	
	(−/+) Predictors	R^2	(−/+) Predictors	R^2	(−/+) Predictors	R^2
Perceptiveness						
by Mother						
at 4.5 yrs	(+) **Compliant**	.13	(+) **Compliant**	.06	(+) **Compliant**	.08
	(+) Expressive	.03	(+) Control [t]	.03	(+) Expressive	.03
	(+) Control [t]	.03				
at 3.5 yrs	(+) Positive Affect [t]	.03	None		None	
by Father						
at 4.5 yrs	(+) **Compliant**	.04	(+) **Compliant**	.25	(+) **Compliant**	.07
			(+) Expressive	.06	(+) Control [t]	.02
			(+) Positive Affect [t]	.03		
at 3.5 yrs	(+) Positive Affect [t]	.03	(+) Positive Affect [t]	.02	None	

continued on next page

	by Mother		by Father		by Familiar Adult	
	(-/+) Predictors	R^2	(-/+) Predictors	R^2	(-/+) Predictors	R^2
Perceptiveness						
by Teacher						
at 4.5 yrs	(+) **Compliant**	.05	(+) **Compliant**	.04	(+) **Compliant**	.07
					(+) Control [t]	.02
at 3.5 yrs	None		None		None	
Acceptance						
by Mother						
at 4.5 yrs	(+) Compliant	.12	None		(+) Compliant	.02
	(+) Expressive	.04				
	(−) Disruptive	.02				
at 3.5 yrs	(+) Positive Affect [t]	.04	None		None	
by Father						
at 4.5 yrs	(−) Disruptive	.03	(+) Expressive	.09	(+) Compliant	.05
	(+) Expressive	.02				
at 3.5 yrs	None		(+) Compliant	.03	None	
at 4.5 yrs	None		(+) Positive Affect [t]	.04	None	

122

by Teacher			
at 4.5 yrs	(−) Disruptive .03	(+) Compliant .04 (+) Control[t] .02	(+) Compliant .07
at 3.5 yrs	None	None	(−) Negative Affect[t] .02
Rejection			
by Mother			
at 4.5 yrs	(+) Disruptive .10 (−) Expressive .05	(−) Compliant .02	None
at 3.5 yrs	(+) Disruptive .02	(−) Compliant .04	None
at 4.5 yrs	(+) Negative Affect[t] .07	None	None
at 3.5 yrs	(−) Positive Affect[t] .02	None	None
by Father			
at 4.5 yrs	(+) Disruptive .03	(+) Disruptive .12 (−) Expressive .03	(−) Compliant .05
at 3.5 yrs	None	(−) Compliant .04 (−) Expressive .02	None
at 4.5 yrs	None	(+) Negative Affect[t] .03	None
by Teacher			
at 4.5 yrs	(+) Disruptive .04	None	(−) Compliant .04

continued on next page

	by Mother		by Father		by Familiar Adult	
	(−/+) Predictors	R^2	(−/+) Predictors	R^2	(−/+) Predictors	R^2
by Teacher *(continued)*						
at 3.5 yrs	(+) Disruptive	.02	None		(−) Disruptive	.03
Isolation						
by Mother						
at 4.5 yrs	(−) Expressive	.16	(−) Expressive	.05	(−) Expressive	.03
	(+) Disruptive	.05				
by Father						
at 4.5 yrs	(−) Expressive	.04	(−) Expressive	.12	(−) Expressive	.03
	(+) Disruptive	.02	(+) Disruptive	.02	(+) Negative Affect [t]	.02
at 3.5 yrs	None		(−) Expressive	.02		
by Teacher						
at 4.5 yrs	None		None		(−) Expressive	.03
Victimization						
by Mother						
at 4.5 yrs	(−) Expressive	.05	None		None	
at 3.5 yrs	None		(−) Expressive	.03	(+) Compliant	.02
					(−) Expressive	.02

by Father			
at 4.5 yrs	None	(−) Expressive .06 (−) Positive Affect[t] .07 (+) Negative Affect[t] .03	None
at 3.5 yrs	None	(+) Control[t] .02 (−) Positive Affect[t] .02	
by Teacher			
at 4.5 yrs	(−) Expressive .03 (+) Compliant .03 (+) Control .01	(−) Disruptive .04 (−) Expressive .04	(+) Compliant .03 (−) Expressive .02
at 3.5 yrs	None	None	(+) Control[t] .03 (−) Positive Affect[t] .03

Note. (+/−) refers to the sign of Beta.
The results for each outcome measure are first divided by respondent; then results are presented by order of entry of the predictors (social maturity variables at 4.5 yrs., social maturity variables at 3.5 yrs., temperament variables at 4.5 yrs., temperament variables at 3.5 yrs.).
No entry in the table for one of these four sets of variables indicates that there were no significant predictors.
The final regressions were significant at p < .05.
[t] specifies temperamental predictors.

ized across all three informants. For example, maternal ratings of disruptiveness consistently predicted peer acceptance ratings of mothers, fathers, and
teachers, but paternal or familiar adult caregiver ratings of disruptiveness did
not predict peer acceptance ratings. Rather, familiar adult ratings of compliance consistently predicted peer acceptance ratings by mothers, fathers, and
teachers, but compliance ratings of mothers and fathers predicted only their
own ratings of peer acceptance. Thus, positive dimensions of peer relations
such as peer acceptance and perceptiveness were predicted by compliance
and disruptiveness ratings.

An examination of temperamental predictors of positive dimensions of
peer relations, denoted by t superscripts in Table 6.5, speaks to the contextual
specificity in predictions. For example, maternal and paternal ratings of temperamental positive affectivity predicted peer perceptiveness and acceptance,
but only when these two peer measures were also rated by mothers and fathers. Familiar adult caregiver ratings of control predicted teacher's ratings of
perceptiveness whereas their negative affectivity ratings predicted teacher
acceptance ratings. In other words, although some temperament dimensions
emerged as independent predictors of positive dimensions of peer relations,
these temperament dimensions did not show extensive cross-informant consistency as predictors.

Turning to the more negative dimensions of peer relations (rejection, isolation, and victimization), social maturity prior to kindergarten showed a moderate degree of cross-informant consistency in prediction. Maternal ratings of
disruptiveness consistently predicted peer rejection ratings of all three informants; paternal disruptiveness ratings predicted paternal reports of rejection, and familiar adult disruptiveness ratings predicted later teacher reports
of rejection. Thus, the link between early disruptiveness and kindergarten rejection was fairly robust. Familiar adult caregiver ratings of socially appropriate emotional expressiveness consistently predicted peer isolation ratings of
mothers, fathers, and teachers. Socially appropriate emotional expressiveness ratings of mothers and fathers also predicted peer isolation ratings but
only for maternal and paternal ratings of this peer dimension. In fact, none of
the parental predictors were associated with teacher reports of peer isolation
(see later analyses on CBQ shyness). Finally, socially appropriate emotional
expressiveness ratings of mothers, fathers, and familiar adult caregivers consistently predicted maternal and teacher ratings of victimization by peers.

Table 6.5 also reveals several instances in which temperament composites
predict the problematic peer relations residuals, after the effects of social maturity are considered. In some cases, the effect was substantial; for instance,
maternal reports of negative affect accounted for 7% of the residual variance
in maternal reports of later rejection. Considering all of the results, however,
the independent predictive power of temperamental characteristics for negative peer relations over and above social maturity ratings showed low

cross-informant consistency. For example, maternal and paternal ratings of negative affectivity emerged as predictors of rejection ratings but only for mothers' and fathers' own ratings of later peer rejection. Similarly, only negative affectivity ratings of familiar adult caregivers predicted paternal ratings of peer isolation, whereas both maternal and familiar adult caregiver ratings of control predicted teachers' peer victimization ratings.

Taken together these findings suggest that children low in socially appropriate emotional expressiveness tend to be victimized by peers following the transition to kindergarten, whereas those who are rated as compliant and less disruptive tend to be rated as perceptive, less likely to be rejected or isolated, and more accepted by their peers. Thus, our findings replicate and extend previous findings in showing that children who are relatively more mature in their social interactions prior to kindergarten experience more positive peer relations following the transition (Alexander et al., 1997). Although the evidence often did not generalize across informants, incremental effects (beyond the effects of social maturity) of earlier positive affectivity and behavioral control were associated with higher peer perceptiveness and acceptance, lower rejection, and lesser victimization.

These regressions of peer relations outcomes on temperament controlled for the effects of prior social maturity at 3.5 and 4.5 years, and the results mainly highlight the strength of social maturity ratings in predicting peer relations. It is also possible that temperament plays an indirect role on these outcome measures through its direct effects on social maturity as assessed by the ASBI. A similar indirect role for temperament has been demonstrated in the development of internalized behavior and attachment (Kochanska, 1991, 1995). To further explore this possibility, we carried out stepwise regressions predicting dimensions of peer relations from temperamental characteristics without controlling for the effects of social behavior scales assessed by the ASBI. These regressions (not presented) showed temperamental characteristics had a direct effect on peer perceptiveness, acceptance, and rejection ratings but the same dimensions of temperament did not emerge consistently as predictors across informants. For example, maternal and caregiver ratings of positive affectivity predicted mothers' ratings of acceptance, but only control ratings predicted teacher ratings of acceptance. On the whole, our findings support a cross-situationally consistent yet indirect role for temperament. However, temperament dimensions that appear to have indirect effects on peer outcomes often do not show cross-informant (cross-context) consistency.

Predicting Internalizing and Externalizing Tendencies Following the Kindergarten Transition

We next analyzed within- and across-informant consistency in predicting internalizing and externalizing tendencies using both social maturity ratings and temperamental characteristics. Table 6.6 presents the stepwise regressions wherein the outcome variables are HBQ internalizing and externalizing tendencies reported following the transition into kindergarten by mothers, fathers, and teachers. We predicted these outcomes by the socially appropriate expressiveness, compliance, and disruptiveness scales of the ASBI and by temperament composites obtained from mothers, fathers, and familiar adult caregivers at 4.5 and 3.5 years of age. The order of entry in these regressions was identical to the stepwise regressions presented in Table 6.5, where ASBI scales at 4.5 and 3.5 years were entered as blocks in the first and second steps, followed by temperament composites at 4.5 and 3.5 years entered as blocks in the third and fourth steps, respectively. A stepwise selection algorithm was used within each block with $p = .05$ for entry and $p = .10$ for removal.

Internalizing.   First, we examined Internalizing as an outcome. Table 6.6 shows several significant predictors, each of which had a sensible direction, with less adaptive social behaviors and more negative temperament associated with later internalizing problems. As in other results, the predictors were more numerous and stronger when the same informant supplied both predictor and outcome measures. Perhaps the most informative outcome measure was the teachers' ratings of Internalizing, from the school context. As Table 6.6 shows, this measure of problem behavior was predicted by maternal, paternal, and other familiar adult ratings of socially appropriate emotional expressiveness at age 4.5 years. This longitudinal prediction, unconfounded by common raters, might be very noteworthy. In fact, low expressiveness predicted Internalizing in 6 of the 9 possible within- and across-informant contexts in Table 6.6. Temperamental negative affect also predicted significant residual variance in Internalizing in several instances in Table 6.6 although there were also instances of lack of cross-informant consistency. Despite these positive findings, the overall evidence for cross-informant consistency in predictors of internalizing tendencies was modest, and there were fewer replicated associations than in the results on peer relations presented earlier in the chapter.

Externalizing.   Results for Externalizing are presented in the lower section of Table 6.6. At the outset, we acknowledge that the prekindergarten social maturity predictors Disruptive and Compliant hold much in common conceptually with the later measure of Externalizing. In a sense, we can view the prediction of externalizing from earlier ratings on how disruptive the child was and how little the child complied as straightforward continuity of externalizing problems across the kindergarten transition.

The results of regressions on externalizing tendencies showed that compliance ratings, whether obtained from mothers, fathers or caregivers, consistently emerged as predictors of externalizing tendencies, whether rated by mothers, fathers, or teachers. The results also showed that maternal ratings of disruptiveness predicted externalizing tendencies but fathers' ratings of disruptiveness predicted only their own ratings of externalizing tendencies. Thus, the cross-informant consistency in predictors of externalizing tendencies was much stronger than that found for internalizing tendencies and is comparable to the degree of cross-informant consistency we found between temperament and social maturity ratings of the ASBI, reported in Table 6.3. This finding of greater cross-informant consistency of externalizing tendencies relative to internalizing tendencies replicates previous research (Hinshaw et al., 1992). The additional contribution of temperament ratings to the prediction of externalizing tendencies were negligible, with the exception that maternal and paternal ratings of negative affectivity helped predict their own ratings of later externalizing tendencies (and powerfully so in the case of mothers).

As in the prior analyses of peer relations, we also examined the possible indirect contribution of temperamental differences to internalizing and externalizing problems without controlling for the effects of social maturity. These regressions (not shown) revealed that, when the effects of social maturity prior to kindergarten were uncontrolled, temperament had a direct influence on externalizing tendencies. However, once again, the temperament dimensions that emerged were inconsistent across informants (contexts). For example, preschool-age negative affectivity ratings of mothers and fathers consistently predicted later externalizing ratings of all three informants, but the negative affectivity ratings of familiar caregivers did not predict later externalizing. On the other hand, the familiar caregivers were capable of detecting temperament correlates of later externalizing because their control ratings did consistently emerge as a predictor of later externalizing. Shifting our attention to internalizing tendencies, the influence of temperament was less consistent. For example, maternal and paternal ratings of temperament at preschool age consistently predicted internalizing ratings of mothers and fathers but not of teachers. This suggests that when the predictions are within the same context, such as home, there is a consistent effect of temperament on internalizing tendencies, without controlling for social maturity. Together, these findings support an indirect role for preschool-age temperament in influencing externalizing tendencies following the transition to kindergarten, through its direct influence on social maturity and specifically on disruptiveness. The evidence for a similarly indirect role for temperament or a direct role for social maturity in predicting internalizing problems is mixed.

The Special Case of Shy Children

We found that structural characteristics of the kindergarten experience such as class size and hours spent in kindergarten were not associated with out-

TABLE 6.6 Predicting Internalizing and Externalizing Tendencies Following the Kindergarten Transition From Temperament and Social Behavior at 3.5 and 4.5 years

	by Mother		by Father		by Familiar Adult	
	(−/+) Predictors	R^2	(−/+) Predictors	R^2	(−/+) Predictors	R^2
Outcome Measures: Internalizing						
by Mother						
at 4.5 yrs	(+) Disruptive	.10	(−) Expressive	.09	None	
	(−) Expressive	.05				
at 3.5 yrs	(+) Disruptive	.03	None		None	
at 4.5 yrs	(+) Negative Affect [t]	.07	None		None	
at 3.5 yrs	(+) Negative Affect [t]	.05	None		None	
	(+) Control [t]	.03				
by Father						
at 4.5 yrs	(+) Disruptive	.05	(−) Expressive	.12	(−) Compliant	.05
	(+) Negative Affect [t]	.02	(+) Disruptive	.08	(+) Negative Affect [t]	.03
at 3.5 yrs	None		(+) Disruptive	.03	None	
at 4.5 yrs	None		(+) Negative Affect [t]	.05	None	

130

by Teacher

at 4.5 yrs	(−) Expressive	.04	(−) Expressive	.04	(−) Expressive	.03
at 3.5 yrs	None		None		(+)Control[t]	.02

Outcome Measures: Externalizing

by Mother

at 4.5 yrs	(+) Disruptive (−) Compliant (+) Negative Affect[t]	.35 .03 .12	(−) Compliant	.10	(−) Compliant	.04
at 3.5 yrs	None		None		(+) Disruptive	.04

by Father

at 4.5 yrs	(+) Disruptive (−) Compliant	.14 .04	(+) Disruptive (−) Compliant	.28 .09	(−) Compliant	.05
at 3.5 yrs	None		(−) Compliant	.01	(−) Compliant	.02
at 4.5 yrs	None		(−) Negative Affect[t]	.03	None	

by Teacher

at 4.5 yrs	(+) Disruptive (−) Compliant	.09 .03	(−) Compliant	.07	(−) Compliant (−) Control[t]	.11 .01
at 3.5 yrs	(+) Disruptive	.01	None		None	

Note. (+/−) refers to the sign of Beta.   In all of these regressions, the overall regressions were significant at p < .05.
[t] specifies temperamental predictors.

131

come measures rated by either parents or teachers. To study one rather specific measure of context and one focal dimension of temperament more closely, we examined whether having friends in the same class on entry to kindergarten affected shy and bold children's experiences differentially. It seemed conceivable that, for shy children, the presence of known peers on entry into kindergarten would render the experience much less intimidating, and perhaps even make their overall adjustment in the spring semester more positive. To examine this possibility, we used maternal ratings of the CBQ Shyness scale along with presence of friends on entry to examine mean differences in teacher outcomes ratings. We used a criterion of one standard deviation to create three groups of children who were shy, intermediate, or bold on the CBQ Shyness scale. Because only mothers provided CBQ ratings we could not examine cross-informant consistency in these analyses. Two-way between subject ANOVAs with shyness and presence of friends on entry as predictors (levels: no friends on entry and friends on entry) revealed a two-way interaction effect on peer perceptiveness, acceptance, and externalizing ratings, $p < .05$, and a marginal interaction effect on peer isolation, $p < .10$. Figure 6.1 shows the means for peer perceptiveness, Fig. 6.2 for peer acceptance, Fig. 6.3 for peer isolation, and Fig. 6.4 for externalizing ratings. As can be seen from these figures, shy children who did not have friends on entry relative to those with friends on entry were rated lower in perceptiveness, acceptance, and higher in peer isolation. On the other hand, bold children who had friends on entry were rated higher on externalizing relative to other bold children who did not have friends on entry. The presence of previously known friends on entry to kindergarten might not be the causal agent affecting shy children's adjustment to kindergarten in these findings. For example, perhaps

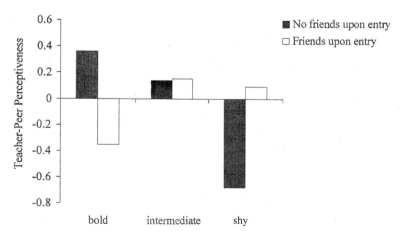

FIG. 6.1.   Mean differences in teacher ratings of peer perceptiveness for bold, intermediate, and shy children either with previously known friends or no previously known friends at entry to kindergarten.

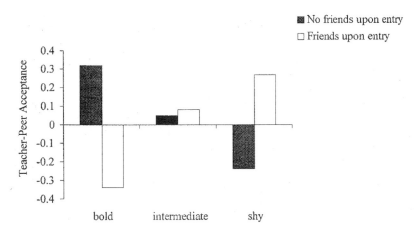

FIG. 6.2.   Mean differences in teacher ratings of peer acceptance for bold, intermediate, and shy children either with previously known friends or no previously known friends at entry to kindergarten.

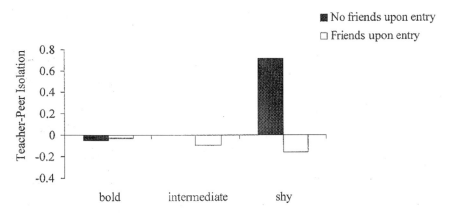

FIG. 6.3.   Mean differences in teacher ratings of peer isolation for bold, intermediate, and shy children either with previously known friends or no previously known friends at entry to kindergarten.

parents who have strong community ties are more likely to have children who know other children their age on entry to kindergarten.

CONCLUSIONS

Our findings support previous research and extend our understanding of temperament and context interrelations in several ways. For example, prior to the kindergarten transition, temperament had a cross-situationally consis-

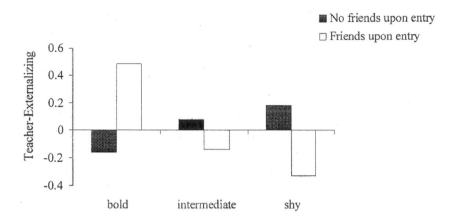

FIG. 6.4.   Mean differences in teacher ratings of externalizing tendencies for bold, intermediate, and shy children either with previously known friends or no previously known friends at entry to kindergarten.

tent effect on social maturity ratings both within the family and outside the family as observed by adults in nonparental roles. Following the transition to kindergarten, temperament had a consistent, indirect influence on some dimensions of peer relations and externalizing tendencies. Prior social maturity, rather than temperament, showed a cross-situationally consistent influence on peer and emotional outcomes during the second semester of kindergarten. In other words, social maturity appeared to mediate the influence of temperament on children's adjustment to kindergarten. When we did not control for the effects of social maturity, temperamental characteristics helped predict predicted peer perceptiveness, acceptance, and rejection but not isolation or victimization. Similarly, temperament indirectly predicted externalizing to a greater extent than internalizing tendencies across the transition to kindergarten. Furthermore, the role of structural characteristics such as time spent and class size did not appear to modify the cross-informant or context predictions from social maturity or temperament on adjustment measures. Unlike these structural variables, presence of friends in the same class on entry appeared to differentially influence the eventual adjustment of shy children to kindergarten in the spring semester as rated by their teachers. For example, shy children with friends on entry experienced less isolation and more acceptance by their peers as perceived by their teachers.

    This indirect and sometimes inconsistent role for temperament in predicting adjustment to kindergarten stands in stark contrast to its direct effect on social maturity. Temperamental characteristics as observed in different contexts showed remarkable consistency in predicting social maturity (which might be thought of as internalized behavioral patterns) before the kindergarten transition. Thus, whereas our results support the contextual specificity of temperamental characteristics, they also show a complex role for temperament in adjusting to the transition. Our results need to be interpreted within the framework of a larger literature on temperament and adjustment, which is reviewed by Rothbart and Bates (1998). This literature is fairly definitive in establishing concurrent and antecedent links between temperament and adjustment, despite lingering questions about contamination of predictor and outcome measures. Several investigators have explained processes that could explain the link between temperament and adjustment measures (Clark, Watson, & Mineka, 1994; Rothbart & Bates, 1998; Rothbart, Posner, & Hershey, 1995).

Our findings suggest that behavioral characteristics that are social rather than temperamental in nature such as compliance, disruptiveness, and socially appropriate emotional expressiveness have a direct bearing on both peer relations and emotional/behavioral problems following the transition to kindergarten. Consistent with previous research, children who engage in socially appropriate emotional expressiveness and who are compliant and less disruptive are rated as perceptive in their peer interactions; as less likely to be rejected, victimized, or isolated; and as more likely to be accepted by peers. As noted earlier, these social characteristics are considered indicators of social maturity in previous research, and are targeted by socialization efforts (Alexander et al., 1997). Our findings also suggest that temperamental characteristics influence these social characteristics. For example, children who are high in attentional and behavioral control tend to be compliant, whereas children high in negative affectivity tend to be disruptive. Temperamental positive affectivity promotes the development of socially appropriate emotional expressiveness. Although previous research on socialization shows that temperamental characteristics are not the only predictors of social maturity or internalized behavior, they play a decisive role along with attachment and parenting styles (Kochanska, 1991, 1995; Kochanska & Aksan, 1995; Kochanska, Murray, Jacques, Koenig, & Vandegeest, 1996).

Our results perhaps hold some implications for interpreting other existing research and planning new studies. For example, the results demonstrate the importance of maintaining distinctions between positive and negative affect, as we have also emphasized in our genetics of temperament research (Goldsmith, Buss, & Lemery, 1997). This distinctiveness was illustrated in Table 6.5, where the predictive power of positive affect was not always mirrored by negative affect, and vice-versa.

The transition to kindergarten is perhaps the first major life event outside the family that involves a social role transition and is common to most children. Our findings suggest that temperamental characteristics conceptualized as primarily emotional in nature play an important role in negotiating the demands of this role transition and underscore the importance of better understanding the predictors of successful socialization. Our findings are consonant with previous research in highlighting the complex role individual differences in temperament or personality are likely to play in positive psychological adjustment.

We emphasize, however, that our results only address one of three interesting questions about the link between earlier temperament and the kindergarten transition. Another question is how earlier temperament affects emotional and social reactions during the initial stages of the kindergarten transition. Our observations, taken a few months later, probably reflect an adaptation after this initial reaction. The third question is how temperament itself changes across the kindergarten transition. As emphasized in psychopathology research, inflexibility of personality across situations that hold different environmental presses is maladaptive, and the same principle probably holds for temperament. Unfortunately, we do not have temperament measures during the kindergarten year, but we hope to address this issue with further longitudinal follow-up of the sample.

ACKNOWLEDGMENTS

The Wisconsin Maternity Leave and Health Project was supported by National Institute of Mental Health Grant No. MH44340 to Marilyn J. Essex and Janet S. Hyde, Co-Principal Investigators, with Roseanne Clark, H. Hill Goldsmith, Marjorie H. Klein, Nancy A. Smider, and Deborah Lowe Vandell. Additional funding was provided by the John D. and Catherine T. MacArthur Foundation Research Network on Depression and the Network on Psychopathology and Development (David J. Kupfer, Chair), the Wisconsin Center for Affective Science (NIMH P50-MH53254, Richard J. Davidson, Director), the University of Wisconsin Graduate School, and the Wisconsin Psychiatric Research Institute.

Special thanks are extended to Jeff Armstrong and Will Shattuck for their central role in the overall management and quality assurance of the project, and to specialized project staff Roy Barnes, Laura Haugen, Francine Horton, Tracy Kryshak, Ashby Plant, Mary Jo Ryan, and Stephanie McNeil. The researchers also thank the interviewers and many students and other staff who coded the interviews, entered data, and performed the many other tasks central to the project. Special thanks are extended to the families who have committed their time and energy for participating in this research program since its inception.

REFERENCES

Achenbach, T. M., McConaughy, S. H., & Howell, C. T. (1987). Child/adolescent behavioral and emotional problems: Implications of cross-informant correlations for situation specificity. *Psychological Bulletin, 101,* 213–232.

Ahadi, S. A., & Rothbart, M. K. (1994). Temperament, development and the Big Five. In C. Halverson, G. Kohnstamm, & R. Martin (Eds.), *The developing structure of temperament and personality from infancy to childhood,* (pp. 189–208). Hillsdale, NJ: Lawrence Erlbaum Associates.

Ahadi, S. A., Rothbart, M. K., & Ye, R. M. (1993). Children in the U.S. and China: Different yet the same. *European Journal of Personality, 7,* 359–377.

Alexander, K. L., Entwisle, D. R. & Horsey, C. S. (1997). From first grade forward: Early foundations of high school dropout. *Sociology of Education, 70,* 87–107.

Baron, R. M., & Kenny, D. A. (1986). The moderator-mediator variable distinction in social psychological research: Conceptual, strategic and statistical considerations. *Journal of Personality and Social Psychology, 51,* 1173–1182.

Bates, J. E., Pettit, G. S., Dodge, K. A., & Ridge, B. (1998). Interaction of temperamental resistance to control and restrictive parenting in the development of externalizing behavior. *Developmental Psychology, 34,* 982–995.

Bayley, N. (1993). *Bayley scales of infant development* (2nd ed.). San Antonio, TX: Harcourt Brace.

Behar, L., & Stringfield, S. (1974). A behavior rating scale for the preschool child. *Developmental Psychology, 10,* 601–610.

Campos, J. J., Barrett, K. C., Lamb, M. E., Goldsmith, H. H., & Stenberg, C. (1983). Socioemotional development. In M. M. Haith & J. J. Campos (Eds.), P. H. Mussen (Series Ed.), *Handbook of Child Psychology: (Vol. 2). Infancy and developmental psychobiology,* (pp. 783–915). New York: Wiley.

Clark, L. A., Watson, D., & Mineka, S. (1994). Temperament, personality, and the mood and anxiety disorders. *Journal of Abnormal Psychology, 103,* 103–116.

Cowan, P. A., Cowan, C. P., Heming, G., & Miller, N. (1995). *The child adaptive behavior inventory.* Unpublished manuscript, University of California, Berkeley

Entwisle, D. R., & Alexander, K. L. (1998). Facilitating the transition to first grade: The nature of transition and research factors affecting it. *The Elementary School Journal, 4,* 351–364.

Goldsmith, H. H. (1994). Parsing the emotional domain from a developmental perspective. In R. Davidson & P. Ekman (Eds.), *Questions about emotion* (pp. 68–73). New York: Oxford University Press.

Goldsmith, H. H., Buss, K. A., & Lemery, K. S. (1997). Toddler and childhood temperament: Expanded content, stronger genetic evidence, new evidence for the importance of environment. *Developmental Psychology, 33,* 891–905.

Goldsmith, H. H., Buss, A. H., Plomin, R., Rothbart, M. K., Thomas, A., Chess, S., Hinde, R. A., & McCall, R. B. (1983). Roundtable: What is temperament? Four approaches. *Child Development, 58,* 505–529.

Goldsmith, H. H., & Campos, J. J. (1990). The structure of infant temperamental dispositions to experience fear and pleasure: A psychometric perspective. *Child Development, 61,* 1944–1964.

Herbert, N. (1985). *Quantum reality.* New York: Doubleday.

Hinshaw, W. P., Han, S. S., Erhardt, D., & Huber, A. (1992). Internalizing and externalizing behavior problems in preschool children: Correspondence among parent and teacher ratings and behavior observations. *Journal of Clinical Child Psychology, 21,* 143–150.

Hogan, A. E., Scott, K. G., & Bauer, C. R. (1992). The adaptive social behavior inventory: A new assessment of social competence in high-risk 3-year-olds. *Journal of Psychoeducational Assessment, 10,* 230–239.

Hyde, J. S., Klein, M., Essex, M. J., & Clark, R. (1995). Maternity leave and women's mental health. *Psychology of Women Quarterly, 19,* 257–285.

Kochanska, G. (1991). Socialization and temperament in the development of guilt and conscience. *Child Development, 62,* 1379–1392.

Kochanska, G. (1995). Children's temperament, mothers discipline, and security of attachment: Multiple pathways to emerging internalization. *Child Development, 66,* 597–615.

Kochanska, G. (1998). Individual differences in emotionality in infancy. *Child Development, 68,* 94–112.

Kochanska, G., & Aksan, N. (1995). Mother–child mutually positive affect, the quality of child compliance to requests and prohibitions, and maternal control as correlates of early internalization. *Child Development, 66,* 236–254.

Kochanska, G., Murray, K., Jacques, T. Y., Koenig, A. L., & Vandegeest, K. A. (1996). Inhibitory control in young children and its role in emerging internalization. *Child Development, 67,* 420–507.

MacArthur Research Network on Psychopathology and Development. (1998). *A middle childhood assessment battery: Development of the health and behavior questionnaire.* Unpublished manuscript

Offord, D. R., Boyle, M. H., & Racine, Y. (1989). Ontario Child Health Study: Correlates of disorder. *Journal of the American Academy of Child and Adolescent Psychiatry, 28,* 856–860.

Patterson, C. R. (1982). *A social learning approach: Coercive family process.* Oregon: Castalia.

Plomin, R., DeFries, J. C., & Loehlin, J. C. (1977). Genotype-environment interaction and correlation in the analysis of human behavior. *Psychological Bulletin, 84,* 309–322.

Rothbart, M. K., & Bates, J. E. (1998). Temperament. In W. Damon (Series Ed.) & N. Eisenberg (Vol. Ed.), *Handbook of child psychology* (Vol. 3). *Social, emotional, and personality development.* (5th ed., pp. 105–176). New York: Wiley.

Rothbart, M. K., Posner, M. I., & Hershey, K. L. (1995). Temperament, attention, and developmental psychopathology. In D. Cicchetti & D. J. Cohen (Eds.), *Manual of Developmental Psychopathology* (Vol. 1, pp. 315–340). New York: Wiley.

Scarr, S., & McCartney, K. (1983). How people make their own environments: A theory of genotype environment effects. *Child Development, 54,* 424–435.

Wachs, T. D. (1992). *The nature of nurture.* Newbury Park, CA: Sage.

Watson, D., Clark, L. A., & Harkness, A. R. (1994). Structures of personality and their relevance to psychopathology. *Journal of Abnormal Psychology, 103,* 18–31.

Watson, D., Clark, L. A., & Tellegen, A. (1988). Developmental and validation of brief measures of positive and negative affect: The PANAS scales. *Journal of Personality and Social Psychology, 54,* 1063–1070.

7 Culture as a Context for Temperament: Suggestions From the Life Courses of Shy Swedes and Americans

Margaret Kerr
Örebro University

When people live and work together closely and have a common history, they begin to share basic assumptions about the way things are and, indeed, should be (e.g., whether children should work, whether people should marry for love, or whether children should sleep with their parents) (Schweder et al., 1998). These shared assumptions also concern what the best, or most admirable, personality traits are—in general and for certain subgroups within a society.

In this chapter, I suggest a goodness of fit model that builds on previous models (Lerner, 1983; Lewis, 1987). I suggest that, in any given culture, there are both psychological and practical features of the environment that reflect people's shared assumptions about behavior. As a result, the environment favors some temperamentally based behaviors over others, and the favored behaviors are then more likely to be associated with good developmental outcomes. I draw examples of the various links in this model from the literature on shyness, inhibition, and anxiety, and compare findings from two studies of the life courses of shy people: one using an American sample (Caspi, Elder, & Bem, 1988) and the other using a Swedish sample (Kerr, Lambert, & Bem, 1996).

A GENERAL MODEL OF CULTURE AS A CONTEXT
FOR TEMPERAMENT

There are at least two processes through which culturally shared preferences
ɔr certain temperamental and personality characteristics can affect the con-
ɹuity and life course sequelae of temperament. One involves people's inter-
ions with each other (interpersonal processes), and the other involves
tₗ 'r dealings with the culture's institutions and customs (institutional processes). Both are depicted in Fig. 7.1. Interpersonal processes, shown on the
left side of the figure, mainly concern the psychological environment. Culturally shared notions influence how people perceive and respond to temperamentally based behaviors. Their responses, in turn, help to determine how
stable those behaviors will be over time and how easily people will accomplish various goals. Institutional processes, shown in the right side of the figure, concern the more practical aspects of the environment. Cultures develop

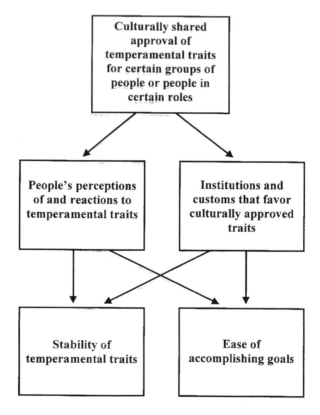

FIG. 7.1.   Proposed model of the role in culture in the stability of temperament and
its life course sequelae.

institutions, or established ways of doing things (e.g., the job interview, dating, going away to college), that favor the culturally admired behaviors. This benefits those whose temperaments are consistent with the culturally admired behaviors and hinders those whose temperaments are inconsistent. These processes might ultimately strengthen the shared assumptions by allowing those with the valued traits to accomplish the goal of reproduction more readily, thus making the valued traits more common (Lewis, 1989).

Interpersonal Processes

Cultural values determine how people perceive and respond to temperamental traits—the first step in the interpersonal processes sequence. There is a sizable literature that suggests that North Americans' perceptions of shy, inhibited people are generally negative. They judge shy people as less friendly and likable than nonshy people (Jones & Russell, 1982; Zimbardo, 1977) and consider them less poised (Jones, Cavert, & Indart, 1983), and less affectionate, warm, and happy (Jones & Carpenter, 1986). One could argue that these traits might actually correlate with shyness, and thus these findings reveal no culturally shared attitude; however, Americans also rate shy people as less talented (Jones, Cavert, & Indart, 1983) and less physically attractive (Jones & Carpenter, 1986). Because these are characteristics that have no inherent relation to shyness, it is difficult to explain these relations without inferring a culturally shared negative attitude toward shyness. Apparently, children also share this negative attitude toward shy, inhibited behavior. In research with North American children, socially wary children are at risk for being rejected by their peers (Rubin, Chen, & Hymel, 1993). It has been suggested that this is a common attitude among individualistic, competitive North American and Western European cultures, but not among collectivist cultures such as China (Chen et al., 1998; Rubin, 1998). Chinese children's socially wary behavior is valued and encouraged by adults and other children (Chen, Rubin, & Li, 1995, 1997). Additionally, mothers' warm and accepting attitudes have been positively linked to inhibition in Chinese toddlers, but negatively linked in Canadian toddlers (Chen et al., 1998).

Even within a given culture, however, the same behavior can be viewed as more appropriate or desirable for some people than it is for others. In some studies of Western cultures, negative attitudes toward shyness in childhood seem to apply more to boys than girls. Parents have been found to respond more favorably to shy girls than shy boys (Radke-Yarrow, Richters, & Wilson, 1988; Stevenson-Hinde, 1988; Stevenson-Hinde & Hinde, 1986). In one study, mothers of shy boys expressed irritation or dissatisfaction that their sons had not already outgrown this behavior; mothers of shy girls expressed pleasure that their daughters wanted to be at home with them

(Stevenson-Hinde & Hinde, 1986). Additionally, shyness in boys, but not girls, seems to become less acceptable with age (Stevenson-Hinde & Shouldice, 1993). These differences suggest that people's responses to shy children are guided by some culturally-shared notion that the trait is less desirable for boys than girls.

These culturally influenced reactions to temperamentally based behaviors, in turn, determine how stable the behaviors will be and whether the developmental outcomes will be good or bad—the second step in the interpersonal processes sequence. In a number of studies, mothers' emotional responses to children have been linked to changes over time in children's temperamental characteristics such as sociability and negative emotionality (Engfer, 1993; Grusec & Lytton, 1988; Matheny, 1986; Van den Boom, 1994; Washington, Minde, & Goldberg, 1986). Studies also suggest that the way mothers respond to shy, inhibited, or anxious children can influence the stability of the behavior. In one study, anxious kindergarten boys became less anxious by fifth grade if their mothers were overprotective (Bowen, Vitaro, Kerr, & Pellitier, 1995). In another study, babies who cried a lot as newborns cried less at 5 months if they had mothers who were especially sensitive and responsive (Fish, Stifter, & Belsky, 1991). In addition to these apparent effects on stability, parents' expectations and responses also influence children's later adjustment. Children have better developmental outcomes if, for example, they choose toys that are consistent with their mothers' sex role orientations (Lewis, 1987). This finding also appears for shy, inhibited behavior. In the study mentioned above in which mothers viewed girls' shyness positively and boys' negatively (Stevenson-Hinde & Hinde, 1986), girls' shyness was related positively to measures of good adjustment and negatively to poor adjustment. For boys it was exactly the opposite. Furthermore, different developmental outcomes appear in cultures that have different views of shy, inhibited behavior. Inhibited North American children have low opinions of their social skills and peer relationships (e.g., Boivin, Hymel, & Bukowski, 1995) and are prone to loneliness and depression (Boivin et al., 1995; Rubin, Chen, McDougall, Bowker, & McKinnon, 1995). Inhibited Chinese children, in contrast, have good relationships with their peers (Chen et al., 1995; Chen, Rubin, & Sun, 1992) and think of themselves as socially competent (Chen, Rubin, & Li, in press).

Results from longitudinal studies also reveal long-term consequences of temperament-related interpersonal processes. In a longitudinal study of Americans from the Berkeley Guidance Study, shy boys, but not shy girls, married and had children later than their peers (Caspi et al., 1988). Although interpersonal and institutional explanations probably both apply, one can easily imagine that the interpersonal processes would be as follows: People thought that boys should be bold in establishing romantic relationships. Shy boys fell short of this expectation and were, thus, less desirable. This interfered with their abilities to form relationships. In a previous study of the present Swedish sample, girls who were inhibited at about 2 years tended to remain more inhibited than average through 16 years, whereas boys did not (Kerr, Lambert, Stattin, & Klackenberg-Larsson, 1994). Similarly, in an American sample, boys were more likely than girls to shift from being very inhibited at 21 months to very uninhibited at 5.5 years (Kagan, Reznick, & Snidman, 1987). One interpretation of these sex differences in stability is that boys were more pressured than girls were to change their inhibited behavior. Taken together, these studies suggest that shared assumptions partly determine how people will respond to certain temperamentally based behaviors, and those responses partly determine how stable those traits will be.

Institutional Processes

Cultures develop institutions and customs that fit their assumptions about how people should behave. This idea is borrowed from S. Bem's (1993) argument about American culture and gender. Bem proposed that Americans historically have assumed that women should take on traditional roles, and they have developed certain institutions and practices that build on that assumption. For example, the fact that the work day does not match the school day reveals an assumption that families will have a stay-at-home mom to take care of the children during the nonoverlapping hours. As another example, the fact that firefighting equipment is so big and heavy that most women cannot use it reveals an assumption that only men will fight fires. Naturally, people who exhibit the favored behaviors find those institutions and customs easier to deal with (e.g., stay-at-home moms are untroubled by the fact that the work day does not match the school day, and women who do not try to be firefighters are not put off by the minimum size requirements). The assumptions determine the institutions and customs, but with different assumptions, the customs that now seem so natural could be completely different and yet seem equally natural. For example, if only women were available to fight fires, and everyone assumed that firefighters would be women, equipment would be manufactured to be light enough that the average woman could use it effectively. A similar argument can be made concerning culturally shared assumptions about temperament and personality. We used such an argument to understand the similarities and differences between findings from our study of the life courses of shy people in Sweden (Kerr, Lambert, & Bem, 1996) and findings from an earlier study of Americans (Caspi, Elder, & Bem, 1988). We identified two salient differences in culturally shared assumptions. They concerned attitudes about shy behavior and about the role of women in society.

COMPARING THE LIFE COURSES OF SHY SWEDES
WITH THOSE OF SHY AMERICANS

Cultural Context: Shyness

We argued that Americans have less favorable views of shyness and, in fact, assume that people should not be shy unless something is wrong. Consequently, the customs and institutions surrounding many of the important life transitions that Americans make, by convention, require outgoing, assertive behavior. A case in point is career transitions. Job seekers get advice that speaks to the importance of assertiveness, personal charm, and making personal contacts, "You have to sell yourself." and "It's not what you know, but who you know." Self-help books recommend daring, aggressive self-promotional measures, as though these qualities, alone, will insure success on the job market. And they might. Some have argued that by the 1950s personality had become more important than technical skill in the American workplace (Mills, 1956, p. 187), and American parents, recognizing this fact (Miller & Swanson, 1958, p. 229), had begun teaching their children to develop unusual personalities rather than skills or talents (Miller & Swanson, 1958, p. 23). What is suggested is that Americans have a general assumption that people should be outgoing, and that assumption is reflected in the customs and institutions surrounding career entry. Outgoing people should benefit from these customs and institutions and shy people should be hindered.

Sweden is a society that has, in many ways, been very similar to the United States throughout recent history. It is not a collectivist culture like China. Yet, unlike the United States, Sweden has a long social and political history of valuing humility and reserve, and devaluing the bold, self-promoting behavior that is so highly valued by Americans (Daun, 1989, p. 265; Daun, Mattlar, & Alanen, 1989; Hendin, 1964, p. 43). It is difficult to say why this philosophy—that people should never think of themselves as better than anyone else—evolved and became an explicit political goal. Perhaps it grew out of the combined influences of the Lutheran church and the hierarchical society that once existed in Sweden, although similar factors existed elsewhere in Europe. Perhaps it was influenced by the fact that, among European countries, Sweden had one of the highest rates of emigration to the New World, and many people emigrated because they wanted better treatment from their employers (as suggested by one Swedish historian, A.-S. Ohlander, personal communication, February 3, 1999). Thus, there might have been some selective migration in which the people who were the least willing to be humble and reserved left for a more congenial climate: the United States. It might be going too far to say that shyness is highly valued in Sweden. It is, however, less inconsistent with the valued behavior in Sweden than in the United States, and, as such, is less devalued. This is reflected in some of the customs and institutions. Scholars argue that assertive, competitive behavior is unnecessary for dealing with most Swedish institutions and customs (Dahl, 1984; Enquist, 1984; Zetterberg, 1984), or for succeeding in the workplace (Daun, 1989). Consequently, the experiences of a temperamentally inhibited person facing many Swedish institutions and customs would most likely differ greatly from those of a temperamentally inhibited person facing American institutions and customs.

Cultural Context: Women's Roles

At the time when the data were collected for the American and Swedish samples referred to in this paper, Swedish and American societies differed in another important way, namely in their philosophical beliefs about the role of women in society. The American sample matured during the 1940s, a time when women typically assumed traditional homemaking roles. The Swedish sample matured in the early 1970s, just after sweeping legislative changes concerning women had occurred. Until then, Swedish women had assumed traditional roles in even larger numbers than American women (Sandlund, 1971). However, during the late 1960s the Swedish government set out to create equality between the sexes as part of a larger equality program (Sandlund, 1971), based on the idea that economic equality would pave the way for equality in other domains. Consequently, women were urged into the workforce. This social change occurred when the participants in our sample were young adolescents; therefore, they would have been affected directly.

Life Courses of Shy Americans

Caspi et al. (1988) used data from the Berkeley Guidance Study (Macfarlane, Allen, & Honzik, 1954) to examine the life courses of shy American children who were born in the late 1920s. They identified shy children from mothers' reports of behavior at ages 8–10 and then compared them with nonshy children on adult measures. They found that shy boys were slow in making certain life transitions. They married and had children later than nonshy boys, and they entered into stable careers later than nonshy boys. Shy girls were not slow to marry or have children, but they tended to drop out of the workforce when they married and then never return to work. Many of the nonshy girls also quit working when they married, but later returned to work.

Life Courses of Shy Swedes

We reasoned that in Sweden, where shyness is relatively more accepted, various support systems might allow people to travel the paths to education and career without being outgoing or assertive (e.g., teachers might watch for talented students and offer them advice and assistance concerning education or job placement; professors might approach students with offers of graduate study). Until the late 1960s, most of the people who traveled those paths were males. Without the same established supports, Swedish females would have faced a different set of institutions and practices—a set similar to those faced by American males in the Berkeley sample. If so, then we should see shy Swedish women's careers being affected much as American men's careers were, but we should see no effects on Swedish men's careers.

The participants in the Swedish study were from a suburb of Stockholm and have been part of a longitudinal study since they were born in the mid 1950s. More complete details of this study can be found in Kerr et al. (1996). The participants are representative of people in Swedish urban communities on a variety of physical, socioeconomic, and behavioral measures (Karlberg et al., 1968; Stattin & Klackenberg-Larsson, 1990). The children were seen every year until age 16 and then again at about ages 25 and 35. Of 212 original subjects, 169 (80%) are included in the present analyses. Attrition was unrelated to shyness, socioeconomic status, sex, intelligence, or education.

We chose childhood shyness measures that were comparable to those used by Caspi and colleagues: mothers' ratings at ages 8, 9, and 10. Mothers in our study answered two questions about shyness every year: "Is your child shy with strange peers?" and "Is your child shy with strange adults?" They used a scale from 0 *(never)* to 4 *(always)*. For these analyses, we used a dichotomized measure of shyness in which the children who had received the most extreme rating at least once were placed in the shy group. The shy group contained 32 subjects (14 females, 18 males); the nonshy group contained 147 subjects (63 females, 84 males). Thus 18% of males and 18% of females for whom data were present at ages 8–10 were identified as shy. We compared these shy and nonshy children on measures that were taken later in life when the subjects were about 35 years old. We looked at age of marriage, age at birth of first child, and several measures of career progress, including attained education and monthly income. In Table 7.1 a summary of these findings is compared with the parallel findings from the American study.

There were two major findings from the Swedish study. One was that shy girls attained less education than nonshy girls ($t(66) = 2.9$, $p = .005$, two-tailed). Not one of the shy girls earned a university degree, but 44% of the nonshy girls did. Furthermore, this link between childhood shyness and later education was independent of two powerful determinants of education: family socioeconomic status and intelligence. Shyness predicted attained education even with family socioeconomic status and intelligence controlled in a multiple regression model ($b = -.29$, $p = .004$). For boys, on the other hand, shyness did not seem to affect educational choices or incomes. Shy and nonshy boys achieved equal levels of education and they were earning equivalent age-35 incomes. A second major finding was that shy boys were slower to

TABLE 7.1   **Similarities and Differences in Findings From Studies of the Life Courses of Shy Swedish and American People**

		Swedish study[a]	*American study*[b]
Education and career			
	Males	Shy and nonshy boys are similar on all education and career measures	Shy boys enter stable careers about 3 years later than nonshy boys
	Females	Shy girls attain less education— 0% of shy girls earn university degrees versus 44% of nonshy girls	Most women leave the workforce at marriage, but shy women are less likely to return later
Marriage and family			
	Males	Shy boys marry and have children about 3–4 years later than nonshy boys	Shy boys marry and have children about 3–4 years later than nonshy boys
	Females	Shy and nonshy girls marry and have first child at similar ages	Shy and nonshy girls marry and have first child at similar ages

Note. [a]Kerr, Lambert, & Bem (1996); [b]Caspi, Elder, & Bem (1988).

marry and start families. They married 4 years later and had their first child 3 years later, on average, than those with no histories of shyness (t (39) = -2.15, $p = .04$ and t (58) = -1.9, $p = .05$ for age at marriage and age at birth of first child, respectively). There were no such delays for shy girls.

The findings concerning education and career are consistent with an institutional processes explanation. In the American study (Caspi et al., 1988), there is evidence that shyness hindered both boys' and girls' careers, and this is what would be predicted. American culture values boldness, especially in the workplace, and the official and unofficial institutions and customs that determine career entry and success also favor bold, assertive behavior. In other words, the things one needs to do to be successful are difficult for shy people. Thus the shy people who go into the workplace (men, in the Berkeley sample) are not as successful as the nonshy people. Swedish culture, on the other hand, values reserved behavior. Its career-related institutions and customs are consistent with that value, perhaps providing support systems to smooth the path through education and career. But, traditionally only males had taken that path; therefore, the same supports might not have been offered to the females in our sample who were among the first to be expected to enter the workforce in large numbers. Consequently, shy Swedish females might have had as much difficulty navigating this system as did shy American males.

The results concerning marriage and parenthood are consistent with both institutional- and interpersonal-process explanations. In both studies, shyness was associated with delayed marriage and parenthood for males but not females. This probably reflects the fact that traditional sex roles concerning sexual and romantic relationships were dominant for males and females in both Sweden and the United States. In Sweden, shyness was generally more acceptable than in the United States, but boys were still expected to take the initiative in establishing romantic relationships, as they were in the United States. This would have been more difficult for shy boys than for nonshy boys (an institutional-process explanation). Consequently, perhaps the shy boys were older before they summoned the courage to initiate their relationships with girls, or perhaps they had awkward early experiences with girls. Either of these factors could have delayed their progression into more serious relationships. On the other hand, perhaps shy boys were not seen as the most desirable partners because they were not behaving as expected in this domain (an interpersonal-process explanation).

The reader will, no doubt, recognize several ways in which the Swedish study is limited as a replication of Caspi et al. (1988). Some of these—namely, that the two samples were from different countries and historical times—are the very basis for inferring what I have called interpersonal and institutional processes. However, other factors might provide alternative explanations of the results. Different measures of childhood shyness were used in the two studies (although both relied on mothers' ratings) and different proportions of the samples were identified as shy. In addition, our measure of age at marriage was not ideal, in that we only know what age subjects were when they entered the marriage they were in at age 35. Some might have married, divorced, and then remarried, but divorce data are not available. Furthermore, marriage itself did not have the same meaning in the two times and places. For Swedes of that generation, many couples who would eventually marry lived together for a number of years and then married after they started having children. The same could not be said for Americans in the 1940s. Swedes, then, were marrying later in the courses of their relationships and marriage was not the pivotal step that it was among Americans of the 1940s.

The measures, however, would not have been exactly comparable even if they had appeared so, because Swedish mothers were probably not thinking about the same thing as American mothers were when they judged their children's shyness. Supporting this hypothesis, Swedish mothers seemed to be less willing than American mothers to rate their children as extremely shy. Thirty percent of the American sample fell above the midpoint on combined shy and reserved scales averaged over ages 8 to 10. (The midpoint was shy/reserved around some people, not around others.) In the Swedish sample, only 12% fell above the midpoint on a mean score of the age 8–10 shyness measures described above. (The two endpoints were never and always.) The interpersonal-process interpretation of this would be that the cultural value on shyness influences how mothers perceive behavior. Specifically, if Swedish mothers were untroubled by shyness, they might have been less likely to notice it or to label a given behavior as shyness.

These problems should reduce the likelihood of finding any similarities in the life courses of shy people in the two samples. However, some of the most notable results replicated in spite of these differences. The findings regarding transitions to marriage and parenthood replicated those found in the American sample with an effect of shyness for males and not females and with differences between shy and nonshy boys that were almost identical in the two samples. Additionally, other results differed in the ways that we predicted. Shyness did not seem to affect Swedish males' careers, but it affected Swedish females' careers as it had American males' (albeit not in quite the same way). The very fact that these effects were not dependent on the exact shyness or outcome measures provides the strongest basis for inferring that the same processes were at work in both times and places.

CONCLUSIONS

Culture could affect the lives of people with different temperaments through at least two possible mechanisms. One involves the ways people respond to each other. The other involves the official and unofficial institutions that people must deal with. These explanations are consistent with the existing literature in one temperament domain. However, this is a simple model of processes that are, in reality, complex. The questions remain whether specific predictions can be made and supported from this model, and whether such predictions will apply to other temperament dimensions.

It is clear that the study of childhood temperament should not ignore the context in which individuals develop. A growing body of research suggests that culture is one important context to consider. The interesting questions are: why and how? The question *why* cultural values develop has been the subject of speculation. Chen et al. (1992, 1995, in press) have suggested that inhibited behavior is valued in China because it is better for the group. Casiglia, Lo Coco, & Zappulla (1998) have suggested that aggression might be more accepted in Southern Italy than in North America because historically it has been used as a social tool. These speculations should be documented empirically, if at all possible. Certainly the question *how,* which deals with mechanisms such as those that I have proposed, can and should be investigated empirically. A systematic investigation of mechanisms could start with several cultures or subcultures in which attitudes about a given temperament driven behavior are thought to differ. Those attitudes should be operationalized and measured. One should then be able to make testable predictions about the structuring of customs and institutions relevant to specific important areas of life such as childhood peer relationships or transitions to school, adult work, or one's own family. These results would provide a foundation for looking at people's responses, the stability of temperament, and the developmental outcomes associated with individual differences in temperament. For developmental researchers, cultural assumptions about behavior are important for another reason. In focusing on the mechanisms that are responsible for cultural differences, we are forced to examine the assumptions that we are making about why developmental outcomes are as they are in our own culture. We then confront the possibility that we are wrong in assuming that certain behaviors are generally adaptive and others are generally maladaptive.

ACKNOWLEDGMENTS

I thank Håkan Stattin and Ingrid Klackenberg-Larsson for facilitating work with the Swedish data and offering insights into Swedish culture and values. The research described was supported by a grant from the William T. Grant Foundation to William W. Lambert and a Jacob K. Javits Graduate Fellowship to Margaret Kerr.

REFERENCES

Bem, S. (1993). *The lenses of gender: Transforming the debate on sexual inequality*. New Haven, CT: Yale University Press.

Boivin, M., Hymel, S., & Bukowski, W. M. (1995). The roles of social withdrawal, peer rejection, and victimization by peers in predicting loneliness and depressed mood in childhood. *Development and Psychopathology, 7,* 765–785.

Bowen, F., Vitaro, F., Kerr, M., & Pellitier, D. (1995). Childhood internalizing problems: Prediction from kindergarten, effect of maternal overprotectiveness, and sex differences. *Development & Psychopathology, 7,* 481–498.

Casiglia, A. C., Lo Coco, A., & Zappulla, C. (1998). Aspects of social reputation and peer relationships in Italian children: A cross-cultural perspective. *Developmental Psychology, 34,* 723–730.

Caspi, A., Elder, G. H., Jr., & Bem, D. J. (1988). Moving away from the world: Life-course patterns of shy children. *Developmental Psychology, 24,* 824–831.

Chen, X., Hastings, P. D., Rubin, K. H., Chen, H., Cen, G., & Stewart, S. L. (1998). Childrearing attitudes and behavioral inhibition in Chinese and Canadian toddlers: A cross-cultural study. *Developmental Psychology, 34,* 677–686.

Chen, X., Rubin, K. H., & Li, D. (1995). Social and school adjustment of shy and aggressive children in China. *Development and Psychopathology, 7,* 337–349.

Chen, X., Rubin, K. H., & Li, D. (1997). Maternal acceptance and social and school adjustment: A 4-year longitudinal study. *Merrill-Palmer Quarterly, 43,* 663–681.

Chen, X., Rubin, K. H., & Li, D. (in press). Adolescent outcomes of social functioning in Chinese children. *International Journal of Behavioral Development*.

Chen, X., Rubin, K. H., & Sun, Y. (1992). Social reputation and peer relationships in Chinese and Canadian children: A cross-cultural study. *Child Development, 63,* 1336–1343.

Dahl, H. F. (1984). Those equal folk. *Dædalus: Journal of the American Academy of Arts and Sciences, 113,* 93–108.

Daun, Å. (1989). *Svensk mentalitet: Ett Jämförande perspektiv [Swedish Mentality: A comparative perspective].* Stockholm; Rabén & Sjögren.

Daun, Å., Mattlar, C.-E., & Alanen, E. (1989). Personality traits characteristic for Finns and Swedes. *Ethnologia Scandinavica, 19,* 30–50.

Engfer, A. (1993). Antecedents and consequences of shyness in boys and girls: A 6-year longitudinal study. In H. Rubin & J. B. Asendorpf (Eds.), *Social withdrawal, inhibition, and shyness* (pp. 49–79). Hillsdale, NJ: Lawrence Erlbaum Associates, Inc.

Enquist, P. O. (1984). The art of flying backward with dignity. *Dædalus: Journal of the American Academy of Arts and Sciences, 113,* 61–74.

Fish, M., Stifter, C. A., & Belsky, J. (1991). Conditions of continuity and discontinuity in infant negative emotionality: Newborn to 5 months. *Child Development, 62,* 1525–1537.

Grusec, J. E., & Lytton, H. (1998). *Social development.* New York: Springer-Verlag.

Hendin, H. (1964). *Suicide and Scandinavia.* New York: Grune & Stratton.

Jones, W. H., & Carpenter, B. N. (1986). Shyness, social behavior, and relationships. In W. H. Jones, J. M. Cheek, & S. R. Briggs (Eds.), *Shyness: Perspectives on research and treatment* (pp. 227–238). New York: Plenum Press.

Jones, W. H., Cavert, C. W., & Indart, M. (1983, August). Impressions of shyness. Paper presented at the meeting of the American Psychological Association, Anaheim, CA.

Jones, W. H., & Russell, D. (1982). The social reticence scale: An objective instrument to measure shyness. *Journal of Personality Assessment, 46,* 629–631.

Kagan, J., Reznick, J. S., & Snidman, N. (1987). The physiology and psychology of behavioral inhibition in children. *Child Development, 58,* 1459–1473.

Karlberg, P., Engstrom, I., Klackenberg, G., Klackenberg-Larsson, I., Lichentenstein, H., Stensson, J., & Svennberg, I. (1968). The development of children in a Swedish urban community. A prospective longitudinal study. *Acta Paediatrica Scandinavica* (Suppl. 187).

Kerr, M., Lambert, W. W., & Bem, D. J. (1996). Life course sequelae of childhood shyness in Sweden compared with the United States. *Developmental Psychology, 32,* 1100–1105.

Kerr, M., Lambert, W. W., Stattin, H., & Klackenberg-Larsson, I. (1994). Stability of inhibition in a Swedish longitudinal sample. *Child Development, 65,* 138–146.

Lerner, J. V. (1983). A goodness of fit model of the role of temperament in psychosocial adaptation in early adolescence. *Journal of Genetic Psychology, 143,* 149–157.

Lewis, M. (1987). Early sex role behavior and school age adjustment. In J. M. Reinish, L. A. Rosenblum, & S. A. Sanders (Eds.), *Masculinity/femininity: Basic perspectives* (pp. 202–226). New York: Oxford University Press.

Lewis, M. (1989). Culture and biology: The role of temperament. In P. Zelazo & R. Barr (Eds.), *Challenges to developmental paradigms.* Hillsdale, NJ: Lawrence Erlbaum Associates.

Macfarlane, J. W., Allen, L., & Honzik, M. P. (1954). *A developmental study of the behavioral problems of children between twenty-one months and fourteen years.* Berkeley: University of California Press.

Matheny, A. P., Jr. (1986). Stability and change in infant temperament: Contributions from the infant, mother, and family environment. In G. Kohnstamm (Ed.), *Temperament discussed* (pp. 49–58). Berwyn, PA: Swets North America.

Miller, D. R., & Swanson, G. E. (1958). *The changing American parent: A study in the Detroit area.* New York: John Wiley & Sons.

Mills, C. W. (1956). *White collar: The American middle class.* New York: Oxford University Press.

Radke-Yarrow, M., Richters, J., & Wilson, W. E. (1988). Child development in a network of relationships. In R. A. Hinde & J. Stevenson-Hinde (Eds.), *Relationships within families: Mutual influences* (pp. 48–67). Oxford: Clarendon Press.

Rubin, K. H. (1998). Social and emotional development from a cultural perspective. *Developmental Psychology, 34,* 611–615.

Rubin, K. H., Chen, X., & Hymel, S. (1993). Socioemotional characteristics of aggressive and withdrawn children. *Merrill-Palmer Quarterly, 49,* 518–534.

Rubin, K. H., Chen, X., McDougall, P., Bowker, A., & McKinnon, J. (1995). The Waterloo longitudinal project: Predicting adolescent internalizing and externalizing problems from early and midchildhood. *Development and Psychopathology, 7,* 751–764.

Sandlund, M. B. (1971). The status of women in Sweden: Report to the United Nations 1968. In E. Dahlström (Ed.), *The changing roles of men and women* (pp. 209–302). Boston: Beacon Press.

Schweder, R. A., Goodnow, J., Hatano, G., LeVine, R. A., Markus, H., & Miller, P. (1998). The cultural psychology of development: One mind, many mentalities. In W. Damon (Ed.-in-Chief) & R. M. Lerner (Vol. Ed.), *Handbook of child psychology* (5th ed., pp. 865–937). New York: John Wiley & Sons, Inc.

Stattin, H., & Klackenberg-Larsson, I. (1990). The relationship between maternal attributes in the early life of the child and the child's future criminal behavior. *Development and Psychopathology, 2,* 99–111.

Stevenson-Hinde, J. (1988). Individuals in relationships. In R. A. Hinde & J. Stevenson-Hinde (Eds.), *Relationships within families: Mutual influences* (pp. 68–80). Oxford: Clarendon Press.

Stevenson-Hinde, J., & Hinde, R. A. (1986). Changes in associations between characteristics and interactions. In R. Plomin & J. Dunn (Eds.), *The study of temperament: Changes, continuities, and challenges* (pp. 115–129). Hillsdale, NJ: Lawrence Erlbaum Associates.

Stevenson-Hinde, J., & Shouldice, A. (1993). Wariness to strangers: A behavioral systems perspective revisited. In K. H. Rubin & J. B. Asendorpf (Eds.), *Social withdrawal, inhibition, and shyness in childhood* (pp. 101–116). Hillsdale, NJ: Lawrence Erlbaum Associates.

van den Boom, D. C. (1994). The influence of temperament and mothering on attachment and exploration: An experimental manipulation of sensitive responsiveness among lower-class mothers with irritable infants. *Child Development, 65,* 1457–1477.

Washington, J., Minde, K., & Goldberg, S. (1986). Temperament in preterm infants: Style and stability. *Journal of the American Academy of Child Psychiatry, 25,* 493–502.

Zetterberg, H. L. (1984). The rational humanitarians. *Dædalus: Journal of the American Academy of Arts and Sciences, 113,* 75–92.

Zimbardo, P. G. (1977). *Shyness: What it is, what to do about it.* Reading, MA: Addison-Wesley.

8 The Role of Temperament as a Moderator of Stress

Jan Strelau
University of Warsaw
Silesian University, Poland

INTRODUCTION

According to Nebylitsyn (1972) and Strelau (1983) the functional significance of temperament can be demonstrated when individuals are confronted
with excessive situations or demands. Understanding the role played by temperament as a moderator of physiological and psychological stress is a central
theme of this chapter.

In several temperament theories the assumption that temperament plays
an important role in moderating stress is incorporated as a major postulate.
Probably Pavlov (1951–1952) was one of the first who demonstrated that behavior under extreme conditions, such as an unexpected flood in his laboratory, depends on individual differences in temperament. Following the flood,
behavior disorders occurred for dogs classified as having a weak nervous system, whereas for dogs with a strong nervous system such excessive experience did not lead to disturbances in behavior. Later studies conducted by
neo-Pavlovian researchers using extreme natural settings, such as a simulated
breakdown in a power plant, have shown that operators characterized as having a weak nervous system showed an increased number of mistakes, a lack of
self-control and withdrawing reactions (Gurevich & Matveyev, 1966). Such
behavior was not present in individuals with a strong and well balanced nervous system who were able to cope with these extreme situations.

Forty years ago Thomas and Chess (1957) in their New York Longitudinal
Study (NYLS) showed that the functional significance of temperamental

traits comes to force when the child is confronted with difficult situations and extreme demands. Since then dozens of studies have demonstrated a higher likelihood of behavioral disturbances as a function of difficult temperament interacting with predisposing environmental conditions (poorness of fit). More recently Kagan (1983) has described inhibited and uninhibited temperaments as representing different vulnerability to experienced stress, particularly involving situations of unexpected or unpredictable events.

In arousal-oriented theories of temperament, which refer to the concepts of optimal level of arousal or stimulation, temperament characteristics are regarded as moderators in experiencing the state of stress under extreme levels of stimulation, as exemplified in the domains of extraversion (Eysenck, 1970; Eysenck & Eysenck, 1985), stimulus screening (Mehrabian, 1977), reactivity (Strelau, 1983, 1988) or sensation seeking (Zuckerman, 1994). For example, in his initial research on sensation seeking, Zuckerman (1964) came to the conclusion that some individuals are resistant to sensory deprivation, whereas others react in a way that suggests perceptual isolation is stressful. In his later writings Zuckerman's definition of sensation seeking involves a willingness to take physical and social risks (Zuckerman, 1979, 1994).

The statement that the role of temperament in regulating the relationship between individuals and their external world is especially evident in difficult situations and extreme behaviors has become one of the main postulates in the regulative theory of temperament (RTT; Strelau, 1996). Taking RTT as a point of departure, several reasons for considering temperamental traits as important variables moderating stress phenomena may be mentioned. First, temperament refers to more or less unspecific, rather formal, characteristics that penetrate all kinds of behavior, whatever the content or direction of this behavior. In so doing they interact with a variety of stress phenomena. Second, by being connected mainly with energetic and temporal characteristics of behavior, temperament characteristics act as moderators in all stress phenomena that may be characterized by energy and time. Third, temperament characteristics are related to emotions, as expressed in an individual-specific tendency to generate emotional processes (Strelau, 1987), especially in the domain of negative emotions. As commonly accepted (see e.g., Lazarus, 1991, 1993), emotions are one of the core constructs in the state of stress.

STRESS PHENOMENA DEFINED

Before entering the temperament-stress relationship some explanations are needed regarding different conceptualizations of stress. These explanations take into account the most basic distinction between stressors, the state of stress, coping with stress, and consequences of stress.

Psychological stress is understood here as a state characterized by strong negative emotions, such as fear, anxiety, anger, hostility, or other emotional states evoking distress. Such emotional states are accompanied by physiological and biochemical changes that evidently exceed a baseline level of arousal. For example, neuroendocrine changes are inherent attributes of emotions (Frankenhaeuser, 1986; Zuckerman, 1991) and so they cannot be ignored as components of psychological stress.

A fundamental question involves causes determining *the state of stress*. In my own view (Strelau, 1988, 1995), a state of stress is caused by the lack of equilibrium (occurrence of discrepancy) between demands and the individual's capability (capacity) to cope with them. Such a conceptualization of stress can also be found elsewhere (see Krohne, 1986; McGrath, 1970; Schulz & Schönpflug, 1982). The magnitude of the state of stress is a function of the degree of discrepancy between demands and capacities, assuming the individual is motivated to cope with the demands with which he or she is confronted. Within this framework demands are regarded as stressors or stress-inducing situations. The following factors may be considered as demands: unpredictable and uncontrollable life events, daily hassles, significant life changes, and situations of extreme high or extreme low stimulative value.

Demands can exist in two forms: objective and subjective. Subjective demands are the result of individual-specific appraisal of a given situation. Demands that exist objectively act independently of the individual's perception. Examples of objective demands include traumatic or extreme life changes, such as death, bereavement, disaster and war. As shown by Holmes and Rahe (1967), and confirmed in our own research, there is a very high degree of consensus between groups and among individuals about the significance of life events. The fact that there exist high correlations (about .9) across age, sex, marital status, and education in the intensity and time necessary to accommodate to specific life events speaks in favor of the existence of objective, universal stressors (see Aldwin, Levenson, Spiro III, & Bosse, 1989; Freedy, Kilpatrick, & Resnick, 1993; Pellegrini, 1990).

The individual's capability to cope with demands depends on the following characteristics: intelligence, special abilities, skills, knowledge, personality including temperamental traits, features of an individual's physical makeup, experience with stress-inducing situations, coping strategies, and the actual (physical and psychic) state of the individual. Depending on the specificity of the demands, different individual characteristics influence an individual's capability. Capabilities may occur in two forms. Capabilities exist objectively, and as such they may be subject to measurement. Capabilities may also be subjectively experienced, based on individual-specific appraisal.

An imbalance between demands and capacities (whether objective or subjective) may be considered a source of psychological stress. What is to be emphasized here is the fact that the state of stress is the outcome of interaction between real or perceived demands and the individual's response capability as it really exists or is perceived by the given individual.

The consequences of being in a state of stress are inseparable from coping. *Coping* with stress is understood in this chapter as a regulatory function that consists of maintaining an adequate balance between demands and capacities, or of reducing the discrepancy between demands and capacities. Efficient coping, which results in a match or goodness of fit between demands and capacities, reduces the state of stress, whereas inefficient coping leads to an increase in the state of stress (see Vitaliano, DeWolfe, Maiuro, Russo, & Katon, 1990). In addition: "Coping is highly *contextual*, since to be effective it must change over time and across different stressful conditions" (Lazarus, 1993, p. 8).

According to Chess and Thomas (1986), absence of stress may constitute a developmental risk factor. "New demands and stresses, when consonant with developmental potentials, are constructive in their consequences" (p. 158; see also Chess & Thomas, 1989, 1991). As Chess and Thomas point out, it is excessive stress resulting from a demand the individual is unable to cope with that leads to maladaptive functioning. Maladaptive functioning and behavior disorders, including pathology resulting from excessive or chronic stress are regarded here as consequences or costs of stress. *Excessive stress* consists of extremely strong negative affects accompanied by unusually high elevation of the level of arousal. *Chronic stress* is regarded as a state of stress, not necessarily excessive, but experienced permanently or frequently. Looking at the consequences of excitatory effects, because of the effects of summation long-lasting weak stimuli may have an effect that is comparable to strong short-lasting stimuli. As a consequence of both excessive and chronic stress, changes in the organism occur that may result either in psychological maladaptive functioning, such as an increased level of anxiety and depression, or in physiological or biochemical disturbances expressed in psychosomatic diseases or other health problems (Strelau, 1995, 1998).

However, not all excessive or chronic states of stress lead to the negative consequences described above. A low discrepancy between demands and capacities, assuming it is not a chronic state, may result in positive changes as measured by efficiency of performance or developmental shifts. Stress should be regarded as one of the many risk factors (external and internal) contributing to maladaptive functioning and disorders. When the state of stress interacts with other factors that decrease or dampen the consequences of stress, maladjustment or behavioral disturbances may not occur.

THE TEMPERAMENT-STRESS RELATIONSHIP: THEORETICAL CONSIDERATIONS

Having now defined the major constructs of stress phenomena, I shall concentrate on the relationships between temperament and stress. Because temperament plays the role of a moderator in all stages producing stress and its consequences, these relationships are very complex, as illustrated in Fig. 8.1. As shown in Fig. 8.1 temperament has been given the status of a *moderator*. Following Folkman and Lazarus (1988) this means that temperament occurs as an antecedent condition that interacts with other conditions in producing stress phenomena. As opposed to a moderator, a mediator is considered as a condition that occurs when stress phenomena are already present, as for example social support given when an individual already experiences the state of stress.

The specific relationships between temperament and different aspects of stress phenomena broadly discussed elsewhere (Strelau, 1995) are selectively presented in the following sections. The model presented in Fig. 8.1 is temperament-centered, but the place of temperament as a moderator can be filled by other personality dimensions, such as, hardiness (Kobasa, 1979; Kobasa & Puccetti, 1983), locus of control (Ormel & Schaufeli, 1991), and a sense of coherence (Antonovsky, 1987). Temperament, however, occupies a specific position among individual characteristics moderating stress. This is due to the very fact that temperament is present from infancy and thus moderates stress phenomena from early ontogenesis on, which is not the case in respect to other personality dimensions.

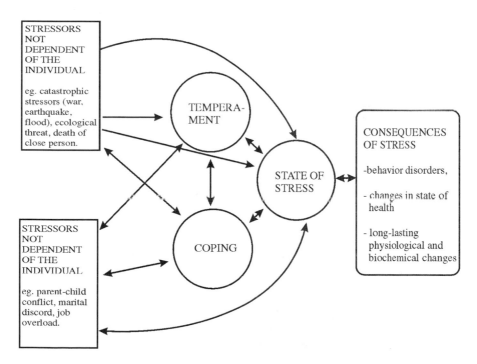

FIG. 8.1.   Hypothesized relationships between temperament and different aspects of stress.

Temperament and the Consequences of Stress

By tradition most of the studies centered on the functional significance of temperament although not referring directly to the construct of stress, refer to consequences of stress. The constructs of difficult temperament, goodness of fit, and temperament risk factor may be mentioned here as examples.

The concept of *difficult temperament* emerged as a result of clinical observations. Integrating across the multiple definitions of difficult temperament found in the literature led me to the conclusion that extremes of certain temperament traits, or a configuration of these traits found in a normal population, are regarded by parents or caretakers as causal factors for a child's inappropriate behavior and maladjustment (Strelau, 1998). They may result in behavior disorders, especially when in interaction with an adverse environment (Thomas & Chess, 1977).

The construct *goodness of fit* implies that the adequacy of the individual's functioning is dependent on the degree to which environmental demands are in accord with the individual's own characteristics. The numerous case studies described by Thomas and Chess (1977; Chess & Thomas, 1986, 1991; Thomas, Chess & Birch, 1968) showed that, when there is an adequate interaction (goodness of fit) between the child's difficult temperament and parental or other caretaker practices and demands, behavior disorders may not occur. Thus there is no direct relationship between difficult temperament and behavior disorders or maladjustment. Further, poorness of fit between the child's temperament characteristics and parental (caretaker's) practices or other environmental demands, enhances the risk that difficult temperament will lead to behavioral disturbances.

To underline the fact that disturbances of behavior and pathology in children occur only when temperament characteristics predisposing a child to poor fit interact with an unfavorable environment, Carey (1986, 1989) introduced the concept of temperament risk factor. However, he limited this concept to excessive interactional stress experienced by children. Extending this concept my definition of *temperament risk factor* (TRF) refers to any temperamental trait, or configuration of traits, that in interaction with other factors acting excessively, persistently, or recurrently (e.g., physical and social environment, educational treatment, situations, the individual's characteristics) increases the risk of developing behavior disorders or pathology, or favors the shaping of a maladjusted personality (Strelau 1989, 1995; Strelau & Eliasz, 1994).

Rutter (1979), has shown how the probability of behavior disorders increases with the number of risk factors taken into account. The rate of behavior disorders was, in practice, the same for an individual with only one risk factor as for an individual free of this risk factor. But when the number of jointly acting risk factors extended to four or more, the rate of behavior disorders increased to 20%. Within a cumulative risk framework temperament may be viewed as one of the many possible risk factors contributing to psychological, psychophysiological, and pathological consequences of stress.

Temperament as a Moderator of Stressors and the State of Stress

When considering such concepts as difficult temperament, poorness of fit or temperament risk factor in relationship to behavior disorders or pathology it has to be taken in mind that it is not temperament that leads to these disorders or changes in health status. As underlined in the model presented above (see Fig. 8.1) it is the state of stress that leads to these changes and behavioral disturbances. Temperament is considered in this model as a moderator of stressors. The state of stress indirectly raises or lowers the risk of developing stress consequences by increasing or decreasing, augmenting or dampening the value of stressors and level of the state of stress.

Temperament may contribute significantly to determining the state of stress from at least three perspectives:

1. intensity characteristics (stimulative value) of demands
2. optimal level of arousal as a standard for normal functioning
3. emotion-oriented temperamental traits as expressed in tendencies to elicit emotions, especially negative ones.

Temperament Traits as Moderators of the Intensity Characteristics of the Demand-Capability Relationship.   As postulated by Selye (1975, p. 21) "Deprivation of stimuli and excessive stimulation are both accompanied by an increase in stress, sometimes to the point of distress." Amongst others Lundberg (1982), McGrath (1970), Strelau (1988), and Weick (1970) also considered intensity of demands as stressors. All life events that can be interpreted in terms of intensity of stimulation and, as a consequence, in terms of arousal effects may be regarded as factors subject to moderation by different temperamental traits (Rahe, 1987). Which of the specific temperament characteristics plays the role of moderator, by elevating or reducing the stimulative value of life events, depends on the kind of event. Ursin (1980) has pointed out that, under a high level of arousal, the tolerability of high intensity life events is lowered. This is caused by the process of augmentation of acting stimuli. Under a low level of arousal there is a decrease in tolerability of low stimulative life events value (e.g., deprivation, isolation). This results from suppression processes in relation to acting stimuli.

In several publications (Strelau, 1983, 1988, 1994) I have developed the idea that arousal-oriented temperament dimensions are based on the assumption that there exist more or less stable individual differences in the level of arousal. There are at least a dozen temperament traits for which the construct of arousal has been used when referring to their biological background (Strelau, 1994). Temperament traits that refer to low arousability, as for example extraversion, high sensation seeking, endurance, or strong type of nervous system, when interacting with life events of low stimulative value, such as deprivation or isolation, act as moderators that increase the state of stress, leading in extreme cases to excessive stress. Temperament traits characterized by high arousability, such as introversion, low sensation seeking, reactivity, or weak type of nervous system, interacting with life events characterized as having high stimulation value, as for example, death, disaster, or traumatic stressors, act as moderators to increase the state of stress, again leading in extreme cases to excessive stress as illustrated in Fig. 8.2.

As can be seen from Fig. 8.2 the same temperament trait, depending on the kind of environment (demand), may or may not operate as a moderator of stress. Furthermore, opposite poles of the same trait may be considered as moderators of stress, depending on the specificity of the demands with which they interact. For example, highly reactive individuals or introverts (both characterized by high arousability), when confronted with high stimulation, experience a state of stress not present for extraverts or low reactive individuals under such conditions. In turn, for individuals characterized by low arousability (e.g., extraverts or low reactives), low stimulation (e.g., deprivation, isolation) leads to a state of stress.

A good example to start with is neuroticism (treated by Eysenck as a synonym of emotionality), one of the most representative activation-sensitive traits. Eysenck (1983, p. 126) postulated "that *ceteris paribus* high N individuals live a more stressful life, not in the sense that they necessarily encounter more stressful stimuli (although that may be so) but because identical stress-

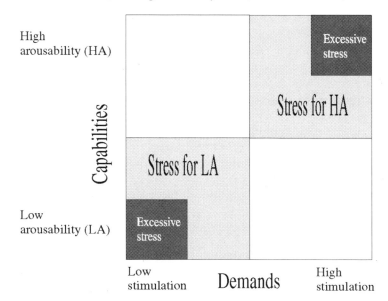

FIG. 8.2.   Arousability and the state of stress.

ful stimuli produce a greater amount of strain in them." Strain, according to Eysenck, reflects the individual's state of stress. A life event that produces a state of stress of low intensity may be moderated by emotionality or other temperament traits in such a way as to increase the state of stress. Thus, the same state of stress, in terms of intensity, may result from low intensity life events interacting with high emotionality, as well as from high intensity life events interacting with low emotionality.

The Deviation From Optimal Level of Arousal, Moderated by Temperament, as a Source of Stress.   As shown more than a century ago by Wundt (1887), the sign of emotion depends on the strength of sensory stimuli and this relationship has an inverted-U shape (see also Schneirla, 1959). The fact that intensity of stimuli is a source of positive or negative hedonic tones has been applied to the concept of optimal level of arousal (Berlyne, 1960), where hedonic tone functions as an affective-motivational process regulating the need for stimulation. A low level of arousal is the result of weak stimulation; a very high level of arousal is the result of high intensity stimulation. Both low and high levels of arousal are regarded as sources of negative hedonic tone, the increase of which results in the state of stress. An intermediate level of arousal, evoked by stimuli of average intensity, is a source of positive hedonic tone. However, depending on the position an individual holds on a given temperament dimension, life events that are objectively the same intensity may be a source of positive or negative hedonic tone. This relationship can be attributed without much simplification to such traits as extraversion (Eysenck, 1970; Eysenck & Eysenck, 1985), sensation seeking (Zuckerman, 1979, 1994) and reactivity (Strelau, 1983, 1988). Under high intensity stressors individuals characterized by high arousability experience a negative hedonic tone (state of stress). On the other hand, in response to the same stressors, low arousability individuals may not experience distress; in fact, they may even experience a positive hedonic tone, as exemplified by sensation seekers (Zuckerman, 1994).

Temperamentally Determined Tendency to Express Negative Emotions Under Stress-Inducing Situations.   Temperament traits moderate the state of stress by regulating the intensity (arousal) component of stress or by sharing in the regulation of optimal level of arousal and subsequent hedonic tone. Certain traits such as neuroticism, emotionality, and emotional reactivity also operate as moderators of the state of stress by increasing or decreasing the individual's emotional response to stressors. Whether there is an increase or decrease depends on the position an individual occupies on emotion-oriented temperament dimensions (see Strelau, 1987). This is especially evident in relation to temperamental traits that refer to negative emotions. As vividly expressed by Buss and Plomin (1984, p.

54), "Emotionality equals distress, the tendency to become upset easily and intensely."

From another point of view it could be said that a given neurophysiological basis predisposes the individual to experience more negative emotions than others. For example, Gray (1994) argued that a high level of reactivity in the behavioral inhibition system (BIS) predisposes the individual to experience anxiety even when stressors are absent. As a consequence of chronically high reactive BIS, individuals are more prone to develop personality disorders under traumatic life events than are individuals with low-reactive BIS.

The three mechanisms by which temperament moderates stressors: temperament-intensity characteristics influencing demand-capability relationship, deviation from optimal level of arousal, and tendency to express negative emotions, do not act in isolation. As a consequence it is not easy, if possible at all, to separate them in studies aimed at examining the temperament-stress relationship. In the next section studies are presented that show the role of temperamental traits in moderating selected stress phenomena, as proposed by the regulative theory of temperament.

THE TEMPERAMENT-STRESS RELATIONSHIP: SELECTED DATA

There have been a number of studies conducted in our laboratory that have shown that temperament understood in terms of Pavlovian constructs and measured by means of the Strelau Temperament Inventory (STI) is related to different aspects of stress, especially when extremely high or low levels of stimulation are taken into account (Strelau, 1983; 1995). During the last decade RTT as developed by Strelau has undergone essential changes. One conceptual change involves our understanding of the quality and number of traits of which the structure of temperament is composed (Strelau, 1996, 1998). One result of this conceptual change is the construction of a new measure of temperament—the Formal Characteristics of Behavior—Temperament Inventory (FCB-TI; Strelau & Zawadzki, 1993, 1995). Evidence showing a relation between temperament, as measured by means of the FCB-TI, and stress is not yet very rich although some studies have been already conducted that show a promising perspective in treating temperament from the view of RTT.

Temperament as a Moderator of the Relationship Between Stress and Psychometric Measures of Mental Health

In two studies conducted in our laboratory the relation between stressors and mental health status was examined. In these two studies we tested whether relations between stress and mental health is moderated by temperament, especially those dimensions involving characteristics that refer to the construct of arousal. The hypothesis underlying both studies was that vulnerability to behavior disorders is a function of both temperament and environment, with temperament influencing sensitivity to the environment. Specific temperament traits regarded here as temperament risk factors (TRF) act to moderate the intensity of stressors by elevating sensitivity to stress-inducing situations. As a consequence of increased sensitivity to the predisposing environment, vulnerability to behavior disorders is expected to be higher in individuals in whom TRF are present (Strelau, 1995).

In both studies temperament was measured by means of the Formal Characteristics of Behavior—Temperament Inventory (FCB-TI), which is composed of the following scales: Briskness, Preservation, Sensory sensitivity, Emotional reactivity, Endurance, and Activity. Stressors were estimated by using the Recent Life Changes Questionnaire (RLCQ; Rahe, 1975), which measures stressors using two indicators: (a) Subjectively weighted experienced stressors (life changes: LC) as expressed in the intensity and length of time necessary for an individual to accommodate to a life event, and (b) normative weights that consists of relating weights derived in step (a) to weights given to 75 life changes (parallel to the number and quality of events listed in the RLCQ), as measured by means of the Social Readjustment Rating Scale (SRRS; Holmes & Rahe, 1967). This scale has been revised for a Polish population by Sobolewski, Strelau, and Zawadzki (1999), the authors of the Polish adaptation of the RLCQ.

In both studies different measures of health status were taken. In a study conducted by Trzcińska (1996) a short version of the General Health Questionnaire composed of 30 items (GHQ-30; Goldberg & Williams, 1988) was administered together with the Questionnaire of Neurotic Symptoms (S-II; Aleksandrowicz et al., 1981). The GHQ-30 measures one common factor described as mental health, whereas S-II measures the intensity of neurotic symptoms. Subjects were 200 adults (115 women and 85 men) aged from 21 to 69 years ($M = 32.4$; $SD = 11.92$), most of them with high school or college education.

In a second study conducted by Cupas (1997) using a group of 93 subjects (44 men and 49 women) aged from 22 to 75 ($M = 44.3$; $SD = 13.87$), the Mental Health Inventory (MHI) constructed by Veit and Ware (1983) was utilized. MHI includes five scales—Anxiety, Depression, Loss of behavioral/emotional control, General positive affect and Emotional ties. Additionally two more general scales were constructed by the authors: Psychological distress, composed of anxiety, depression, and loss of behavioral/emotional control, and Well-being, composed of general positive affect and emotional ties.

In both studies results indicated that measures of stressors (subjective and normative weights) show low to moderate correlations with different aspects of health (see Table 8.1). From our point of view the most important question was the role temperament plays as a moderator of the stressor-mental health relationship. Taking into account all three measures of mental health results indicated that among the six temperamental traits assessed by means of the FCB-TI emotional reactivity was the one trait that functions as a moderator, as illustrated in Table 8.1.

As shown in Table 8.1 subjective as well as normative weights of stressors show low to moderate correlations with different aspects of mental health status. If emotional reactivity is included as a moderator of these relationships multiple correlations show greater prediction of mental health from life events. This is evident in respect to both measures of stressors (subjective and normative) and to all assessments of mental health status. Multiple correlations (R) vary from .39 to .58 supporting the importance of emotional reactivity as a moderator.

Taking into account the results of both studies, one may say that emotional reactivity constitutes a temperament risk factor for behavior/mental disorders as measured by means of the GHQ-30, S-II and MHI. According to RTT emotional reactivity is defined as a tendency to react intensively to emotion-generating stimuli, expressed in high emotional sensitivity and in low emotional endurance (Strelau & Zawadzki, 1993).

TABLE 8.1   Correlation Between Mental Health and Life Events Moderated by Emotional Reactivity

Index of life changes (LC)	Correlation		Significance of R	
	r	*R*	*F*	*p*
GHQ-30: General mental health				
Subjective weights of LC	.27	.41	19.64	.0001
Normative weights of LC	.22	.39	17.99	.0001
S-II: Intensity of neurotic symptoms				
Subjective weights of LC	.21	.58	49.95	.0001
Normative weights of LC	.13	.57	48.00	
MHI: Psychological well-being				
Subjective weights of LC	− .23	.44	10.88	.0001
Normative weights of LC	− .03	.48	13.12	.0001

Note. LC—life changes, GHQ-30—General Health Questionnaire (30-item version), S-II—Questionnaire of Neurotic Symptoms, MHI—Mental Health Inventory. The Psychological well-being factor is composed of two scales: General positive affect and Emotional ties.

In the study conducted by Trzcińska (1996) emotionality and endurance showed the highest correlations with scores of general mental health, as measured by means of the GHQ-30. A high score in the latter inventory is an indicator of mental disturbances. According to RTT endurance is defined as the ability to react adequately in situations demanding long-lasting or high stimulative activity and involving intensive external stimulation (Strelau & Zawadzki, 1993). A further test was done to examine whether the status of mental health depends on the interaction between one of these two temperamental traits and life changes. Taking the median score of normative weights of life changes as a criterion, subjects ($N = 200$) were divided into two groups with high and low normative weights. The same procedure was applied to divide both groups into two subgroups based on criterion scores on the Emotional Reactivity (ER) and Endurance (EN) scales from the FCB-TI. As a consequence four subgroups differing in emotional reactivity—high (ER +) and low (ER–), and in endurance—high (EN +) and low (EN–) were created.

When emotionality was taken into account the ANOVA on general mental health produced two significant main effects, of normative weights of life changes (LC) ($F_{1,196} = 13.425$; $p < .0001$) and emotional reactivity ($F_{1,196} = 9.214$; $p = .003$) with no LC · ER interaction ($F_{1,196} = .994$; $p = .32$). This result, illustrated in Fig. 8.3, indicates that mental health status is an additive function of emotional reactivity and normative weights of life changes.

The ANOVA on general mental health, with endurance taken as the temperament variable also produced two significant main effects—normative

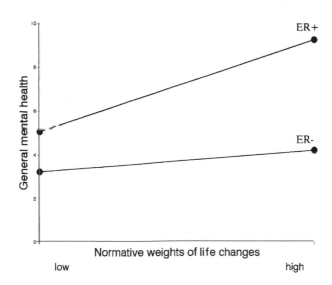

FIG. 8.3.   Mental health as a function of emotional reactivity and normative weights of life changes with additive effects of both.

weights of LC ($F_{1,196} = 8.512$; $p = .004$), and endurance ($F_{1,196} = 15.531$; $p < .0001$) with a strong tendency for an LC · EN interaction ($F_{1,196} = 3.362$; $p = .068$). As with emotional reactivity, the results for endurance (see Fig. 8.4) suggest mental health status is a function of additive effects of both stressors and endurance, although a synergistic effect of both variables cannot be excluded.

To summarize, results indicate that emotional reactivity and endurance can be regarded as temperament risk factors for general mental health. The interactional effect of these temperamental traits with intensity of stressors, as measured by means of normative weights of LC has not been documented. However an interactive influence involving endurance cannot be excluded.

Temperament and Affective Disorders

When considering the consequences of stress and temperament for the development of psychopathology it is often difficult to identify the specific role of temperament as a moderator in the chain of stress phenomena—stressor, state of stress, and consequences of stress (see Fig. 8.1). In part this difficulty reflects the transactional multidirectional relationship between stress phenomena and temperament.

Especially in the case of affective diseases excessive or chronic states of stress could be essential risk factors (Bidzińska, 1984). If so, one may expect that temperamental traits based on the construct of arousal and/or linked to emotional characteristics should be related to affective disorders. The importance of temperament in the understanding of affective disorders has been

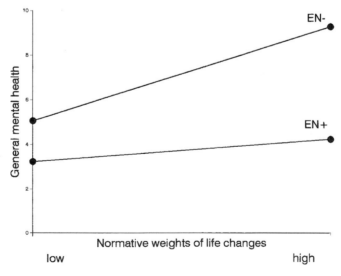

FIG. 8.4.   Mental health as a function of endurance and normative weights of life changes with additive effects of both.

underlined by Akiskal (1994a, 1994b) who has proposed a temperament-based classification of depression.

Habrat (1997), taking as a point of departure the assumption that there exists a relationship between affective disorders and temperament characteristics has undertaken a study in which temperament as described by RTT (Strelau, 1996) was related to depression. The main hypothesis of this study was that patients with a depressive disorder differ from normal subjects in their temperament characteristics and that these differences will be less obvious after clinical treatment (remission).

Subjects were patients in the psychiatric hospital at the Institute of Psychiatry and Neurology in Warsaw, diagnosed in accordance with DSM-IV as having a depressive disorder. Among the 47 adult patients ($M = 48.6$; $SD = 9.80$), 30 were women and 17 were men. The control group consisted of 49 subjects matched for gender, age, and education. Subjects in the control group never suffered from psychiatric diseases or other psychological disturbances and during examination no somatic illness was recorded. Among other measures, the FCB-TI was administered 3 to 4 days after entering the hospital. A second examination by means of the FCB-TI was conducted during remission (3.5 ± 2.5 months after the first examination), when symptoms of depression either disappeared or were below the level considered as a criterion for identifying depressive disorders. During the stay in the hospital patients were treated by means of psychotherapy, and antidepressive drugs were administered. The FCB-TI was administered only once to the control group. Because of tiredness and difficulties in concentration observed in depressive patients all examinations, including those of the control group, were conducted before noon. The results of this study are summarized in Table 8.2.

As can be seen, the patterns of temperament for patients in the stage of depression and remission, and between patients and the control group are clearly in the hypothesized direction. As compared with controls, patient's score higher in respect to perseveration and emotional reactivity—two traits that are directly related to the emotional domain. Patients also have lower scores in briskness, endurance, and activity, that is, in traits that are typical for individuals low in arousability. Also sensory sensitivity of patients with a depressive disorder is higher as compared to the controls. Most interesting, however, is the fact that after remission the temperament scores, although significantly different from those seen in the state of depression and from controls (except sensory sensitivity), represent an intermediate position as might be expected from the theory.

Although ANOVA was not applied in analyzing the data, the study suggests that an interaction effect between depression, temperament, and treatment cannot be excluded. Given that under medical treatment both states of depression and temperamental scores changed, it is possible that only the behavioral expression of temperamental traits changed. Behavioral change in

TABLE 8.2   **Temperament Dimensions in Patients with Depressive Disorders and Their Changes Under Clinical Treatment**

Temperamental traits	Patients				Control group (C)		Differences (p)		
	Depres-sion (D)		Remission (R)				D/R	D/C	R/C
	M	SD	M	SD	M	SD			
Briskness	9.7	4.81	12.0	4.71	16.3	2.95	.001	.001	.001
Perseveration	14.7	2.89	13.5	3.51	11.3	4.60	.05	.001	.01
Sensory sensitivity	13.5	4.25	14.8	3.55	15.9	3.19	.01	.05	n.s.
Emotional reactivity	16.6	3.22	14.9	4.76	10.4	4.41	.01	.001	.001
Endurance	5.0	4.55	6.2	4.92	9.8	4.91	.05	.001	.001

underlying temperament may be caused by temporary changes in the level of activation or by changes in the characteristics of neurotransmitters responsible for the regulation of emotional processes. To use a metaphor, the fact that differences in the acceleration of two cars occurs when one car was just tuned and the second car's plugs and carburetor were dirty, does not mean that the two cars differ in acceleration potential.

FINAL REMARKS

One may be left with the impression that temperament is the sole, or the most important individual characteristic moderating different aspects of stress. In many studies the significance of such personality constructs as hardiness, repression-sensitization, self-esteem, locus of control, self-confidence, sense of coherence, and several other personality variables has been brought out. However, my intention is to demonstrate that temperament cannot be ignored for a proper understanding of human functioning under stress. In other words, stress has been viewed here from a temperament perspective to demonstrate the functional significance temperament plays in human life.

ACKNOWLEDGMENTS

Preparation of this chapter was supported by The Foundation for Polish Science (Subsidies for Scientists: NP.-2/1998)

REFERENCES

Akiskal, H. S. (1994a). The temperamental borders of affective disorders. *Acta Psychiatrica Scandinavica, 89,* 32–37.

Akiskal, H. S. (1994b). Toward a temperament-based classification of depressions. *Neuropsychopharmacology, 10,* 724–730.

Aldwin, C. M., Levenson, M. R., Spiro III, A., & Bosse, R. (1989). Does emotionality predict stress? Findings from the normative aging study. *Journal of Personality and Social Psychology, 56,* 618–624.

Aleksandrowicz, J. W., Bierzysńki, K., Filipiak, J., Kowalczyk, E., Martyniak, J. Mazoń, S., Meus, J., Niwicki, J., Paluchowski, J., Pytko, A., & Romeyko, A. (1981). Kwestionariusze objawowe "S" i "O"—Narzędzie służące do diagnozy i opisu zaburzeń nerwicowych [Symptom questionnaires "S" and "O": Tools for diagnosing and description of neurotic disorders]. *Psychoterapia, 37,* 11–27.

Antonovsky, A. (1987). *Unraveling the mystery of health: How people manage stress and stay well.* San Francisco, CA: Jossey-Bass.

Berlyne, D. E. (1960). *Conflict, arousal, curiosity.* New York: McGraw-Hill.

Bidzińska, E. (1984). Stress factors in affective disease. *British Journal of Psychiatry, 18,* 313–318.

Buss, A. H., & Plomin, R. (1984). *Temperament: Early developing personality traits.* Hillsdale, NJ: Lawrence Erlbaum Associates.

Carey, W. B. (1986). The difficult child. *Pediatrics in Review, 8,* 39–45.

Carey, W. B. (1989). Introduction: Basic issues. In W. B. Carey & S. C. McDevitt (Eds.), *Clinical and educational applications of temperament research* (pp. 11–20). Lisse: Swets & Zeitlinger.

Chess, S., & Thomas, A. (1986). *Temperament in clinical practice.* New York: Guilford Press.

Chess, S., & Thomas, A. (1989). Temperament and its functional significance. In S. I. Greenspan & G. H. Pollock (Eds.), *The course of life* (Vol. 2, pp. 163–227). Madison, CT: International Universities Press.

Chess, S., & Thomas, A. (1991). Temperament and the concept of goodness of fit. In J. Strelau & A. Angleitner (Eds.), *Explorations in temperament: International perspectives on theory and measurement* (pp. 15–28). New York: Plenum Press.

Cupas, M. (1997). *Adaptacja inwentarza zdrowia psychicznego MHI C. Veit i J. Ware do warunków polskich* [Adaptation of the mental health inventory (MHI), constructed by C. Veit and J. Ware, to Polish conditions]. Unpublished master's thesis, University of Warsaw, Poland.

Eysenck, H. J. (1970). *The structure of human personality* (3rd ed.). London: Methuen.

Eysenck, H. J. (1983). Stress, disease, and personality: The 'inoculation effect'. In C. L. Cooper (Ed.), *Stress research* (pp. 121–131). London: Wiley.

Eysenck, H. J., & Eysenck, M. W. (1985). *Personality and individual differences: A natural science approach.* New York: Plenum Press.

Folkman, S., & Lazarus, R. S. (1988). Coping as a mediator of emotion. *Journal of Personality and Social Psychology, 54,* 466–475.

Frankenhaeuser, M. (1986). A psychobiological framework for research on human stress and coping. In M. H. Appley & R. Trumbull (Eds.), *Dynamics of stress: Physiological, psychological, and social perspectives* (pp. 101–116). New York: Plenum Press.

Freedy, J. R., Kilpatrick, D. G., & Resnick, H. S. (1993). Natural disasters and mental health: Theory, assessment, and intervention. *Journal of Social Behavior and Personality, 8,* 49–103.

Goldberg, D., & Williams, P. (1988). *A user's guide to the general health questionnaire.* Windsor: NFER-Nelson

Gray, J. (1994). Framework for a taxonomy of psychiatric disorder. In S. H. M. van Goozen, N. E. V. de Poll, & J. A. Sergeant (Eds.), *Emotions: Essays on emotion theory* (pp. 29–59). Hillsdale, NJ: Lawrence Erlbaum Associates.

Gurevich, K. M., & Matveyev, V. F. (1966). On the professional fitness of operators and methods of assessment. In B. M. Teplov & K. M. Gurevich (Eds.), *Problems of professional fitness of power plants operation section staff* (pp. 3–96). Moscow: Prosveshcheniye [in Russian].

Habrat, E. (1997). *Reaktywność i zapotrzebowanie na stymulację w depresjach w przebiegu choroby afektywnej dwubiegunowej* [Reactivity and need for stimulation during depressive phase in bipolar affective disorders]. Unpublished doctoral dissertation, Institute of Psychology, Polish Academy of Sciences, Warsaw.

Holmes, T. H., & Rahe, R. H. (1967). The social readjustment rating scale. *Journal of Psychosomatic Research, 11,* 213–218.

Kagan, J. (1983). Stress and coping in early development. In N. Garmezy & M. Rutter (Eds.), *Stress, coping, and development in children* (pp. 191–216). New York: McGraw-Hill.

Kobasa, S. C. (1979). Stressful life events, personality and health: An inquiry into hardiness. *Journal of Personality and Social Psychology, 37,* 1–11.

Kobasa, S. C., & Puccetti, M. C. (1983). Personality and social resources in stress resistance. *Journal of Personality and Social Psychology, 45,* 839–850.

Krohne, H. W. (1986). Coping with stress: Dispositions, strategies, and the problem of measurement. In M. H. Appley & R. Trumbull (Eds.), *Dynamics of stress: Physiological, psychological, and social perspectives* (pp. 209–234). New York: Plenum Press.

Lazarus, R. S. (1991). *Emotion and adaptation.* New York: Oxford University Press.

Lazarus, R. S. (1993). From psychological stress to the emotions: A history of changing outlooks. *Annual Review of Psychology, 44,* 1–21.

Lundberg, U. (1982). Psychophysiological aspects of performance and adjustment to stress. In H. W. Krohne & L. Laux (Eds.), *Achievement, stress, and anxiety* (pp. 75–91). Washington: Hemisphere.

McGrath, J. E. (Ed.). (1970). *Social and psychological factors in stress.* New York: Holt, Rinehart, & Winston.

Mehrabian, A. (1977). A questionnaire measure of individual differences in stimulus screening and associated differences in arousability. *Environmental Psychology and Nonverbal Behavior, 1,* 89–103.

Nebylitsyn, V. D. (1972). *Fundamental properties of the human nervous system.* New York: Plenum Press.

Ormel, J., & Schaufeli, W. B. (1991). Stability and change in psychological distress and their relationship with self-esteem and locus of control: A dynamic equilibrium model. *Personality and Social Psychology, 60,* 288–299.

Pavlov, I. P. (1951–1952). *Complete works* (2nd ed.). Moscow: SSSR Academy of Sciences [in Russian].

Pellegrini, D. S. (1990). Psychosocial risk and protective factors in childhood. *Journal of Developmental and Behavioral Pediatrics, 11,* 201–209.

Rahe, R. H. (1975). Epidemiological studies of life change and illness. *International Journal of Psychiatry in Medicine, 6,* 133–146.

Rahe, R. H. (1987). Recent life changes, emotions, and behaviors in coronary heart disease. In A. Baum & J. E. Singer (Eds.), *Handbook of psychology and health* (Vol. 5, pp. 229–254). Hillsdale, NJ: Lawrence Erlbaum Associates.

Rutter, M. (1979). Protective factors in children's responses to stress and disadvantage. In M. W. Kent & J. E. Rolf (Eds.), *Primary prevention of psychopathology* (Vol. 3, pp. 49–74). Hanover, NH: University Press of New England.

Schneirla, T. C. (1959). An evolutionary and developmental theory of biphasic processes underlying approach and withdrawal. In M. J. Jones (Ed.), *Nebraska Symposium on Motivation* (Vol. 7). Lincoln, NE: University of Nebraska Press.

Schulz, P., & Schönpflug, W. (1982). Regulatory activity during states of stress. In H. W. Krohne & L. Laux (Eds.), *Achievement, stress, and anxiety* (pp. 51–73). Washington: Hemisphere.

Selye, H. (1975). *Stress without distress.* New York: New American Library.

Sobolewski, A., Strelau, J., & Zawadzki, B. (1999). Kwestionariusz zmian życiowych (KZŻ)—*Polska adaptacja kwestionariusza recent life changes questionnaire (RLCQ) R. H. Rahe'a* [Polish adaptation of Rahe's recent life changes questionnaire (RLCQ)]. *Przegląd Psychologiczny, 42, 27–49.*

Strelau, J. (1983). *Temperament, personality, activity.* London: Academic Press.

Strelau, J. (1987). Emotion as a key concept in temperament research. *Journal of Research in Personality, 21,* 510–528.

Strelau, J. (1988). Temperamental dimensions as codeterminants of resistance to stress. In M. P. Janisse (Ed.), *Individual differences, stress, and health psychology* (pp. 146–169). New York: Springer.

Strelau, J. (1989). Temperament risk factors in children and adolescents as studied in Eastern Europe. In W. B. Carey & S. C. McDevitt (Eds.), *Clinical and educational applications of temperament research* (pp. 65–77). Lisse: Swets & Zeitlinger.

Strelau, J. (1994). The concepts of arousal and arousability as used in temperament studies. In J. E. Bates & T. D. Wachs (Eds.), *Temperament: Individual differences at the interface of biology and behavior* (pp. 117–141). Washington: APA Books.

Strelau, J. (1995). Temperament and stress. Temperament as a moderator of stressors, emotional states, coping, and costs. In C. D. Spielberger & I. G. Sarason (Eds.), *Stress and emotion: Anxiety, anger, and curiosity* (Vol. 15, pp. 215–254). Washington: Taylor & Francis.

Strelau, J. (1996). The regulative theory of temperament: Current status. *Personality and Individual Differences, 20,* 131–142.

Strelau, J. (1998). *Temperament: A psychological perspective.* New York: Plenum Press.

Strelau, J., & Eliasz, A. (1994). Temperament risk factors for Type A behavior patterns in adolescents. In W. B. Carey & S. C. McDevitt (Eds.), *Prevention and early intervention: Individual differences as risk factors for the mental health of children* (pp. 42–49). New York: Brunner/Mazel.

Strelau, J., & Zawadzki, B. (1993). The formal characteristics of behavior—Temperament inventory (FCB-TI): Theoretical assumptions and scale construction. *European Journal of Personality, 7,* 313–336.

Strelau, J., & Zawadzki, B. (1995). The formal characteristics of behavior—Temperament inventory (FCB-TI): Validity studies. *European Journal of Personality, 9,* 207–229.

Thomas, A., & Chess, S. (1957). An approach to the study of sources of individual differences in child behavior. *Journal of Clinical and Experimental Psychopathology and Quarterly Review of Psychiatry and Neurology, 18,* 347–357.

Thomas, A., & Chess, S. (1977). *Temperament and development.* New York: Brunner/Mazel.

Thomas, A., Chess, S., & Birch, H. G. (1968). *Temperament and behavior disorders in children.* New York: New York University Press.

Trzcińska, M. (1996). *Wpływ temperamentu i stresu na stan zdrowia. Adaptacja Inwentarza Zdrowia GHQ* [Influence of temperament and stress on health status: Adaptation of the General Health Questionnaire]. Unpublished master's thesis, University of Warsaw, Warsaw, Poland.

Ursin, H. (1980). Personality, activation, and somatic health: A new psychosomatic theory. In S. Levine & H. Ursin (Eds.), *Coping and health* (pp. 259–279). New York: Plenum Press.

Veit, T. C., & Ware, J. E., Jr. (1983). The structure of psychological distress and well-being in general populations. *Journal of Consulting and Clinical Psychology, 51,* 730–742.

Vitaliano, P. P., DeWolfe, D. J., Maiuro, R. D., Russo, J., & Katon, W. (1990). Appraised changeability of a stressor as a modifier of the relationship between coping and depression: A test of the hypothesis of fit. *Journal of Personality and Social Psychology, 59,* 582–592.

Weick, K. E. (1970). The ess in stress. Some conceptual and methodological problems. In J. E. McGrath (Ed.), *Social and psychological factors in stress* (pp. 287–347). New York: Holt, Rinehart & Winston.

Wundt, W. (1887). *Grundzüge der physiologischen Psychologie* [Outlines of physiological psychology, Vol. 2, 3rd ed.]. Leipzig: Verlag von Wilhelm Engelmann.

Zuckerman, M. (1964). Perceptual isolation as a stress situation: A review. *Archives of General Psychiatry, 11,* 225–276.

Zuckerman, M. (1979). *Sensation seeking: Beyond the optimal level of arousal.* Hillsdale, NJ: Lawrence Erlbaum Associates.

Zuckerman, M. (1991). *Psychobiology of personality.* New York: Cambridge University Press.

Zuckerman, M. (1994). *Behavioral expressions and biosocial bases of sensation seeking.* New York: Cambridge University Press.

9 Adjustment Style in Childhood as a Product of Parenting and Temperament

John E. Bates
Indiana University
New York University

This chapter explores the origins of children's adjustment, especially stable differences in externalizing behavior problems. Externalizing behavior can be seen as a dimensional array of adjustment styles, with aggressive and uncooperative behavior on one side and nonaggressive and cooperative behavior on the other side (Achenbach, 1982). Origins of externalizing adjustments can be traced to social-experiential processes, such as qualities of parenting (Bates, Bayles, Bennett, Ridge, & Brown, 1991; Patterson, Reid, & Dishion, 1992; Pettit, Bates, & Dodge, 1997). Its roots can also be traced to temperament. Temperament roots of adjustment can be traced not only to behavioral measures of temperament, but also to psychophysiological and genetic correlates of the behaviors and behavior patterns underlying both temperament and adjustment (Caspi, 1998; Kagan, 1998; Newman & Wallace, 1993; Reiss, 1997; Rothbart & Bates, 1998). Of course, almost any translation of early-appearing personality traits into adjustment must involve particular kinds of transactions with the environment across the span of development. This chapter, therefore, considers origins of adjustment in both parent–child transactions and child temperament, as well as in the interaction of these two factors.

The chapter's specific focus in the temperament realm is a particularly relevant, but not-often-studied temperamental dimension, resistance to control. This dimension is conceived of as one aspect of early appearing regulatory tendencies (Rothbart & Bates, 1998), especially as seen in uninhibited children (Caspi, 1998; Kagan, 1998). It is operationalized here as mothers' reports of their children's tendencies to ignore or resist ordinary parental restrictions, such as not stopping when the parent demands it. This dimension appears to be a specific antecedent of externalizing problems and thus, an early part of externalizing adjustment style (Bates, 1989; Rothbart & Bates, 1998); its assumed temperamental underpinnings are considered more specifically later in the chapter.

The research described here is a further step based on several years of preliminary efforts to model temperament-environment interactions in the development of adjustment. This next step was spurred by two things, first, a somewhat systematic look at relevant interaction effects in the literature since my last reviews of that topic (see Bates, 1989; Rothbart & Bates, 1998), and second, an invitation by the editors of this volume to think about temperament in context. The goal in this kind of research is to gradually make improved lenses for seeing the complexities of social development, through the grinding together of a rough theoretical model and empirically measured child development.

The first of two kinds of lenses to be described here is pattern of adjustment, which I refer to as adjustment style. The term *style* has complex, incompletely defined meanings, but in the current context, I especially refer to a system of individual differences in how people adapt in the social world. This includes distinct facets of adjustment, such as externalizing problems (aggressive, disruptive) versus internalizing (inhibition, dysphoria) problems. It also includes developmental trajectories, such as increasing or decreasing trends on a dimension of adjustment (e.g., McFadyen-Ketchum, Bates, Dodge, & Pettit, 1996) versus stability of one's rank order relative to others. The focus of the chapter is on the externalizing patterns and their stability.

The second lens describes the developmental origins of stable patterns of adjustment. This includes environment-individual transactions—between child and parents, peers, and teachers. Ideally this list of transactions should also involve the emerging self, one's sense of values and competencies, and ultimately, character (Eisenberg, 1998). The list should also include transactions between the environment and genetically-based reaction tendencies of the individual. Genetic information would range from the level of family resemblances to the level of genetic codes for a particular protein with a known function in the brain and a known reactivity to stimuli (Bates, Wachs, & Emde, 1994; Boomsma, Anokhin, & de Geus, 1997). The present chapter cannot consider information about either self or genetics, but it does assume that both kinds of influences are present in adjustment styles. The chapter's special focus is how parental control style might alter developmental trajectories of linkage between early temperament and later adjustment style.

CORE CONCEPTS

Adjustment Style

This chapter focuses on the stable components of behavioral adaptations over development, not the description of change. This is not due to a lack of interest in the increasingly important research on questions of change in adjustment (see, e.g., Keiley, Bates, Dodge, & Pettit, 2000; McFadyen-Ketchum, et al., 1996; Stoolmiller, 1995). Rather, it is due to a special interest in stability of adjustment. Stability is a phenomenon large enough to deserve more than cursory attention. The chief example of such stability is externalizing problem behavior and the styles of adaptation that are so often associated with such behaviors. As Olweus (1979) pointed out, and others have since confirmed many times, children who are aggressive, disobedient, and destructive are often found to continue having problems of that general sort, even if the particular forms of externalizing do change with development (Patterson, 1993). However, as Caspi (1998) has emphasized, there are still many interesting questions to ask about continuity in personality. This is analogous to the important point made by the social historian Fischer (1989), writing about four waves of British emigrants to America: Having richly described continuities of particular, ethnically based styles of cultural adaptations across centuries of history, Fischer argued, "Many things must *happen* if a culture is to be transmitted from one generation to the next." (p. 896, italics original). This must be equally true of the transmission of individuals' personality and adjustment from one era of development to another. It will be important, for example, to learn more about how genetics, such as those underlying temperament, constrain children's development via reactive and evocative transactions with the social environment. The present question is what happens, in child–mother transactions, that might maintain or change a pattern of resistant, externalizing behavior from toddlerhood to middle childhood. How might maternal control styles moderate linkages between child temperamental resistance to control and later externalizing behavior?

Studies with mathematically modeled trajectories of children's adjustment seem to be increasingly common. Such models provide one way to operationalize an adjustment style, in terms of slopes and intercepts of behavior problem scores across years of development. However, simpler questions can be asked of growth curves, too. These are less rigorous, but perhaps still practical in this early stage of attempts to describe pathways of adjustment style. The present chapter considers a visual analysis of growth curves, aiming at a general description of the salient patterns across development. Partly based on the growth curve patterns, which are described later, we chose to focus on a measure of the average or stable component of middle childhood adjustment.

Adjustment style is a term that implies stylistic concepts of personality. In his classic monograph, Shapiro (1965) gave a rich, clinical description of the perceptual and cognitive styles conceptually underlying obsessive-compulsive, dissociative, antisocial and other "neurotic styles." In a formerly vigorous area of research, Witkin, Dyk, Faterson, Goodenough, & Karp (1962), empirically described a variety of personality styles, with implications for a range of perceptual, cognitive, and behavioral tendencies, notably field dependence versus independence. As used here, the concept of adjustment style ultimately implies a configural approach to understanding child psychopathology (e.g., see findings of Bates, Pettit, & Dodge, 1995). For the sake of manageability, the research described in this chapter followed the simpler choice of focusing on only one dimension of adjustment style—externalizing problems measured on multiple occasions in middle childhood, one dimension of temperament—resistance to control, and one environmental transactional process—maternal efforts to control the very young child's explorations.

Parenting

In describing origins of adjustment style, the research described here looks configurally at child and parent characteristics as antecedents. The major emphasis of research on the origins of children's behavior problems throughout the present century has been on parenting traits. Many studies have confirmed theoretical expectations of associations between adverse parenting and the concurrent presence of child adjustment problems (e.g., Hetherington & Martin, 1986; Rothbaum & Weisz, 1994). Recent longitudinal research has also showed that parenting characteristics such as harsh and ineffective discipline are predictive of later behavior problems (e.g., Bates, Bayles, Bennett, Ridge, & Brown, 1991; Dodge, Pettit, & Bates, 1994; McFadyen-Ketchum et al., 1996; Patterson et al., 1992; Shaw, Keenan, & Vondra, 1994). Research has shown that characteristics of warmth and educationally stimulating involvement, on the other hand, are often associated with lower levels of behavior problems (Pettit & Bates, 1989; Pettit, Bates, & Dodge, 1997; Rothbaum & Weisz, 1994).

The amounts of variance in child adjustment accounted for by the parenting variables have been statistically significant, but relatively modest, with even concurrent correlations typically in the .2 to .4 range (e.g., Rothbaum & Weisz, 1994). This can reflect poor measurement of the key constructs. However, it can also suggest a need to consider interactive models beyond the main-effects models dominant in previous studies. Implications of a parenting variable may depend on the context provided by some other variable. Child characteristics, especially temperament traits, have been often mentioned as possible moderators of parenting.

Temperament

Research on temperament has a shorter history in developmental psychopathology than research on parenting, but in the past 20 years or so research has begun to confirm the theoretical expectation that adverse temperament traits forecast adjustment difficulties (Bates, 1989; Rothbart & Bates, 1998). As with parenting traits, temperament traits have not accounted for large enough portions of the variance to be useful in practice, although some studies find they account for portions of variance comparable to those of parenting measures (e.g., Bates et al., 1991).

Temperament is defined as biologically based, early appearing, relatively stable personality characteristics. The term encompasses specific traits, each of which concerns different kinds of behaviors and different biological roots. Biological basis can mean a variety of things, but for most temperament traits it probably means genetic predispositions, and implies variations in numbers and types of nerve cells and their neurotransmitter chemicals in characteristic locations of the brain. These variations influence responses to particular classes of stimuli (Kagan, 1998). The biological basis of temperament goes beyond initial genetic codes. Experiences such as traumatic stress, intellectual stimulation, and nurturance affect brain organization, too. Despite this fuzzy boundary for concepts of the specific biological roots of temperament, biological concepts of temperament can help account for the tendency of temperament traits to be relatively stable. Of course, stable environments may also help account for stability of temperament, as may social-cognitive structures internal to the individual, such as self-concept (Caspi, 1998). Theoretically, there are multiple forces on any phenotypic behavior trait, and environmentally triggered changes are even possible at the levels of neural organization and the expression of genes (Rothbart & Bates, 1998). As particular sets of genes supporting particular responses to specific environments are identified, it may be possible to more precisely separate the phenotype and the genotype. In the meantime, although behavior genetics designs can statistically model multiple components in a phenotype, I do not think it is feasible to draw sharp empirical distinctions between the phenotype and the genotype of temperament, nor between its biological and its experiential roots.

Specific Temperament Traits.   There are many names for temperament traits, but, in accord with recent research in the tradition of the factorial models of adult personality, these many dimensions can be summarized in three or five, second-order dimensions (Goldberg, 1993; Halverson, Kohnstamm, & Martin, 1994; Rothbart, Derryberry, & Posner, 1994; Slotboom et al., 1996). Conceptual links have been advanced between various temperament concepts and adult personality dimensions, including extraversion, agreeableness, conscientiousness, neuroticism, and openness to experience (Caspi, 1998; Rothbart & Bates, 1998). As previously mentioned, the specific temperament concept of focus here is resistance to control, a variable identified as consistently distinct from negative emotionality and inhibition to the unfamiliar (Bates & Bayles, 1984). Resistance to control can be conceptually defined as a joint function of the early temperamental roots of several broad personality dimensions, including especially extraversion, agreeableness, and conscientiousness (Bates, Pettit, Dodge, & Ridge, 1998). Each of these dimensions has evidence for temperamental roots (Caspi, 1998), especially in genetic heritability. Roots of conscientiousness are less established in infants and very young children than the other two kinds of traits, for obvious, developmental reasons. However, it seems plausible that resistance to control might represent an early component of that trait. Links between Big-5-type models of personality and established models of temperament are more conceptual at this stage than empirical at present. However, empirical links are starting to appear (Lanthier & Bates, 1995), and I predict that future research will more clearly establish such links. One should not expect all temperament traits to appear early in infancy. Some traits, such as ones based on an ability to executively direct attention (Rothbart et al., 1994), will not be visible early, because they depend on further brain development. More specifically, one would probably not see a trait of resistance to control in a young infant, but by walking age, the trait could start to emerge.

THE SEARCH FOR MODERATOR EFFECTS

The interaction or moderator effect interpretation has been a leading component of models of social development for many years. Thomas, Chess, & Birch (1968), pioneering researchers in the area of temperament and psychopathology, emphasized that the effect of a given temperament would depend on the fit between the child's characteristics and the parent's predilections for dealing with the child. For example, the social development of an inhibited child might be shaped by parents' skillful efforts to expose the child to novelty in gently challenging doses. More recently, Wachs (1992; Wachs & Plomin, 1991) has drawn attention to child-environment moderator processes as shapers of development. However, considering the theoretical dominance of the assumption of interaction effects between temperament and parenting environment, there have been surprisingly few relevant findings compared to the findings of direct, main effects of temperament and parenting variables. Of the relatively few interaction effect findings, very few have been replicated (Rothbart & Bates, 1998; Wachs, 1992).

There are at least three reasons for the relative dearth of solid findings. The first, probably true in part, but not very interesting, is that researchers lack incentives for replication research. The second, more interesting possibility is that the assumption that developmental forces interact with one another is wrong. This sends us back to better measurement of hypothetical factors, finding new factors to measure, and the use of simple, linear or additive models to account for developmental outcomes (Wiggins, 1973). This interpretation may conceptually elegant, but it also requires nature to be simpler than most of us believe it to be; and it is also daunting to think of new factors and measures that will overcome the deficiencies of the ones used to date. The third, most interesting interpretation is that there are special methodological problems that interfere with the reliable detection of interaction effects. Aside from difficulties in getting a large enough sample for adequate power to detect interaction effects, especially the likely modest-sized effects (see Wachs & Plomin, 1991), there is also the problem emphasized by McClelland and Judd (1993): Common deviations from normal in the distributions of predictor variables typically do not cause major problems in simple, linear analyses. However, in nonlinear analyses evaluating interaction effects, these same deviations from normal in a predictor and a moderator variable can cause extreme reductions in efficiency in detecting an interaction effect. So, even if one assumed sufficient statistical power and adequate measurement of constructs, distributional properties of predictor and moderator variables make it likely that some interaction effects that exist will be undetected, and that some of the ones that have been detected are spurious. One practical answer to these problems, as pointed out by Rutter (1983), is replication of interaction effects.

Thomas et al. (1968) supported their interpretation of moderator effects in large part through idiographic analyses of their longitudinal, quasi-clinical data. However, this research and the wider influence of the systems zeitgeist subsequently inspired a number of more empirical findings of moderator effects.

One relevant effect in the recent literature is from Henry, Caspi, Moffitt, & Silva (1996). In this study of the Dunedin longitudinal sample, there was a direct linkage between externalizing-like behavior in laboratory testing sessions at ages 3 and 5 years in predicting convictions for crimes by age 18. There was also an interaction effect: Highly impulsive, uncooperative children who had been in single-parent homes at age 13 were more likely to have received a conviction than those who lived in two-parent homes. Assuming that children in single-parent homes received less supervision and control of their behavioral predispositions, this interaction finding may mean that the implications of a temperament-like predisposition was moderated by the level of control experienced in early adolescence. This may resemble the interaction to be described in the present chapter—between temperamental resistance to control and levels of maternal control in predicting later externalizing adjustment. A number of other, very interesting Temperament × Environment interaction effects were reviewed by Rothbart and Bates (1998), but for this chapter, the focus is on the few that have been replicated in some way.

First, Wachs (1992) describes a replicated effect in the literature, going back to Escalona (1968), in which children who are highly active are less adversely affected by psychologically impoverished environments than inactive children. Wachs (1992) also summarizes replicated findings of other adverse effects of stressful environments on temperamentally difficult children.

Also relevant are Kochanska's recent findings. Kochanska (1991) showed in a sample of 2- to 4-year-olds followed for 6 years that fearful children later displayed less highly developed conscience when their mothers had used power-assertive discipline techniques than when they had used gentler discipline. However, nonfearful children's conscience development was not associated with the mother discipline style. Theoretically, gentle discipline works by keeping a fear-prone child's anxiety levels low, and thus increasing the child's ability to attend to feedback regarding limits and to internalize these limits. Kochanska (1995) reported converging results in a preschool sample. Highly fearful children's behaviors indicating internalized self-control were more frequent when their mothers were gentle in their discipline and less frequent when their mothers were power-assertive. Nonfearful children's levels of conscience were not associated with the gentle versus power-assertive discipline index, but rather by the presence of a secure attachment relationship between mother and child, as indexed by the mother's report on a Q-sort. Kochanska (1997) has replicated this effect longitudinally in the same sample at a later age. Furthermore, Colder, Lochman, and Wells (1997) found that teacher ratings of aggression were higher in temperamentally fearful children whose parents used harsh discipline than in temperamentally nonfearful children with harsh parents or highly fearful children with gentle parents.

Another pair of studies can be interpreted as providing an additional, replicated interaction effect. There is a general linkage between high reactivity in infancy and later behavioral inhibition in response to novelty (Kagan, 1998). Arcus and Gardner (1993) found, however, that parental limit setting moderated the linkage between reactivity in infancy and behavioral inhibition in toddlerhood (see also chapter by Arcus, this volume). Specifically, highly reactive infants whose mothers were high in limit setting were less likely to become inhibited than those whose mothers were low in limit setting. Very low-reactive infants tended to become noninhibited toddlers, independent of the way their mothers controlled them. This set of findings is conceptually similar to the later findings of Park, Belsky, Putnam, and Crnic (1997), who followed children from age 1 to age 3. Temperamentally negative 1-year-olds turned out to be less inhibited at age 3 when their parents were more affectively negative in their home behavior at ages 2 and 3 than when their parents were less negative. Low negativity infants' outcomes were not related to the negativity of the parents.

Background Findings on Temperament

As background for my own findings on Temperament-by-Environment inter-action, I present a brief summary of directly relevant prior research. Mean-ings of data depend on the web of previous results and theoretical interpretations in which they are found. The web's basic methodological, empirical nature provides important context for a theoretical story. The con-cepts and measures of temperament and environment that are used in the re-search to be described here are based on prior work done by students, colleagues, and myself, beginning in 1975. Among the many influences for this work was the work of Thomas et al. (1968), which gave rich, clinical in-terpretation of the interaction of temperament and parenting in the develop-ment of adjustment differences of children.

One of the key bases for the chapter's viewpoint is the Infant Characteris-tics Study (Bates, Freeland, & Lounsbury, 1979). This study provided the orig-inal form of our multidimensional measure of adverse temperament traits in infancy. A second basis was the Infant Cries Study (Lounsbury & Bates, 1982), which provided some important clues as to the nature of difficult tem-perament in infants. Third, the Bloomington Longitudinal Study (BLS; Bates, Olson, Pettit, & Bayles, 1982; Bates et al., 1991) provided a rich stream of fol-low-through data. There were other, smaller studies, too, but these three were the most relevant ones for the study of temperament. The following section lists a number of findings and methodological concerns arising in rela-tion to the findings and their interpretations. This review will provide con-text for appreciating (or rejecting) the newer findings to be presented here. The focus of the background given here is the meaning of temperament mea-sures. There exist comparable findings regarding meaningfulness of the other measures in the present studies, including child adjustment (Achenbach, 1991a, 1991b) and our observational measures of parent–child interaction (Frankel & Bates, 1990; Lee & Bates, 1985; Pettit & Bates, 1989; Pettit, Bates, & Dodge, 1997).

Operational Definitions of Temperament.   Our three tempera-ment studies suggested a structure of adverse temperament traits: The difficultness concept, according to mothers' and fathers' reports on a number of infant traits is most clearly defined by the tendency to fuss and cry fre-quently and intensely (Bates et al., 1979). Lounsbury and Bates (1982) showed, through both expert ratings and spectral analyses, that the cries of the most difficult infants, compared with the easier infants, were more irri-tating to listeners and contained longer pauses between cry sounds and higher pitch at volume peaks, suggesting more aversive demandingness and more urgency. A second dimension found in the research was called unadaptability. This corresponds conceptually to the Thomas and Chess concepts of approach and adaptability, as well as to the important concept of be-havioral inhibition (Kagan, 1998). A third dimension—the focus of the present research—was the concept of resistance to control (a name suggested by G.A. Kohnstamm, based on the content of the scales). Some children are relatively unmanageable, in the sense that they do not respond readily or co-operatively to the verbalizations that caregivers use to modulate children's activity (Rothbart & Bates, 1998). Conceptually, unmanageability can arise from an active ignoring or openly uncooperative stance, or from deficits in cognitive processing of inhibitory cues or from difficulty inhibiting domi-nant, especially reward-seeking responses. This third dimension is the focus of the present research.

Social Perception Measures.

The previous research also supported the position that parental ratings of child temperament (and adjustment) should be conceived of as social perceptions, containing objective and subjec-tive components, as well as psychometric error (Bates, 1980; Bates & Bayles, 1984; Bates et al., 1979). The objective components can be seen in the correla-tions between parent perceptions of temperament and independently ob-served, conceptually relevant traits of the child, such as frequency of crying (Bates et al., 1979) or qualities of the cry (Lounsbury & Bates, 1982), and many other measured qualities (Bates & Bayles, 1984). The subjective com-ponents can be seen in the correlations between perceived characteristics of the child and the parent's own characteristics, such as social desirability re-sponse bias (Bates & Bayles, 1984). When we learn more precisely how the parent's characteristics bias the view of the child's temperament relative to a more objective source, we may be able to correct for such biases (Bates, 1989).

Clearly, for the time being one should not see parent perceptions of tem-perament as equivalent to objective assessments. However, validity of obser-vation measures is also far from perfect (Rothbart & Bates, 1998), and one need not go to the other extreme of totally rejecting the use of parent report measures (see Kagan, 1998, for an opposing view). For the measurement of temperament, the key issue in observational measures is adequacy of the be-havior sample. It will be difficult for outside observers to assess all of the rele-vant situations that parents can relatively easily, if not perfectly, report on. In contrast to the assumptions some may make, so far, subjective components have not been dominant over the objective ones—in other words, amounts of variance explained by subjective factors have not overall been stronger or more numerous than amounts explained by objective measures (Bates & Bayles, 1984). This is especially interesting in light of the likely genetic over-lap between temperament of child and parent personality, which might be expected to inflate correlations between parents' ratings of self and child (Plomin & Bergeman, 1991; Reiss, 1997). In short, I recognize the likelihood of perceptual biases in parents' perceptions, and I also recognize that observational measures have some key shortcomings (Rothbart & Bates, 1998). At the same time, I recognize the likelihood of objective components of parents' reports as well as the potentially great value of direct observations.

To dwell a bit longer on the methodological issues about subjective components in parent reports, what kind of bias would there be in parents' perceptions of their children's behavior? Would bias be a momentary phenomenon, not the same from age to age? Or would it color reports in similar ways across development? If bias were continuous, would it be a simple, good–bad/hopeful–depressed kind of evaluative coloring that persists over time, or something more complex than that?

Differential Continuity.   If the parental bias components of temperament perceptions and later adjustment perceptions are global and not just momentary correlates, one might expect parent reports on the various scales at one age to correlate in substantially indiscriminant ways with their later counterparts. However, this does not appear to be the case. In fact, findings from the BLS suggest a differential pattern of continuity. Early difficultness showed its strongest links to later difficultness; and the same was true for early unadaptability and resistance to control (Bates & Bayles, 1984). Moreover, the pattern extended to behavior problem outcomes in the preschool and early elementary years (Bates & Bayles, 1984; Bates et al., 1991). In overview, the pattern shows that early difficultness, which contains subelements of social demandingness (related to coerciveness) and irritability, and which logically could pertain to either externalizing or internalizing adjustment, predicted both kinds of adjustment well. In addition, early unadaptability—conceptually related to negative affectivity and fearfulness—predicted later internalizing problems such as anxiety better than it predicted externalizing problems. Finally, early resistance to control predicted later externalizing problems better than it did internalizing problems.

The differential linkage pattern may be due to the stability of objective characteristics of the children. It is probably not due to the stability of a simple, global parental bias; but it could conceivably be due, in addition to stability of actual child characteristics, to a complex, multifactorial perceptual and reporting bias, a more complex combination of biases than has yet been described in personality research. My preferred interpretation at this time is that this differentiation is due, partly, to objectively perceived characteristics of children being a somewhat consistently structured system of traits that threads through the development of children. This interpretation does not preclude the likely operation of environmental processes supporting continuity, such as repeating social patterns and concepts of personality held by both caregivers and children (Caspi, 1998). Future methodological advances are needed to address our current difficulty in discerning true variance from biased variance. There are practical limits on the range of variables that can be assessed in multivariate, multisource ways over time. A strength of the study to be summarized in detail, however, is that we did consider more than one source of information about children's environments and outcomes.

The Question of "Contamination."   There is another conceptual point of relevance to any study of the possible implications of early temperament for later adjustment: Sanson, Prior, and Kyrios (1990) pointed out that the contents of temperament and behavior problem scales have similarities, and that this content overlap, which they referred to as contamination, could account for much of the predictive relation between temperament and adjustment. There are two answers to this concern. The first is that content overlap may be theoretically meaningful (Bates, 1990; Caspi, 1998). This is certainly the implication of the notion of adjustment style being advanced in this chapter. The second is that the content overlap may, in fact, not account for a huge portion of the linkage. As shown by Sheeber (1995) in an intervention study, children's perceived behavior problem traits can change without the perceived temperament traits changing. The basic conclusion for the moment is that temperament and adjustment probably are distinguishable concepts. However, it is to be expected that some of the behaviors used to index adjustment styles will be similar in qualities and temporal patterns of behavior to those used to index temperament, just as personality can be seen as a structure underlying particular adjustment styles. One can point to many differences in the concepts of temperament and adjustment, and the distinctions are mostly useful, but there is also considerable overlap. The overlap can be seen as meaningful rather than merely measurement contamination.

Preliminary Explorations of Temperament-Environment Interaction.   Having established some basic, empirically grounded definitions of adverse temperament traits, we next began to look for possible Temperament-by-Environment interactions. The BLS gave hints of a Temperament-by-Environment interaction pattern. The earliest indications came through the 1st-year research project by my student Mariana delaFlor. We divided mothers of the BLS according to their levels of warmth/positive involvement and control. Extending from Baumrind (1967), we thought there might be an interaction between the two parenting dimensions in addition to an interaction between parenting and temperament. The pattern actually found was for the correlations between temperament and later adjustment to be stronger and more consistent for the dyads with high involvement but low control than for the other dyads. This relationship held fairly well for ages 3, 4, 5, and 6, based on a visual analysis of bar graphs of the size of correlations for the different variables within each group. Statistical modeling of this pattern was deferred, because of the small sample size (only 13–24 per group). In subsequent analyses, we learned that the pattern was not due to obvious confounds, such as a strong correlation between temperament and parenting, big differences in the ranges of variables, child gender, or socioeconomic status (SES). The pattern appeared to apply to the adjustment reports of both mothers and teachers. However, the pattern did not replicate fully in the age 7 to 10 followups. The mother warmth/involvement measure no longer played an obvious interactive role. What did remain similar was the interactive role played by level of maternal control—behaviors such as warning, prohibiting, removing objects, and occasionally scolding, and even more rarely, a little swat. When mothers were observed to be high on control their children's temperament was more predictive of later adjustment than when mothers were observed to be low on control (Bates & Marvinney, 1993; Bates, 1994). This was seen in the pattern of correlations of early temperament scores at 12 to 24 months of age with later externalizing and internalizing adjustment scores, as reported by both mothers and teachers. The details of this relation and its further replication became the focus of the present analysis.

I had initially expected that early parenting variables would have robust correlations with early child temperament, based both on child effects models and subjective perceptions models. However, in fact, correlations in the first two years of development between indexes of temperament and parenting have been inconsistent, possibly interacting with low social class or stress (Crockenberg, 1987; van den Boom, 1994) and generally modest in size, as summarized by Bates (1989) and Rothbart and Bates (1998). This turns out to be methodologically useful in the present evaluation of Temperament-by-Environment interaction, because it is simpler to interpret interactions between uncorrelated factors (Rutter, 1983).

THE PRESENT STUDY: METHODOLOGY

What follows is a sketch of the methods for the two data sets combined in the present study—the Bloomington Longitudinal Study (BLS) and the Child Development Project (CDP). In the BLS assessments were done at ages 6, 13, and 24 months and 3, 4, 5, 6, 7, 8 and 10 years. In the CDP, assessments were done at ages 5, 6, 7, 8, 9, 10, and 11 years. For details of the methods see Bates et al. (1998).

Subjects

Two, separate, but conceptually linked, longitudinal studies provided the samples for the present work: The BLS consisted of a core group of approximately 90 to 120 families recruited via hospital birth announcements when the babies approached age 6 months. At age 6 months, the babies showed a fairly normal distribution of temperamental difficultness, according to the Infant Characteristics Questionnaire. Based on parents' work, and to some extent education, families in the present BLS core sample were rated as lower (22%), middle (64%,including skilled trades, white collar, and student), and upper middle (15%) socioeconomic level. Children were 56% male and 44% female. All were of European-American background. The CDP provided the second sample—an independent project with some conceptual links to the BLS, conducted in three different cities, Nashville and Knoxville, TN, and Bloomington, IN. The CDP sample began with a community sample of families with children registering for kindergarten. From the initial 585 families, 156 were selected prior to or early in the kindergarten year to represent children high, medium, and low on parentally perceived aggressiveness. These families showed a wide range of SES, but averaged 40.85 on the Hollingshead (1975) 4-factor index. Children were 49% male and 51% female. Ethnicity was 84% European-American, 15% African-American, and 1% other.

Procedures

In the BLS, temperament was assessed by maternal questionnaires at ages 13 and 24 months. Maternal control behaviors were assessed via naturalistic, home observation at the same ages, using both molecular codes and observer ratings of related constructs, each combined via factor analysis. Child adjustment outcomes were assessed at ages 7, 8, and 10 with questionnaires mailed to mothers and teachers.

In the CDP, temperament was assessed by a retrospective questionnaire completed by the mothers at age 5 years, thinking back to when the child was an infant. Maternal control was assessed in naturalistic home observations at age 5, using events coded from a detailed narrative record. Child adjustment was assessed at ages 7, 8, 9, 10, and 11 with questionnaires mailed to mothers and teachers.

One methodological concern is the meaningfulness of retrospective reports of temperament. Of course, one would not expect the reports to be as accurate as concurrent ones, but we were reassured to learn in the BLS sample that mothers could look back to their infants' temperament traits from the perspective of age 10 years with modest-moderate degrees of validity (Bates et al., 1998). Given that in the CDP the mothers were asked to recall only from age 5 years, one can assume that the validity of their retrospective reports would be no worse than in the BLS. However, even if one makes the unlikely assumption that the retrospective Infant Characteristics Questionnaire (ICQ) reports of the CDP say nothing about the very early characteristics of the child, but only about the child at age 5, one still must note that resistance to control was assessed well before the adjustment outcomes were assessed.

Measures

Resistance to Control.   The temperamental variable of resistance to control conceptually concerns very early unmanageability. It was measured via the ICQ (Bates et al., 1979; Bates & Bayles, 1984). Items concerned the following: (a) persists playing with objects even when told to leave them alone, (b) continues to go even when told "stop," "come here," or "no-no," (c) gets upset when removed from something he or she is interested in but should not be getting into, and (d) snuggles little when held. How does this factor relate to more basic concepts of temperament? Temperament can be defined as encompassing both reactivity and self-regulation (Rothbart & Bates, 1998). Conceptually, then the specific dimension of resistance to control may have two reactivity components: strong attraction to and excitement in response to rewarding stimuli, and weak tendencies toward warm, trusting, helpful responses to people, or low agreeableness. It is also possible that a third reactivity component is involved, a lack of fearful inhibition in response to cues of punishment, but, given the fact that studies show resistance to control to be unrelated to the novelty fear dimension of the ICQ, this does not seem likely. Resistance to control would also conceptually have a self-regulation component related to Rothbart and Bates' (1998) concept of effortful control of attention or Patterson and Newman's (1993) concept of response modulation. Presumably, children differ in their ability to process peripheral information in the environment about future consequences of behaviors, as, for example, in the verbal cues provided by a mother as a child is approaching some kind of risk: "No-no. Put that down." In sum, children who are high on resistance to control may be strongly attracted to rewarding stimuli, weakly connected to the feelings of other people, and poor at detecting cues for inhibition, all of which would put the child at risk for the development of conduct problems. The resistance to control composite scores showed adequate internal consistency, .76 for the BLS index and .83 for the CDP index, especially considering the small numbers of items (Bates et al., 1998).

Maternal Restrictive Control.   In the BLS we measured maternal restrictive control in interaction with the child at ages 13 and 24 months. The restrictive control composite of molecular code and observer rating factors refers to prohibitions, warnings, and scoldings in response to troublesome or risky child actions. This included the possibility of physical punishment, but it is not the equivalent of harsh discipline, because observers seldom saw physical discipline. In the CDP, we measured restrictive control at age 5, using a count of events in which the child misbehaved and the mother restrictively controlled the child in response. Again, the mother behavior was not necessarily highly aversive or punitive. For both indexes, the interobserver reliability estimates were acceptable with correlations of molecular measures in the BLS averaging

.73 and a minimum of 67% agreement on subjective ratings, and in the CDP a kappa of .64 on the nature of the event (Bates et al., 1998).

Methodologically, it is good to remember that the mother's level of control could derive partly from the overall level of explorativeness of the child. The child's explorativeness in turn can derive from a variety of temperamental predispositions, such as level of positive emotional response to stimuli or inhibition in the presence of a strange observer. Child explorativeness can also derive from stable features of the environment, such as level of the mother's active engagement with the child, and temporary features of the environment, such as mother inhibition in response to the presence of an observer. However, in the end, we have to assume provisionally that the measurement biases differ enough from case to case that the data as a whole provide a partially true image of actual, developmental realities. Another possible methodological concern would exist if the child's temperamental resistance to control were tightly linked to the observed levels of mother control. However, this was not actually the case. A child could engage in a high level of trouble behaviors—exploring a lot of things in the forbidden zone—but still be perceived by the mother as not being resistant to control.

Maternal Positive Involvement.   In addition to the dimension of control, there is another parenting dimension repeatedly found in studies of parent–child interaction, that of warmth or positive involvement. As mentioned previously, in early efforts to chart the interactive effects of childrearing environment on the links between child temperament and adjustment, we considered the role of positive involvement in addition to control. The present chapter presents recent results from consideration of the role of positive involvement in interaction with maternal control and child temperament. In the BLS, positive involvement was measured at ages 6, 13, and 24 months through the same kinds of molecular and observer ratings composites as used for the maternal control construct. It included such things as mother affection and educational stimulation of the child. In the CDP, the measure was from a composite of 4 rating items completed by home observers at age 5 years, concerning warmly positive mother behaviors toward the child. Interobserver reliability correlations were adequate, ranging from .58 for the CDP measure to an average of .85 for the BLS codes (for the BLS measures, see Bates et al., 1982; Olson, Bates, & Bayles, 1984; Pettit & Bates, 1984; for the CDP measures see Pettit, Bates, & Dodge, 1997).

In the present analysis, one can think of the environment as encouraging some tendencies in the child and discouraging others. The basic question is what will be the outcome of child tendencies to resist control in transaction with mother tendencies to provide low versus high levels of control of misbehavior. A secondary question is whether levels of mother positive involvement may further moderate the effects of control tendencies.

Externalizing Behavior.   For both the BLS and the CDP, the measures of adjustment were the externalizing scores from the Achenbach (1991a, 1991b; Achenbach & Edelbrock, 1983, 1986) Child Behavior Checklist, for mother report, and the parallel, Teacher Report Form. Two different sets of manuals are cited because of minor changes in the algorithms, that is, lists of items, used in computing scale scores. The earlier, BLS scores were formed with the 1983/1986 algorithms and the later, CDP scores were formed with the 1991 algorithms. Achenbach (1991a, 1991b) reports very high correlation between scores computed with the different algorithms. At this point, I will briefly consider the patterns shown by growth curves of the children's externalizing scores. In viewing the growth curves of either mother or teacher reports of children's externalizing behavior, one sees fluctuations at all levels of externalizing, with a strong tendency of the low externalizing children's scores to fluctuate very slightly, but in the higher externalizing ranges, there are more extreme fluctuations. In the mid to higher reaches the fluctuations are similar across a number of cases in the group, such as the well-documented decline in mother reports of externalizing behavior across the elementary school years (Keiley et al., 2000). There are some, but not many cases in which there is a rise in externalizing behavior that is sustained for more than a few years. More dominant in the mid-high-range cases is a sawtooth pattern in the intensity of the problem behavior. The individual and group change patterns deserve study. They could represent measurement error, but they could also represent true fluctuations in adjustment style. However, it is notable that despite fluctuations over time at the higher reaches of externalizing scores, there is a trend for such a child to remain at least at a moderate level of externalizing.

Individual rates of change on a measure can be analyzed (e.g., Keiley et al., 2000), but for the present project, the decision was to simply use the stable component of externalizing adjustment. The scores from the different ages (three for BLS and five for CDP) were averaged within sources, and children with no score during the middle-childhood period were excluded. The great majority of children had data in the majority of the years, and the internal consistencies of the composite scores ranged from .60 to .92 (details are in Bates et al., 1998).

What are the Direct Correlations Between the Predictors and Outcomes?

The correlations between temperamental resistance to control and externalizing outcome scores in the BLS were .22 ($p = .021$) and .30 ($p = .001$) for teacher- and mother-reported outcomes, respectively; and in the CDP, they were .14 and .32 (both $p = .001$), respectively. [The samples for these CDP analyses were the full, available sample ($N = 509/525$), not just the observed subsample.] The correlations show that mother reports of child temperament did predict later externalizing problems, as perceived both by teachers and mothers. The predictions were stronger for mother-reported outcomes than for teacher reports, as would be expected because of both situational and source of information factors.

The correlations between mother restrictive control and adjustment outcomes were less well replicated across studies. In the BLS, the measure of mother control was not correlated with later adjustment, with correlations of .04 and – .01, for teacher and mother outcome reports, respectively (both ns). However, in the CDP, the corresponding correlations were .28 ($p = .001$) and .14 ($p = .092$). [The sample for the CDP correlations was the home observation sample.] The correlations may have differed because in the BLS parental behavior was measured so early that perhaps it was not highly relevant to the child's developing externalizing pattern, whereas the CDP measure was from age 5 years, when the child's externalizing style may have already become a strong factor in the mothers' control styles. There could be some crucial differences in the meanings of the two measures. Despite their conceptual similarities, the measures were quite different methodologically.

For both sets of correlations, it is worth noting that the prediction correlations were of modest size. This further reinforces the decision to test for interactions between the two predictors in accounting for the outcomes. Wachs (1992) pointed out that in such a situation, there is a greater chance of observing interaction effects than when the predictors are strongly correlated.

Does Maternal Control Moderate the Relation Between Temperament and Adjustment?

The first approach to the question of statistical interaction in these data was to compare the scatterplots of the relations between temperament and adjustment scores within groups formed by splitting the groups at the median of observed maternal control. This provided straightforward evaluation of the possible impact of outlier cases and of differences in distributions on the variables. One example is presented in Figure 9.1. This shows the relations between early resistance to control and middle-childhood externalizing problems at school for the BLS sample, as moderated by the observed levels of mother restrictive control behavior at age 13 to 24 months. As is most easily seen by comparing the two regression lines, the correlation was stronger for the low restrictive control group than for the high restrictive control group. In other words, the child's temperament had a bigger implication for later adjustment at school when the child's mother had been observed relatively infrequently attempting to control the child than when she had been observed controlling often. By comparing the points for the high restrict group to the low restrict group, it can be impressionistically seen that the lowered correlation for the high restrict group can be attributed to a few cases who were high in resistance to control but who ended up with low levels of externalizing behavior, as well as to a few cases who were low in resistance who ended up with high externalizing scores. Remarkably, the same pattern was shown for both teacher and mother outcome scores and in both the BLS and CDP data. This pattern of replication suggested that the moderation pattern, although quite modest in the size of the effect, was likely to be meaningful. The correlations for all groups are shown in Table 9.1.

However, because the visual analysis does not provide a statistical index of the robustness of the observed pattern, we used structural equation modeling in EQS (Bentler, 1995) to compare the fit of a model in which the path coefficients were allowed to vary versus a model in which the key paths were constrained to be equal. The key path coefficients were those between temperamental resistance to control and externalizing outcome. In the first model, they were allowed to be different, and in the second model they were constrained to be equal in the high and low mother restriction groups. In other words, the nested comparison asked whether the data fit better the notion that the relations between temperament and adjustment differed according to the

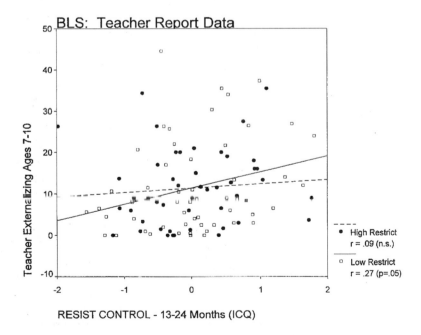

FIG. 9.1. Example of the scatterplots of temperamental resistance to control, reported by the mother, predicting child externalizing adjustment in middle childhood, as moderated by observed maternal restrictive control. In this example, the outcome is teacher-reported externalizing problems.

TABLE 9.1   **Correlations Between Early Temperamental Resistance
to Control and Later Externalizing Adjustment as Moderated
by Level of Maternal Control**

| | Correlations | |
Group	Resist → T Ext	Resist → M Ext
1. BLS Low Control	.27*	.44***
2. BLS High Control	.09	.11
3. CDP Low Control.	24*	.53***
4. CDP High Control	.00	.18

Notes. Resist = Child temperamental resistance to control. T Ext = Teacher reports of externalizing behavior across middle childhood. M Ext = Mother reports of externalizing behavior across middle childhood. *p < .05; ***p < .001. N by group, teacher, mother: 1. 54,54; 2. 47,51; 3. 85,84; 4. 58,57.

level of mother restrictive control or the notion that the paths were, more parsimoniously, essentially the same, and thus there was no moderator effect. The tested models contained all four groups—high and low restrictive control in the BLS and the CDP, and both teacher and mother reports of adjustment outcome. The unconstrained model, the one that allowed the paths to vary freely, provided a good fit to the data (chi-square (2, N = 239) = .705, Comparative Fit Index = 1.000). The constrained model, one that assumed the paths between temperament and adjustment to be equal in the high and low mother restrict groups, that is, no moderator effect, fit the data worse than the model that assumed a moderator effect (chi-square (6, N = 239) = 10.122). The difference between the models had a .053 probability of having occurred by chance. This was small enough that we accepted the moderator effect. We did not insist on a less than .05 difference because the probability estimate did not consider the question of whether the direction of differences between the paths was the same for the four groups. We were interested not only in whether there was a difference but in what direction. In fact, the direction of difference was the same in all four groups and for both teacher and mother report outcomes. We estimate that the actual probability of a spurious difference between the models would be somewhat less than .053. For further details of the analyses and the findings, see Bates et al. (1998).

It appears, then, that levels of maternal control did moderate the implications of children's early temperamental resistance to control for later externalizing adjustment. For both teacher and mother-reported outcomes, there was a stronger linkage between temperament and adjustment for the children whose mothers had been observed to be low in control. This effect was replicated in two, separate studies.

To further evaluate the pattern of findings, we considered, and ruled out, a number of possible confounds of the effect. These included child gender and family SES, differences between the high and low mother restriction groups on distributions of the variables, and nonequivalence of meaning of externalizing scores across the high and low restriction groups (in terms of differences between the convergence between mothers and teachers on externalizing scores). For details, see Bates et al. (1998). Thus, the pattern of correlations is unlikely to be due to chance and it is also unlikely to be due to obvious confounds like distributions of variables or child gender.

Does Maternal Positive Involvement Further Moderate the Moderator Effect of Maternal Restrictive Control?

As mentioned previously, the further moderating effects of maternal positive involvement with the child were evaluated in the BLS sample. However, these moderating effects had not been considered in relation to the stable, middle-childhood outcome measure, and they had not been considered at all in the CDP sample. The samples were further split at their respective medians of relevant maternal warmth or positive involvement variables. Scatterplots and associated correlations between early resistance to control and later externalizing problems in the subsamples formed by the crossed categories of low and high restrictive control and low and high warmth were then examined in the same way as for the moderating effects of restrictive control alone.

The parental warmth dimension did not consistently affect the linkage pattern already described as moderated by restrictive control. The correlations between temperament and adjustment in the low mother restriction groups were higher for the high warmth than for the low warmth dyads in the BLS. In the CDP this pattern held for teachers' reports but not mothers'. The scatterplots, however, did not form a visually compelling case for mother warmth as a moderator. A further subdivision by the sex of the child also did not reveal a consistent pattern of replicated differences. Therefore, for the present, it appears that maternal warmth or positive involvement does not moderate the interaction between maternal restrictive control and child temperament in predicting externalizing adjustment. There may be some pattern yet to be discovered here, as might be predicted by Baumrind's (1967) findings on the developmental advantages of the combination of warmth plus control. However, from the present results, it appears likely that the effect will be quite small or that it will be dependent on some further contextual variables not yet considered in the present research.

Interpretation of the Moderator Effect

The central finding is that child temperamental resistance to control predicts later externalizing adjustment dependent on whether the mother was observed to be high or low in control of the child. If the control was high, temperament did not predict well; if it was low, temperament did predict. What developmental processes might explain this pattern?

First, consider parental control effects on children who were high on resistance to control: If mothers of such children were highly controlling, it is possible that the children's compliance behaviors were shaped and their noncompliance behaviors were pruned. This assumes that the control tactics of the mothers were at least somewhat effective, ultimately. The fact that the interaction effect was far from perfect may reflect ineffective control efforts in many of the mothers. If a resistant child had a mother low in restrictive control, an externalizing adjustment outcome could be explained as simply the continued influence of the child's disposition in the absence of significant counterpressure from the environment. However, there may also have been a more complex process: In cases where mothers of temperamentally resistant children were observed to be low in control, it is possible that this reflected a coercive process. These mothers recognized that their children were resistant to control, and, at least in the presence of the observers, they did not challenge the children by trying to control them. If such a pattern occurred often, this could well be associated with reinforcement of child aversive behavior (Patterson, Reid, & Dishion, 1992). However, even if one does not assume a coercive process, there was at least an absence of the kinds of shaping and modulation that might come from effective control.

Next, consider children who were low in resistance to control: If their mothers were highly controlling, they may have lacked sufficient opportunities for developing internalized self-control. Kochanska's (1997) work suggests that this might have been the result of high levels of anxiety being elicited by negative control, which could have interfered with the kinds of attentional and cognitive events that constitute the internalizing of social controls. It is also possible that the experience of high levels of control in response to ordinary trouble behaviors—not necessarily conflictual or resistant behaviors—produces frustration in the child, and effectively shapes higher levels of aggressive behavior than would have developed on the basis of temperament alone.

FUTURE RESEARCH

It has been gratifying to find a replicated Temperament-by-Environment interaction effect. This provides an unusually rich empirical description of process in the development of psychopathology. However, at the same time, it is clear that the progress in knowledge represented by the interaction effect has been relatively small. There are many degrees of possible complication. Some of the possible complications have been ruled out for now, such as socioeconomic status, sex of child, and the level of maternal warm involvement.

However, even these could be relevant in different samples or with different measures of the constructs. Ultimately, the key question is whether other researchers using methods adequate for detecting a modest effect size can actually replicate the findings of the present study.

Temperament Questions

One possible complication that seems likely to be involved is the nature of the other temperament traits that accompany the child's resistance to control trait. For example, the irritability or negative emotionality dispositions of a child might further moderate the effects of a given level of resistance to control. Perhaps a child who is high in negative reactivity and low in resistance would be disproportionately likely to develop externalizing behavior problems in an environment high in maternal control. It also seems likely that the profile of more basic traits underlying a child's resistance to control could be important in the developmental response to environmental qualities. For example, the phenotype of resistance to control could develop from a high level of positively affective, attraction to "action," from poor executive control of attention to peripheral inhibitory controls when a goal is being pursued, or from a lack of interest in social stimuli, such as a mother's feelings. Children's profiles on these source traits might make big differences in the developmental implications of a given level of resistance to control and a given parent–child relationship environment.

Parenting

Our naturalistic assessments of parent–child interaction were comparable to others in the literature, however, these assessments are probably far from the level of description that will ultimately be needed to understand the developmental process. For example, we have so far not considered the effectiveness of the mothers' control efforts as a possible moderator of the degree to which high restrictiveness modulates a highly resistant child's tendencies away from externalizing problems.

Adjustment Outcomes

There are also remaining questions in the child adjustment domain. For example, one might consider possible differences in the externalizing problems of resistant children who had experienced low levels of maternal control versus the externalizing problems of nonresistant children who had experienced high levels of restrictive control. Perhaps the former would be more likely to show covert symptoms, like stealing, whereas the latter would be more likely to show overt symptoms, like fighting.

CONCLUSION

The main finding of the study was that children's temperamental resistance to control had different implications for future externalizing adjustment style depending on the level of control mothers attempted to exert in the child's early years. For many highly resistant children, high levels of maternal control appeared to deflect their trajectories toward lower levels of externalizing behavior than might have been predicted by the resistance alone. For other resistant children, low levels of maternal control came to be associated with noticeably higher levels of externalizing problems. For a number of nonresistant children, high levels of maternal control forecasted higher levels of externalizing behavior than would have been predicted by temperament alone, and low levels of control were associated with optimal, low-problem outcomes. This effect was replicated in two separate, longitudinal studies and for both mother and teacher reports of externalizing adjustment. This finding is a striking example of temperament in context. When the search for this began a number of years ago, we may not have been able to predict the exact shape the interaction actually took. Nevertheless, it can now be argued that the pattern of data provides a relatively rich, empirical description of developmental process. This description may ultimately have theoretical implications. One caution is that the effect is a modest one: Even assuming further replications of the effect, there are many substrates and intersecting variables that must be explored before the most useful theoretical implications will emerge. Still, the work summarized in this chapter does add to the empirical picture of the development of differences in children's acting-out style of adjustment.

REFERENCES

Achenbach, T. M. (1982). *Developmental psychopathology.* New York: Wiley.

Achenbach, T. M. (1991a). *Manual for the child behavior checklist/4–18 and 1991 Profile.* Burlington: University of Vermont, Dept. of Psychiatry.

Achenbach, T. M. (1991b). *Manual for the teacher's report form and 1991 profile.* Burlington: University of Vermont, Dept. of Psychiatry.

Achenbach, T. M., & Edelbrock, C. (1983). *Manual for the child behavior checklist and revised child behavior profile.* Burlington: University of Vermont.

Achenbach, T. M., & Edelbrock, C. (1986). *Manual for the teacher's report form and teacher version of the child behavior profile.* Burlington: University of Vermont.

Arcus, D., & Gardner, S. (1993, March). *When biology is not destiny.* Presented at conference of Society for Research in Child Development, New Orleans.

Bates, J. E. (1980). The concept of difficult temperament. *Merrill-Palmer Quarterly, 26,* 299–319.

Bates, J. E. (1989). Applications of temperament concepts. In G. A. Kohnstamm, J. E. Bates, & M. K. Rothbart (Eds.), *Temperament in childhood* (pp. 321–355). Chichester, England: Wiley.

Bates, J. E. (1990). Conceptual and empirical linkages between temperament and behavior problems: A commentary on the Sanson, Prior, and Kyrios study. *Merrill-Palmer Quarterly, 36*(2), 193–199.

Bates, J. E. (1994, May). *Alternate pathways between temperament and adjustment in childhood*. Paper presented at the meeting of Midwestern Psychological Association, Chicago.

Bates, J. E., & Bayles, K. (1984). Objective and subjective components in mothers' perceptions of their children from age 6 months to 3 years. *Merrill Palmer Quarterly, 30*, 111–130.

Bates, J. E., Bayles, K., Bennett, D. S., Ridge, B., & Brown, M. M. (1991). Origins of externalizing behavior problems at 8 years of age. In D. Pepler & K. Rubin (Eds.), *Development and treatment of childhood aggression* (pp. 93–120). Hillsdale, NJ: Lawrence Erlbaum Associates.

Bates, J. E., Freeland, C. B., & Lounsbury, M. L. (1979). Measurement of infant difficultness. *Child Development, 50*, 794–803.

Bates, J. E., & Marvinney, D. (1993, March). Temperament, mother–child relations, and marital harmony as predictors of child adjustment at 3–5 years. Presented at Society for Research in Child Development.

Bates, J. E., Olson, S. L., Pettit, G. S., & Bayles, K. (1982). Dimensions of individuality in the mother–infant relationship at 6 months of age. *Child Development, 53*, 446–461.

Bates, J. E., Pettit, G. S., & Dodge, K. A. (1995). Family and child factors in stability and change in children's aggressiveness in elementary school. In J. McCord (Ed.), *Coercion and punishment in long-term perspectives* (pp. 124–138). New York: Cambridge University Press.

Bates, J. E., Pettit, G. S., Dodge, K. A., & Ridge, B. (1998). The interaction of temperamental resistance to control and restrictive parenting in the development of externalizing behavior. *Developmental Psychology, 34*, 982–995.

Bates, J. E., Wachs, T. D., & Emde, R. N. (1994). Toward practical uses for biological concepts of temperament. In J. E. Bates & T. D. Wachs (Eds.), *Temperament: Individual differences at the interface of biology and behavior* (pp. 275–306). Washington, DC: American Psychological Association Press.

Baumrind, D. (1967). Child care practices anteceding three patterns of preschool behavior. *Genetic Psychology Monographs, 75*, 43–88.

Bentler, P. M. (1995). *EQS structural equations program manual*. Encino, CA: Multivariate Software.

Boomsma, D., Anokhin, A., & de Geus, E. (1997). Genetics of electrophysiology: Linking genes, brain, and behavior. *Current Directions in Psychological Science, 6*, 106–110.

Caspi, A. (1998). Personality development across the life course. In W. Damon (Ed.-in-Chief) and N. Eisenberg (Vol. Ed.), *Handbook of child psychology: Vol. 3. Social, emotional and personality development* (5th ed., pp. 311–388). New York: Wiley.

Colder, C. R., Lochman, J. E., & Wells, K. C. (1997). The moderating effects of children's fear and activity level on relations between parenting practices and childhood symptomatology. *Journal of Abnormal Child Psychology, 25*, 251–263.

Crockenberg, S. (1987). Predictors and correlations of anger toward and punitive control of toddlers by adolescent mothers. *Child Development, 58*, 964–975.

Dodge, K. A., Pettit, G. S., & Bates, J. E. (1994). Socialization mediators of the relation between socioeconomic status and child conduct problems. *Child Development, 65,* 649–665.

Eisenberg, N.(1998). Introduction. In W. Damon (Ed.-in-Chief) and N. Eisenberg (Vol. Ed.), *Handbook of child psychology: Vol. 3. Social, emotional and personality development* (5th ed., pp. 1–24). New York: Wiley.

Escalona, S. K. (1968). *The roots of individuality: Normal patterns of development in infancy.* Chicago: Aldine.

Fischer, D. H. (1989). *Albion's seed: Four British folkways in America.* New York: Oxford University Press.

Frankel, K. A. & Bates, J. E. (1990). Mother–toddler problem-solving: Antecedents in attachment, home behavior, and temperament. *Child Development, 61,* 810–819.

Goldberg, L. R. (1993). The structure of phenotypic personality traits. *American Psychologist, 48,* 26–34.

Halverson, C. F., Jr., Kohnstamm, G. A., & Martin, R. P. (Eds.). (1994). *The developing structure of temperament from infancy to adulthood.* Hillsdale, NJ: Lawrence Erlbaum Associates.

Henry, B., Caspi, A., Moffitt, T. E., & Silva, P. A. (1996). Temperamental and familial predictors of violent and nonviolent criminal convictions: Age 3 to age 18. *Developmental Psychology, 32,* 614–623.

Hetherington, E. M., & Martin, B. (1986). Family factors and psychopathology in children. In H. C. Quay and J. S. Werry (Eds.), *Psychopathological disorders of childhood* (3rd ed., pp. 332–390). New York: Wiley.

Hollingshead, A. B. (1975). *Four-factor index of social position.* Unpublished manuscript, Yale University, New Haven, CT.

Kagan, J. (1998). Biology and the child. In W. Damon (Ed.-in-Chief) & N. Eisenberg (Vol. Ed.), *Handbook of child psychology: Vol. 3. Social, emotional, and personality development* (5th ed., pp. 177–235). New York: Wiley.

Keiley, M. K., Bates, J. E., Dodge, K. A., & Pettit, G. S. (2000). A cross-domain growth analysis: Externalizing and internalizing behaviors during 8 years of childhood. *Journal of Abnormal Child Psychology, 28,* 16–79.

Kochanska, G. (1991). Socialization and temperament in the development of guilt and conscience. *Child Development, 62,* 1379–1392.

Kochanska, G. (1995). Children's temperament, mothers' discipline, and security of attachment: Multiple pathways to emerging internalization. *Child Development, 66,* 597–615.

Kochanska, G. (1997). Multiple pathways to conscience for children with different temperaments: From toddlerhood to age 5. *Developmental Psychology, 33,* 228–240.

Lanthier, R. P., & Bates, J. E. (1995, May). Infancy era predictors of the big five personality dimensions in adolescence. Paper presented at the meeting of the Midwestern Psychological Association, Chicago.

Lee, C. L., & Bates, J. E. (1985). Mother–child interaction at age 2 years and perceived difficult temperament. *Child Development, 56,* 1314–1325.

Lounsbury, M. L., & Bates, J. E. (1982). The cries of infants of differing levels of perceived temperamental difficultness: Acoustic properties and effects on listeners. *Child Development, 53,* 677–686.

McClelland, G. H., & Judd, C. M. (1993). Statistical difficulties of detecting interactions and moderator effects. *Psychological Bulletin, 114,* 376–390.

McFadyen-Ketchum, S. A., Bates, J. E., Dodge, K. A., & Pettit, G. S. (1996). Patterns of change in early childhood aggressive-disruptive behavior: Gender differences in predictions from early coercive and affectionate mother–child interactions. *Child Development, 67,* 2417–2433.

Newman, J. P., & Wallace, J. F. (1993). Diverse pathways to deficient self-regulation: Implications for disinhibitory psychopathology in children. *Clinical Psychology Review, 13,* 699–720.

Olson, S. L., Bates, J. E., & Bayles, K. (1984). Mother–infant interaction and the development of individual differences in children's cognitive competence. *Developmental Psychology, 20,* 166–179.

Olweus, D. (1979). Stability of aggressive reaction patterns in males: A review. *Psychological Bulletin, 86,* 852–875.

Park, S.-Y., Belsky, J., Putnam, S., & Crnic, K. (1997). Infant emotionality, parenting, and 3-year inhibition: Exploring stability and lawful discontinuity in a male sample. *Developmental Psychology, 33,* 218–227.

Patterson, C. M., & Newman, J. P. (1993). Reflectivity and learning from aversive events: Toward a psychological mechanism for the syndromes of disinhibition. *Psychological Review, 100,* 716–736.

Patterson, G. R. (1993). Orderly change in a stable world: The antisocial trait as a chimera. *Journal of Consulting and Clinical Psychology, 61,* 911–919.

Patterson, G. R., Reid, J. B., & Dishion, T. J. (1992). *Antisocial boys.* Eugene, OR: Castalia.

Pettit, G. S., & Bates, J. E. (1984). Continuity of individual differences in the mother–infant relationship from 6 to 13 months. *Child Development, 55,* 729–739.

Pettit, G. S., & Bates, J. E. (1989). Family interaction patterns and children's behavior problems from infancy to age 4 years. *Developmental Psychology, 25,* 413–420.

Pettit, G. S., Bates, J. E., & Dodge, K. A. (1997). Supportive parenting, ecological context, and children's adjustment: A 7-year longitudinal study. *Child Development, 68,* 908–923.

Plomin, R., & Bergeman, C. S. (1991). The nature of nurture: Genetic influences on environmental measures. *Behavioral and Brain Sciences, 14,* 373–427.

Reiss, D. (1997). Mechanisms linking genetic and social influences in adolescent development: Beginning a collaborative search. *Current Directions in Psychological Science, 6,* 100–105.

Rothbart, M. K., & Bates, J. E. (1998). Temperament. In W. Damon (Ed.-in-Chief) & N. Eisenberg (Vol. Ed.), *Handbook of child psychology: Vol. 3. Social, emotional, and personality development* (5th ed., pp. 105–176). New York: Wiley.

Rothbart, M. K., Derryberry, D., & Posner, M. I. (1994). A psychobiological approach to the development of temperament. In J. E. Bates & T. D. Wachs (Eds.), *Temperament: Individual differences at the interface of biology and behavior* (pp. 83–116). Washington, DC: American Psychological Association.

Rothbaum, F., & Weisz, J. R. (1994). Parental caregiving and child externalizing behavior: A meta-analysis. *Psychological Bulletin, 116,* 55–74.

Rutter, M. (1983). Statistical and personal interactions: Facets and perspectives. In D. Magnusson and V. L. Allen (Eds.), *Human development: An international perspective* (pp. 295–319). New York: Academic.

Sanson, A., Prior, M., & Kyrios, M. (1990). Contamination of measures in temperament research. *Merrill-Palmer Quarterly, 36,* 179–192.

Shapiro, D. (1965). *Neurotic styles.* New York: Basic Books.

Shaw, D. S., Keenan, K., & Vondra, J. I. (1994). Developmental precursors of externalizing behavior: Ages 1 to 3. *Developmental Psychology, 30,* 355–364.

Sheeber, L. B. (1995). Empirical dissociations between temperament and behavior problems: A response to the Sanson, Prior, and Kyrios study. *Merrill-Palmer Quarterly, 41,* 554–561.

Slotboom, A.-M., Elphick, E., van Riessen, M., van Mill, I., & Kohnstamm, G. A. (1996, October). Continuity in temperament/personality dimensions of children as perceived by parents: Relations between temperament and the Big 5. Presented at The Occasional Temperament Conference, Eugene, OR.

Stoolmiller, M. (1995). Using latent growth curve models to study developmental processes. In J. M. Gottman (Ed.), *The analysis of change* (pp. 104–138) Mahwah, NJ: Lawrence Erlbaum Associates.

Thomas, A., Chess, S., & Birch, H. G. (1968). *Temperament and behavior disorders in children.* New York: New York University Press.

van den Boom, D. (1994). The influence of temperament and mothering on attachment and exploration: An experimental manipulation of sensitive responsiveness among lower-class mothers and irritable infants. *Child Development, 65,* 1457–1477.

Wachs, T. D. (1992). *The nature of nurture.* Newbury Park, CA: Sage.

Wachs, T. D., & Plomin, R. (1991). *Conceptualization and measurement of organism-environment interaction.* Washington, DC: American Psychological Association.

Wiggins, J. S. (1973). Personality and prediction: *Principles of personality assessment.* Reading, MA: Addison-Wesley.

Witkin, H. A., Dyk, R. B., Faterson, H. F., Goodenough, D. R., & Karp, S. A. (1962). *Psychological differentiation.* New York: Wiley.

10 The Bidirectional Nature of Temperament– Context Links

Theodore D. Wachs
Purdue University

Gedolph A. Kohnstamm
University of Leiden

If we were given the task of summarizing the nature of linkages between temperament and context in one word, the word we would choose would be *bidirectional*. Our choice of this term is based in part on evidence illustrating structural bidirectional feedback linkages between context and temperament operating over time (temperament→ context → temperament → context). Whereas individual chapters in this volume have primarily focused either on temperament → context (e.g., Ramsay & Lewis, chap. 2, Goldsmith et al., chap. 6) or on context → temperament links (Arcus, chap. 3, Halverson & Deal, chap. 4, Matheny & Phillips, chap. 5), integrating across these chapters, plus consideration of other findings in the research literature (Crockenberg & McCluskey, 1986; Engfer, 1986; Maccoby, Snow, & Jacklin, 1984; Thoman, 1990; Wachs et al., 1993) illustrates why the structure of context–temperament linkages must be viewed as bidirectional in nature.

Besides structural considerations, our choice of the term bidirectional is also based on evidence contained in this volume (chaps. 9, 7, & 8, by Bates, Kerr, & Strelau, respectively) and elsewhere (as reviewed by Rothbart & Bates, 1998) on developmental processes. Based on available evidence it seems clear that the influence of temperament on development cannot be interpreted without reference to the individual's context, just as the influence of context on development cannot be understood without reference to the individual's temperament.

Although there is a consistent body of literature supporting the operation of structural and process bidirectional linkages between context and temperament it is important to recognize that there is not unanimity on this question. In Chapter 1 (this volume), Costa & McCrae present a conceptual framework based on the assumption that context exerts no influence on individual variability in temperament characteristics, and that context does not interact with temperament to produce individual behavioral-developmental variability (see Fig. 1.2, this volume). In the following sections we will deal both with the challenge posed by Costa & McCrae in chapter 1, as well as with specific issues raised in the various chapters in this volume about the nature and consequences of bidirectional linkages between temperament and context.

TEMPERAMENT INFLUENCES ON CONTEXT

When Does Child Temperament Influence Child Context?

Fundamental to the New York longitudinal study was the assumption that children with specific temperaments will elicit specific patterns of reactivity from their parents (Thomas, Chess, & Birch, 1968). This assumption of child characteristics acting to influence caregiver reactivity is implicit in a number of other central developmental constructs such as the concept of reactive covariance (Plomin, DeFries, & Loehlin, 1977). For example, the control system theory of Bell and Chapman (1986) predicts that parents will react to highly intense difficult infants in ways that will lower the level of the child's behavior, but will act to raise their child's level of behavior if their child is overly passive. However, as discussed by Bates (chap. 9, this volume), findings tend to be inconsistent in regard to the question of when variability in early child temperament leads to systematic variability in caregiver interaction patterns.[1] Depending on the study one can find evidence for either an influence of early temperament on subsequent caregiver interaction patterns, for no relation between early infant temperament and subsequent caregiver behavior patterns, or for a cumulative pattern with the level of relation depending on how long the infant has displayed a particular temperament characteristic (Wachs & Bates, in press). For example, Ramsay and Lewis (chap. 2, this volume) report that greater infant distress at 2 months of age is related to greater maternal soothing at 4 months of age, suggesting that the temperament characteristics of even very young infants can act to influence how their caregivers behave toward them. In contrast, Arcus (chap. 3, this volume) was unable to find relations between child temperament characteristics and caregiver interaction patterns until 9 months of age, suggesting that sys-

---

[1]Although our focus is primarily on early infant temperament and subsequent caregiver reactivity, similar inconsistencies are also found in studies looking at later temperament and subsequent caregiver reactivity as well (Rothbart & Bates, 1998).

tematic differences in caregiver reactivity to infant temperament characteristics may not occur when infants are relatively young.

There have been a variety of explanations for these conflicting results (Wachs & Bates, in press). One possible explanation is that neurologically driven inconsistencies in the expression of early infant temperament makes it difficult for parents to detect a consistent behavioral pattern by their young infant that they can consistently react to. Another possibility is that parents are systematically reacting to temperament characteristics of their young infants, but the pattern of parental adjustment is too subtle to be detected by studies using short-term observational procedures. Although there is little direct evidence for these two hypotheses some studies do suggest the possibility of moderation of relations between infant temperament and subsequent caregiver reactivity as a function of nontemperament factors such as the child's age, gender, maternal attitudes, or parental preferences for certain types of infant behavioral patterns. For example, some studies have shown that experienced mothers or mothers who believe they have the capability to influence their infant's behavior react differently to fussy-difficult infants than do less experienced mothers or mothers who have doubts about their ability to cope with difficult infants (Cutrona & Troutman, 1986; Lounsbury & Bates, 1982).

Given the likelihood that not all caregivers will react in the same way to variability in infant temperament, future studies of temperament fi context links will need to focus more on individual moderators of these linkages. In addition, it will be essential to study such linkages longitudinally, because the bidirectional nature of relations between temperament and context means that we are dealing with moving and not static outcome variables. Thus, to the extent that child temperament influences caregiver behavior patterns, and caregiver behavior patterns influence child temperament our focus needs to be more on change over time, rather than on static correlations between temperament characteristics at time point 1 and caregiver behavior at time point 2 (see chap. 4 by Halverson & Deal for further discussion on this point).

Temperament and the Individual's Subjective Context

Researchers interested in mapping the structure of the environment have made a distinction between the objective environment and the individual's subjective perception of his or her environment (Wachs, 1999). For example, neighborhoods can be classified on objective criteria such as number of people per square mile as a measure of density or number of arrests in the past month as a measure of criminality. However, neighborhoods can also be classified on the basis of the perceptions of individuals living in this neighborhood about how crowded or how safe they feel. While related, the objective and subjective dimensions of the environment are not identical.

For the most part discussion of temperament influences on context have primarily involved the objective environment of the individual, such as caregiver behavior patterns. However, as noted in several chapters in this volume, individual differences in temperament may also act to influence how the individual perceives their objective environment. Goldsmith et al., (chap. 6, this volume) suggest that an individual with a temperamental predisposition toward negative affect may perceive a wider range of contexts as frustrating, whereas Strelau (chap. 8, this volume) has suggested that individual differences in level of sensation seeking may act to influence whether the individual perceives a given level of stimulation as stressful or not. Along the same lines, Rothbart, Derryberry, and Posner (1994) have hypothesized that highly fearful children may be more likely than less fearful children to view neutral stimuli as frightening. Based on clinical case studies Carey (1985) has argued that children whose objective behavioral characteristics place them in the easy temperament category will be at greater developmental risk if their parents perceive them to be temperamentally difficult.

Whereas there is empirical evidence on the specific types of subjective perceptions associated with nontemperament individual characteristics, such as chronic antisocial behavior in childhood (Dodge & Feldman, 1990), there are few parallels to this type of study in the temperament literature. One reason why there has been relatively little study of temperament influences on individual perceptions of their objective environmental context may involve measurement issues. Much of our existing temperament research has focused primarily on infants and toddlers. These are populations for whom it is very difficult to obtain information on how they perceive their environment. With the extension of temperament research into the adult period (e.g., Costa & McCrae; Strelau, chaps. 1 & 8, respectively, this volume) studies of how individual variation in temperament acts to influence individuals' views of their environment would seem to be a logical direction for future temperament → context research in adulthood. For example, given evidence of the role played by individual differences in personality on adult perceptions of physical environmental stressors (Evans, 1999), it would be of interest to investigate whether differences in the adult temperament dimensions discussed by Costa & McCrae and by Strelau (chaps. 1 & 8, respectively, this volume) result in some individuals perceiving high sound levels as noise or high density living conditions as crowded.

The extent to which we can address the question of whether temperament acts to moderate individual's perceptions of their objective environment in infant and preschool age populations is as yet unknown. There is certainly theoretical justification for this line of research, as seen in discussion of the consequences of early individual differences in internal working models of attachment (Belsky & Cassidy, 1994). Further, recent research on suggestibility and the accuracy of young children's recall of past events does suggest that, under certain conditions, preschool children can provide reliable recall information about contextual events and characteristics (Bruck, Ceci, & Hembrooke, 1998). Integrating the procedures used in studies of young children's memory to assess whether child recall or child suggestibility will vary as a function of individual temperament characteristics is a line of inquiry that has the potential to yield interesting findings at both a theoretical and at an applied level of analysis.

CONTEXTUAL INFLUENCES ON TEMPERAMENT

As discussed in the introduction to this volume the fact that temperament is a biologically rooted trait in no way precludes the possibility that contextual factors can influence both the nature and development of individual temperament characteristics. Indeed, some of the strongest evidence showing an influence of context on the expression and nature of temperament comes from the research of biologically oriented temperament researchers (Bates & Wachs, 1994). In considering the role of context as an influence on variability in temperament it is essential to consider the level of temperament we are discussing. As Bates (1989a) has pointed out, temperament can be conceptualized at both a behavioral and a constitutional level. For the most part studies showing context influences on temperament have focused on the behavioral level. Within the limits of such a data base we cannot prove that context has also changed temperament at the constitutional level. However, given evidence cited below documenting contextual influences on the central nervous system (CNS), neither can we exclude the possibility that contextual variability acts on both the behavioral and constitutional levels of temperament. At present this possibility remains a subject for future research, and in our review of this issue we refer primarily to the behavioral manifestations of temperament.

Can Context Influence Temperament?

Chapter 1 by Costa and McCrae (this volume) gives a clearly negative response to this question. Since this "no" is so antipodal to the convictions of the editors we first present our arguments against the Costa and McCrae thesis. Whereas this thesis is provocative it is also problematical, both on empirical and conceptual grounds. Empirically, the major flaw in the Costa and McCrae thesis is seen in the lack of a direct path in their model from external influences to the biological foundations underlying individual differences in basic tendencies (which they equate with personality or temperament). There is, in fact, a large and increasing body of research documenting the role played by contextual influences on individual differences in CNS structure, neurochemistry, individual hormonal characteristics, and even gene action (Wachs, 2000). For example, infrahuman data by Juraska (1990) documents how exposure to either general stimulation or to specific learning experiences results in a larger and denser occipital cortex, as well as more synapses per neuron and greater numbers of dendrites. Similarly, studies have begun to document how the activity of specific regulator genes can be modified by nongenetic factors such as the individual's nutritional status (Natori & Oka, 1997) or even mild levels of variability in sensory stimulation (Mack & Mack, 1992). What this evidence shows is that the conclusion by Costa and McCrae that basic tendencies are unaffected by contextual factors can be accepted only by ignoring a consistent body of evidence documenting how basic biological structures and biological functions are context sensitive.

In addition to evidence showing the contextual sensitivity of the biological foundations of development, other lines of evidence also undermine the validity of Costa and McCrae's thesis. For example, Costa and McCrae argue against context influencing temperament based on factor analytic evidence showing that the Big 5 personality dimensions appear across a number of diverse cultures. However, as has been pointed out in discussions on nature-nurture issues (e.g., Turkheimer, 1991), or on issues involving stability versus change (Halverson & Deal, chap. 4, this volume), very different conclusions can emerge depending on whether analysis of the same data is based on use of correlations or on mean differences. For example, if we focus on the significant correlation between biological parents IQ and the IQ of their adopted-away children our conclusion would emphasize genetic contributions to intelligence. However, if we use the same sample and focus on the significant mean differences in IQ between adopted children and their biological parents our conclusion would emphasize a contextual contribution to intelligence (Wachs, 1995). The same point can be made in regard to Costa and McCrae's argument. Focusing just on cross-cultural similarities in factor structure supports their hypothesis of a strong biological contribution to temperament. However, the supposedly unique contributions of biological influences must be viewed in context, namely evidence on cross-cultural differences in mean level of the Big 5 personality traits (Kerr, chap. 7, this volume; Kohnstamm, Zhang, Slotboom, & Elphick, 1998). Whereas Costa and McCrae do acknowledge that cross-cultural differences in level of personality provide a challenge for their theoretical framework, this acknowledgment is buried in a footnote and does not seem to modify their overall conclusions.

Although Costa and McCrae could argue that the types of results described above involve adaptations rather than basic tendencies, such an argument runs the risk of circularity. How do we know that context-driven influences are impacting on adaptations and not basic tendencies; according to Costa and McCrae this would be because change occurs. Why are changes occurring? According to Costa and McCrae this would be because adaptations and not basic tendencies were involved. The potential for circularity seems all to clear. Whether viewed either empirically or conceptually our conclusion is that the argument by Costa and McCrae against context influencing temperament, or that Context-by-Temperament interactions are a negligible influence on behavioral-developmental variability, has a number of major flaws and in no way weakens the validity of our assumption that contextual characteristics can influence individual variability in temperament. Given this assumption the critical question is, What aspects of context are most salient for temperament variability?

Methodological and Conceptual Issues

Particularly when considered as a proportion of the overall research literature on temperament, there is remarkably little available evidence on contextual contributions to individual variation in temperament. As discussed by Matheny and Phillips (chap. 5, this volume) part of the reason why researchers all too rarely consider contextual contributions to variability in temperament involves the assumption that individual temperament characteristics are highly stable across different contexts. As discussed by Goldsmith et al. (Chap. 6, this volume), the validity of this assumption can be questioned. It is also likely that our emphasis on the biological roots of temperament has shifted research attention away from the contextual roots of temperament. In addition, the methodological requirements needed to document contextual influences, and the complex nature of contextual influences (Wachs, 1999), may have discouraged researchers from attempting to study contextual influences on temperament. One important methodological requirement is the need for repeated observations of the child's environmental context, given evidence indicating both lower stability and less representativeness of caregiver behavior patterns when single as compared to repeated observations are used (Wachs, 1992). Unfortunately, the use of repeated direct analyses of the nature of the child's proximal microenvironment remains the exception rather than the rule in context temperament research. Methodological reviews point to the fact that when less adequate environmental assessments are utilized nonsignificant findings are more likely to occur (Wachs, 1999). Thus, the fact that Arcus (chap. 3, this volume) was able to obtain evidence on contextual influences on temperament, even with a relatively homogenous demographic sample, points to the importance of using direct, repeated assessments of the nature of the child's proximal environment. In contrast, Ramsay and Lewis (chap. 2, this volume) restricted their data base at each age period to a single observation point within a given context and were unable to find significant effects for maternal soothing upon child reactivity.

Temperament Influences on Context: What Is Known

In describing the context of the child, Bronfenbrenner (1989) delineates four linked environmental levels, ranging from the proximal microsystem environment of a child (e.g., the home environment) up to the broader cultural context (macrosystem) within which the family is nested. In addition, each level is further divided into different linked sublevels as well. Not surprisingly, as with other developmental outcomes such as intelligence, attachment, and social interpersonal relationships, most of our knowledge of contextual influences on temperament is based on characteristics of the child's social microsystem as seen in patterns of parent–child transactions (Wachs, 1992).

The Microsystem.   In dealing with the question of microsystem contributions to variation in child temperament we are well aware of the point raised by behavior genetic researchers, namely that correlations between indices of the family environment and children's development may well include genetic as well as environmental components (Plomin, 1994). The fact that some environmental correlations do include genetic components does not mean that environment is irrelevant to development, as some have wrongly concluded (e.g., Rowe, 1994). Rather the inclusion of genetic components in environmental correlations reflects a process of gene–environment correlation, either as a function of children receiving both specific genes and specific environments from their parents or as a function of children with specific genetically driven characteristics having a higher probability of receiving or encountering specific types of environmental input (Wachs, 2000). The occurrence of gene–environment correlations means that development must be viewed as a function of the joint contributions of both biological and contextual influences. Within this framework specific identified environmental factors can act to influence developmental variability either as unique main effect predictors or as the environmental contribution to gene–environment correlation processes.

The importance of the social microsystem is seen in results described by Halverson and Deal (chap. 4, this volume), illustrating how global indices of either positive parent characteristics or family risk characteristics are systematically related to change in individual temperament between the preschool and early school years. Although this information supports the hypothesis that variability in the social microsystem is related to individual differences in temperament, a more critical question is, What specific aspects of a child's proximal social-microsystem environment are most strongly related to such individual differences?

Although the evidence appears to be inconsistent with regard to negative emotionality (Ramsay & Lewis, chap. 2, this volume) two domains of early temperament do appear to be particularly reactive to variations in the child's proximal social microsystem, namely *inhibition* and *resistance to control*. Evidence indicates that there is significantly greater stability of inhibition over time if parents are oversolicitous, and do not set up age appropriate limits on the child's behavior (Arcus, chap. 3, this volume; also see Park, Belsky, Putnam, & Crnic, 1997; Rubin, Hastings, Stewart, Henderson, & Chen, 1997). For resistance to control there is significantly greater stability of this trait when caregivers do little to control or restrict the child's resistant activities (Bates, chap. 9, this volume). Both Arcus and Bates suggest that low control caregivers may be less actively involved in shaping their child's behavior, or may not be exposing their child to minor stresses (e.g., saying "No") that the child can learn to deal with in the relatively safe environment of the home.

Consistency is also seen in regard to another contextual dimension of the child's microenvironment namely the physical microsystem, which refers to physical characteristics of the child's proximal environment. As described by Matheny and Phillips (chap. 5, this volume), a number of studies have reported that less desirable temperament outcomes occur when young children are exposed to chaotic home environments that are poorly scheduled and relatively high in levels of noise and crowding. Whereas both conceptually (Bronfenbrenner, 1999) and empirically (Wachs, 1992) we find linkages between the physical and social dimensions of the child's microenvironment, studies integrating the contributions of physical and social microsystem characteristics with variability in individual temperament characteristics have not yet appeared.

Going Beyond the Microsystem.   Another level of Bronfenbrenner's structural framework of the environment is the exosystem. This level of the environment encompasses contextual characteristics that the child may not directly encounter, but, that nonetheless, influence the child's patterns of development. Although evidence is relatively sparse there are some studies reporting an impact of exosystem influences on variability in child temperament. Halverson and Deal (chap. 4, this volume) have noted the role played by a positive marital relationship as an influence on changes in children's persistence. Similarly, poor quality marital relationships have also been related to increases in infant negative emotionality (Belsky, Fish, & Isabella, 1991; Engfer, 1986). Reductions in negative emotionality have also been related to another exosystem dimension, namely higher levels of maternal social support (Fish, 1997).

Going to the macrosystem level of Bronfenbrenner's environmental structure, group differences in level of temperament have been related both to group differences in socioeconomic level (Fullard, Simeonsson, & Huntington, 1989; Matheny & Phillips, chap. 5, this volume) and to culture (Kohnstamm, 1989; Kohnstamm et al., 1998). Further, as described by Kerr (chap. 7, this volume), systematic shifts in temperament occur as a function of the degree to which cultures value a given temperament trait. Traits that are valued by a culture are more likely to remain stable over time whereas traits that are not valued are more likely to destabilize.

Integrating Contextual Theory and Temperament

Up to the present, most research on contextual influences on variability in individual temperament has been relatively atheoretical. Given the increasing acceptance of Bronfenbrenner's structural model of the environment we would argue that it would be particularly important for future research efforts in this area to generate questions derived from this research framework. For example, a central feature of Bronfenbrenner's model is the fact that there are linkages between different levels and sublevels of the environment. Within this framework characteristics of the child's social microenvironment (e.g., parent–child interactions) may well be a final common pathway through which the environment contributes to variability in children's temperament. However, both the quality and characteristics of parenting will be influenced by a number of other aspects of the overall environmental context such as physical characteristics of the home environment, social support to the family, parental marital relations, neighborhood characteristics, and cultural values (Wachs, 2000). Rather than focusing just on family influences in isolation from the overall context, studies investigating multilevel contextual contributions to temperament variability will be far more informative. Integrating across contextual levels could result in the generation of a number of critical questions. For example, do links between specific parental practices and variability in offspring temperament vary in systematic ways across different cultural or sub-cultural groups? Do parenting practices systematically differ for children with temperament characteristics that are valued or not valued within a given culture? To what degree do contextual characteristics of children's daycare accentuate or attenuate the influence of family environment on children's temperament? What is the validity of structural models wherein high levels of home chaos, poor marital relations, or low social support influence the quality of caregiver behavior patterns, that in turn influence variability in children's temperament?

Questions of this type could be even more illuminating when carried out longitudinally, allowing us to also add a bidirectional component to the research. For example, within a given culture how does children's reactivity to parent pressure to change culturally nonpreferred traits feed back on parents' subsequent attempts to shift their children's behavior patterns. Alternatively, to what extent does children's difficultness, negative emotionality, or resistance to control contribute to high levels of home chaos, poor marital relations, or low outside social support to parents, that in turn feed back on quality of parent caregiving and then onto subsequent variability in children's temperament.

CONTEXT, DEVELOPMENT, AND INDIVIDUAL DIFFERENCES
IN TEMPERAMENT

Whereas temperament is a biologically rooted trait, the perceptions and meanings ascribed to individual differences in temperament go far beyond biology
(Kerr, chap. 7, this volume). In their pioneering work in the New York Longitudinal Study, Thomas, Chess, and Birch (1968) repeatedly emphasized that differences in individual adaptation should not be ascribed either to individual
differences in temperament or to individual differences in context, but rather
to the degree to which the individual's temperament characteristics matched
or fit the characteristics of the context within which the individual lives (the
concept of *goodness of fit*). The best evidence we have supporting the operation
of goodness of fit can be seen at the level of culture. In cultures where
caregiving by multiple siblings is the norm (e.g., Kenya), infants who are less
adaptable are more likely to be considered difficult than are infants with the
same level of adaptability who live in cultures where multiple caregiving is rare.
Similarly, the child's ability to get on a regular schedule (regularity) is of far
more concern to parents in time-driven Western cultures such as the Netherlands (Super & Harkness, 1999), than for parents in cultures such as India
where time demands are not a central cultural value (Malhotra, 1989). Given
that different perceptions and valances are assigned to similar temperament
traits in different cultures it is not surprising to find evidence indicating significantly poorer child or adult adjustment (Ballantine & Klein, 1990; Kerr, chap. 7,
this volume; Korn & Gannon, 1983), or even a reduced chance of survival
(DeVries, 1984; Scheper-Hughes, 1987), for individuals whose temperament
characteristics do not fit the values of their primary culture.

Unfortunately, the problem of defining what is or is not goodness of fit becomes more problematical when we go below the macrosystem level, in good
part because of the lack of a theoretical framework defining what the criteria
are for determining when specific combinations of individual and contextual
characteristics provide a good or a poor fit. Much of the evidence used by
Thomas and Chess in their delineation of goodness of fit was based on clinical
case studies, where goodness of fit was defined by goodness of outcome and
not by prior theoretically driven distinctions (Chess & Thomas, 1991). However, a number of empirical studies have begun to document not only ways to
measure goodness or poorness of fit, but have also replicated interactions between specific child and caregiver characteristics, that offer insights into
what potentially constitutes good or poor Temperament-by-Context fit.

In the area of measurement Lerner and colleagues have described an approach wherein goodness of fit is assessed via the degree of discrepancy between measured parent preferences for specific types of temperament
characteristics and adolescents' ratings of the degree to which they do or do
not possess these characteristics. In a number of studies poor fit between pa-

rental preferences and adolescent characteristics were found to be a stronger predictor than temperament ratings per se of behavioral adjustment problems, lower teacher ratings of academic and social competence and poorer academic performance (Talwar, Nitz, Lerner, & Lerner, 1991).

Although the operation of fit processes are illustrated, these data do not speak directly to the issue of Temperament-by-Context fit because direct measures of context were not assessed. However, although not always presented in a goodness of fit framework, there have been a number of replicated findings of Temperament-by-Context interactions that serve to illustrate how specific temperament and context combinations may or may not fit together. For the infancy and toddler period, Bates (chap. 9, this volume) has described a number of replicated interactions that document how fearful children are less likely to develop internalized self-control when their primary caregiver uses harsh, power-assertive discipline, and how resistant children are more likely to show long-term externalizing behavior problems if their caregivers are low rather than high in limit setting. Put within a goodness of fit framework these results suggest that relatively poor fit occurs for fearful children reared by caregivers who use power-assertive discipline, but relatively good fit occurs for resistant children whose parents are highly controlling. Data reported by Arcus (chap. 3, this volume) and Gunnar (1994) illustrate how the behavioral consequences of having an inhibited temperament are far more obvious in unfamiliar than in familiar settings. Other evidence indicates that environments that are high in stress characteristics (e.g., crowding, parental anger, parental marital problems) provide a relatively poor fit for temperamentally difficult as compared to temperamentally easy infants and children (Wachs, 1992). In adulthood, Strelau (chap. 8, this volume; 1983), has provided a number of examples documenting how poor fit occurs either when individuals with temperaments involving low arousability are placed in less stimulating conditions, or when individuals with temperaments that are characterized as high in arousability are placed in a highly stimulating context.

Whereas there are a number of examples of Temperament-by-Context interactions, supporting the potential operation of goodness of fit processes, as Bates (chap. 9, this volume) has pointed out consistent findings illustrating such interaction patterns are relatively difficult to document. The relatively small number of replicated Temperament-by-Context interactions at the human behavioral level stands in sharp contrast to the far greater number of such interactions found in studies involving infrahuman populations or when biological rather than contextual predictors are used (Rutter & Pickles, 1991). In good part, the paucity of data on Temperament-by-Context interactions at the human behavioral level is most likely related to the multiple methodological problems involved in detecting existing interactions. Identified problems include the need for greater statistical power to detect interactions as opposed to main effects, the underrepresentation of extreme groups in human behavioral studies, the insensitivity of standard statistical techniques to detect interactions, and the use of imprecise measures of either temperament or context (Bates, chap. 9, this volume; McClelland & Judd, 1993; Wachs & Plomin, 1991; Wahlsten, 1990).

However, in addition to these factors there are also additional methodological problems that may be of particular salience when studying Temperament-by-Context or goodness-of-fit interactions. One such problem involves the bidirectional nature of temperament, as discussed above. Temperament-by-Context interactions imply differential reactivity by individuals with different temperaments to similar contexts. However, to the extent that temperament influences context, it may be very difficult to find individuals with different temperaments living in highly similar contexts, either as a function of active or reactive covariance processes. Under these conditions temperament–environment covariation may act to mask Temperament-by-Context interactions (McCall, 1991). In addition, existing Temperament-by-Context interactions may also be masked by higher order interactions (Sackett, 1991). For example, we have noted earlier that there are replicated differences in reactivity to highly chaotic environments for difficult versus easy temperament children. Matheny and Phillips (chap. 5, this volume) have also reported that gender may act to moderate relations between environmental chaos and temperament, with males showing more negative temperament and females more desirable temperament as a function of encountering highly chaotic environments.[2] Putting these two sets of findings together suggests the possibility of a Temperament-by-Chaos-by-Gender interaction. Particularly when viewed in terms of the need for even greater statistical power such second order interactions may make it particularly difficult to detect lower order Context-by-Temperament interactions.

In addition, Bates (chap. 9, this volume) has also noted that even when we find results that look like a Temperament-by-Context interaction we must take care to distinguish between a genuine nonlinear interaction versus linear multiple main effects (additive co-action; Rutter, 1983). For example, Strelau (chap. 8, this volume) has reported that there are poorer mental health outcomes for individuals who are encountering high life changes and who are relatively low in the temperament trait of endurance, as compared to individuals who are encountering such changes and who are higher in endurance. This finding could reflect a greater reactivity of low endurance than high endurance individuals to multiple life changes (interaction), or it may reflect the additive effect of two noninteracting risk factors—high life change and low endurance— compared to only the single risk factor of life change

---

[2]It could be argued that Matheny's findings represent a statistical fluke, except that in an earlier paper we found a similar moderating affect of gender when looking at relations between chaos, gender, and early cognitive performance (Wachs, Uzgiris, & Hunt, 1971).

(additive co-action). There are statistical procedures that can be used to detect whether unique predictive variance occurs when predictors are combined in a nonlinear as opposed to a linear combination, but all too often such critical tests are not made, leaving open the possibility, as suggested by Bates, that we may sometimes be seeing the operation of interactive or poorness of fit processes that are not really there.

Another problem involves a phenomenon we call *contextual specificity,* namely that outcomes associated with specific temperaments or specific predictors of temperament studied in a given context may not generalize when studied in a different context. For example, Halverson and Deal (chap. 4, this volume) report that predictors of a child's temperament in the context of the family do not necessarily act as predictors of the child's temperament in the context of school, whereas Goldsmith et al. (chap. 6, this volume) document how the predictive value of children's temperament for peer relations varies as a function of different informants. The potential operation of contextual specificity means that researchers can not assume generalizability of results across context; rather generalizability is an assumption that must be tested by assessing temperament context linkages across different contexts using different data sources. Where contextual specificity is operating we may wrongly label findings that vary by context as inconsistent, rather than as valid within a given context.

The above methodological concerns do not negate the potential importance of goodness of fit as a mechanism underlying linkages between temperament and context as joint influences on development. What the above does suggest is that we must be very careful ascribing outcomes involving temperament and context combinations to poorness of fit, and that we must be even more careful in designing studies when we are attempting to test for the operation of fit processes.

CONCLUSIONS AND FUTURE DIRECTIONS

Historically, the systematic study of the influence of temperament on behavior and development dates from the early portion of this century (Strelau, chap. 8, this volume), as does the systematic study of contextual influences on development (Wachs, 1992). In contrast, the systematic study of the interface between temperament and context is a relatively new area of investigation, dating back to the pioneering New York Longitudinal Study of Thomas and Chess in the early 1960s. In spite of its relatively recent entrance on to the scientific scene, and in spite of the multiple conceptual and empirical problems involved in the investigation of temperament and context, remarkable progress has been made in a relatively short period of time. The evidence indicating the operation of temperament influences on context allows us to go beyond the general conclusion that biological factors are an important influence on development, by illustrating how biological (temperament) influences on context can serve as a mechanism that acts to influence development. The evidence indicating contextual influences on temperament is consistent with a rapidly growing area of research documenting how context can influence not only individual behavior but also individual biological characteristics. The bidirectional pathways between temperament and context, and concepts such as goodness of fit, both serve to illustrate the centrality of the idea that behavioral development is multidetermined, rather than a function of either biology or context operating in isolation (Wachs, 2000). Going beyond these general conceptual conclusions, the various chapters in this volume have documented the nature of linkages between temperament and context, with specific reference to the types of temperament dimensions that are most important in defining the nature of the individual's context. In addition the various chapters in this volume have also documented the specific types of contextual characteristics that act to influence individual variability in temperament, and the specific combinations of temperament and contextual characteristics that are most salient for individual behavioral developmental variability. In order to maintain this rate of progress in the study of temperament and context certain areas of study seem to be particularly critical for future research investigations.

One general as yet unanswered question is whether bidirectional temperament–context linkages are symmetrical or asymmetrical in nature. That is, are we likely to find stronger effects of temperament on context, context on temperament, or are the bidirectional effects essentially equivalent? What evidence that is available suggests that there is not likely to be a simple answer to this question. The relative strength of the relations between temperament and context may well vary depending on the nature of contextual characteristics considered (e.g., physical vs. social microenvironment; see Matheny & Phillips, chap. 5, this volume), the level of context considered (e.g., temperament influences on higher order context such as culture [Kagan, Arcus, & Snidman, 1993] may well take generations of co-evolution to develop), the age of the individual (e.g., the impact of difficult children on caregiver child transactions may increase as the child gets older; Maccoby et al., 1984; van den Boom & Hoeksma, 1994) and the temperament trait under consideration (e.g., positive vs. negative emotionality; Belsky, Fish, & Isabella, 1991).

Temperament Influences on Context

In the study of temperament influences on context a critical unanswered question is why the research evidence is so inconsistent with regard to young children's temperament characteristics acting to structure caregiver reactivity in the early years of life. It may well be, as suggested earlier, that individual caregiver characteristics such as childrearing experience, or nontemperament child characteristics such as gender, may act to moderate potential child temperament-caregiver behavioral links. However, our knowledge of what these moderating characteristics might be is, as yet, not clear. Future research on the types of moderators that act to influence how caregivers react to children with different temperament characteristics appears to be an essential research step. However, to answer this question we may also need to go beyond the individual's proximal microcontext and look at higher order cultural or even subcultural values. In specific cultural or subcultural groups some temperament traits are particularly valued, and the appearance or lack of appearance of these traits may lead to very different parental caregiving patterns for individuals in these groups. Thus, the degree of fit of child characteristics to culturally driven value systems may act as an additional influence, acting to moderate the nature of caregiver reactivity to early child temperament characteristics.

Along the same lines there is the oft repeated statement that children with extreme temperaments are more likely to influence their context, whereas children with more moderate levels of a given temperament trait are more likely to be influenced by their context (Buss & Plomin, 1984). Although a logical assumption, there has been remarkably little research evidence either verifying or contradicting the truth of this assumption.

A third critical question in the area of temperament influences on context has to do with individual temperament characteristics acting to influence the types of contextual niches that individuals encounter—the concept of active-organism environment covariance. The assumption underlying discussions of active-organism environment covariance seems to be similar to the concept of open markets. That is, it is assumed that there are a variety of contextual niches available and individuals with a given temperament are free to pick and choose which niches are most congenial for their individual characteristics. Far less attention has been given to the possibility that individual temperament characteristics can act to shut down the availability of a variety of potential niches for an individual, so that even if the individual with a given temperament would prefer to be in a certain niche this niche may not be available to them (Wachs, 1996). For example, the behavior patterns associated with children who are low in self-regulation and high in reactivity may serve to alienate the child from his or her peers. (Eisenberg et al., 1995). Peer rejection in turn will limit the types of peer groups the child will be allowed to enter. Far too little is known about how certain types of temperament characteristics act to open up or close down specific contextual niches for individuals, and even far less is known about the implications of niche openings or niche closures for subsequent stability of individual differences in temperament. As a working hypothesis, based on what evidence is available, we would argue that possessing temperament characteristics that are not valued by an individual's cultural context acts to shut down available contextual niches for the individual, which in turn acts to stabilize the undesirable patterns of temperament characteristics that initially led to such niche closures. We would further argue that closing off potential available niches reduces the chances of goodness of fit for the individual and thus increases the likelihood of adjustment problems (Wachs, 2000).

Contextual Influences on Temperament

There is growing interest in the proposition that early temperament characteristics may be a precursor for later individual variability in adult personality (Halverson, Kohnstamm, & Martin, 1994). For the most part discussion of this transitional process has assumed that biological influences act to mediate the transition from infant temperament to adult personality (Costa & McCrae, chap. 1, this volume). Whereas biological influences such as individual genotype undoubtedly play a role in this process, the increasing evidence on contextual contributions to individual biological variability (Wachs, 2000) emphasizes the importance of investigating both the specific contextual processes involved in the transition from infant temperament to adult personality and the context–biology links underlying this type of transition. Of particular importance may be those aspects of context that act to shift young children's temperament characteristics from the extreme to the more moderate range, as discussed by Arcus (chap. 3, this volume). Further, given our increasing knowledge of the complex structure of an individual's context, it is important to broaden our study of contextual influences on individual variability in temperament by going beyond just measuring parent–child transactions. Of particular relevance here might be the study of what Bronfenbrenner has called "mesosystem influences," namely linkages between different proximal microsystems of the individual. As suggested earlier, studies linking contextual characteristics of the child's home and daycare environments would be a potentially fruitful approach to studying mesosystem contributions to individual variability in temperament.

A related issue involves the question of whether contextual influences on biological processes underlying individual variability in temperament are age dependent. A general conclusion drawn from a variety of disciplines is that extrinsic influences on CNS development are more likely to occur when the CNS is developing than when it is essentially developed (Wachs, 2000). This would suggest that contextual influences on biological processes underlying individual variability in temperament are more likely to occur in the early years of life when the CNS is developing. If so, as shown in Fig. 10.1, studies of this type may help to illustrate the bidirectional nature of temperament–context linkages, with early context acting to influence CNS microstructure and biochemical processes early in life, which in turn acts to stabilize individual temperament, which in turn gives parents a more stable set of child behavioral characteristics to react to. Investigation of these types of questions clearly suggests the need for longitudinal collaborative research between contextual, temperamental, and developmental neuroscience researchers.

Goodness of Fit

An understanding of how temperament and contextual variability translate into individual behavioral developmental variability would be greatly facilitated if we had a set of theoretically driven criteria that would allow us to specify, a priori, what specific combinations of contextual and individual characteristics are likely to lead to good versus poor person–context fit. Strelau (chap. 8, this volume) has made a promising start in regard to discrepancies between individual arousability level and intensity of contextual stimuli acting to define goodness of fit, but far more needs to be done in this area. Of particular importance would be attempts to link emerging research on replicated Temperament-by-Environment interactions in ways that allow us to develop a set of common underlying principles defining why child inhibition or resistance to control interacts with caregiver disciplinary strategies, or why difficult temperament children have greater stress reactivity. In generating principles that allow us to frame specific context temperament combinations in terms of providing a good or poor fit, it is essential to pay attention to larger contextual influences such as culture. For example, the consequences of a less than adequate fit may vary depending on the degree of culturally driven tolerance for deviations from the norm. Further, whether viewed conceptually or empirically, it would be important to add on a longitudinal component as well, given that the degree of fit of specific Temperament-by-Context combinations may well vary depending on the age of the individual.

Emphasis on developing culturally relevant age appropriate criteria defining good or poor fit has major practical implications. One such implication involves prevention efforts, based on detecting poor fit combinations before they result in behavioral maladjustment. In addition, there are also treatment implications that follow from conceptualizing children's behavioral problems in terms of fit. For example, re-framing parent–child conflict in terms of problems in fit avoids blaming either parent or child, while also providing cli-

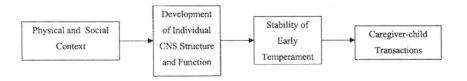

FIG. 10.1. Links between individual context, biology, and temperament.

nicians with approaches to change family dynamics in ways that provide a better degree of fit (Bates, 1989b).

Viewing development as a joint function of temperament and context has implications beyond just clinical interventions. For too long developmental scientists have clung to outmoded dichotomous explanations of behavioral variability, nature versus nurture being the most obvious and notorious example. Hopefully, the continued expansion of theory and research on temperament–context links will help guide researchers away from sterile dichotomies and toward theoretical models that mirror the complexity of multiple influences operating in linked pathways that act to influence individual behavioral developmental variability.

REFERENCES

Ballantine, J., & Klein, H. (1990). The relationship of temperament and adjustment in Japanese schools. *Journal of Psychology, 124,* 299–309.

Bates, J. (1989a). Concepts and measures of temperament. In G. Kohnstamm, J. Bates, & M. Rothbart (Eds.), *Temperament in childhood* (pp. 3–26). Chichester: Wiley.

Bates, J. (1989b). Applications of temperament concepts. In G. Kohnstamm, J. Bates, & M. Rothbart (Eds.), *Temperament in childhood* (pp. 321–355). Chichester: Wiley.

Bates, J., & Wachs, T. D. (Eds.). (1994). *Temperament: Individual differences at the interface of biology and behavior.* Washington, DC: American Psychological Association.

Bell, R., & Chapman, M. (1986). Child effects and studies using experimental or brief longitudinal approaches to socialization. *Developmental Psychology, 22,* 595–603.

Belsky, J., & Cassidy, J. (1994). Attachment: Theory and evidence. In M. Rutter & D. Hay (Eds.), *Development through life* (pp. 373–402). Oxford: Blackwell.

Belsky, J., Fish, M., & Isabella, R. (1991). Continuity and discontinuity in infant negative and positive emotionality. *Developmental Psychology, 27,* 421–431.

Bronfenbrenner, U. (1989). Ecological systems theory. In: R. Vasta (Ed.), *Annals of child development: Six theories of child development* (pp. 187–249). London: Kingsley.

Bronfenbrenner, U. (1999). Environments in developmental perspective. In S. Friedman & T. D. Wachs (Eds.), *Measuring environment across the life span* (pp. 3–30). Washington, DC: American Psychological Association.

Bruck, M., Ceci, S., & Hembrooke, H. (1998). Reliability and credibility of young children's reports. *American Psychologist, 53,* 136–151.

Buss, A., & Plomin, R. (1984). *Temperament: Early developing personality traits.* Hillsdale, NJ: Lawrence Erlbaum Associates.

Carey, W. (1985). Clinical use of temperament data in pediatrics. *Developmental and Behavioral Pediatrics, 6,* 137–142.

Chess, S., & Thomas, A. (1991). Temperament and the concept of goodness of fit. In J. Strelau & A. Angleitner (Eds.), *Explorations in temperament* (pp. 15–28). New York: Plenum.

Crockenberg, S., & McCluskey, K. (1986). Change in maternal behavior during the baby's first year of life. *Child Development, 57,* 746–753.

Cutrona, C., & Troutman, B. (1986). Social support, infant temperament, and parenting self-efficacy. *Child Development, 57,* 1507–1518.

DeVries, M. (1984). Temperament and infant mortality among the Masai of East Africa. *American Journal of Psychiatry, 141,* 1189–1194.

Dodge, K., & Feldman, E. (1990). Issues in social cognition and sociometric status. In S. Asher & J. Coie (Eds.), *Peer rejection in childhood* (pp. 119–155). Cambridge: Cambridge University Press.

Eisenberg, N., Fabes, R., Murphy, B., Maszk, P., Smith, M., & Karbon, M. (1995). The role of emotionality and regulation in children's social functioning. *Child Development, 66,* 1360–1384.

Engfer, A. (1986). Antecedents of perceived behavior problems in infancy. In G. Kohnstamm (Ed.), *Temperament discussed* (pp. 165–180). Lisse: Swets & Zeitlinger.

Evans, G. (1999). Measurement of the physical environment as stressor. In S. Friedman & T. D. Wachs (Eds.), *Measuring environment across the life span* (pp. 249–278). Washington DC: American Psychological Association.

Fish, M. (1997, April). *Stability and change in infant temperament.* Paper presented to the Society for Research in Child Development. Washington, DC.

Fullard, W., Simeonsson, R., & Huntington, G. (1989). Sociocultural factors and temperament. In G. Kohnstamm, J. Bates, & M. Rothbart (Eds.), *Temperament in childhood* (pp. 523–536). Chichester: Wiley.

Gunnar, M. (1994). Psychoendocrine studies of temperament and stress in early childhood. In J. Bates & T. D. Wachs (Eds.), *Temperament: Individual differences at the interface of biology and behavior.* Washington, DC: American Psychological Association.

Halverson, C., Kohnstamm, D., & Martin, R. (1994). *The developing structure of temperament and personality from infancy to childhood.* Hillsdale, NJ: Lawrence Erlbaum Associates.

Juraska, J. (1990). The structure of the rat cerebral cortex. In B. Kolb & R. Tees (Eds.), *The cerebral cortex of the rat* (pp. 483–505). Cambridge: MIT Press.

Kagan, J., Arcus, D., & Snidman, N. (1993). The idea of temperament: Where do we go from here. In R. Plomin & G. McClearn (Eds.), *Nature, nurture, & psychology* (pp. 197–210). Washington, DC: American Psychological Association.

Kohnstamm, G. (1989). Temperament in childhood: Cross-cultural and sex differences. In G. Kohnstamm, J. Bates, & M. Rothbart (Eds.), *Temperament in childhood* (pp. 483–508). Chichester: Wiley.

Kohnstamm, G., Zhang, Y., Slotboom, A., & Elphick, E. (1998). A developmental integration of conscientiousness from childhood to adulthood. In G. Kohnstamm, C. Halverson, I. Mervielde, & D. Havill (Eds.), *Parental descriptions of child personality* (pp. 65–84). Mahwah, NJ: Lawrence Erlbaum Associates.

Korn, S., & Gannon, S. (1983). Temperament, cultural variation, and behavior disorders in preschool children. *Child Psychiatry and Human Behavior, 13,* 203–212.

Lounsbury, M., & Bates, J. (1982). The cries of infants of differing levels of perceived temperamental difficultness. *Child Development, 53,* 677–686.

Maccoby, E., Snow, M., & Jacklin, C. (1984). Children's disposition and mother–child interaction at 12 and 18 months. *Developmental Psychology, 20,* 459–472.

Mack, K., & Mack, P. (1992). Induction of transcription factors in somatosensory cortex after tactile stimulation. *Molecular Brain Research, 12,* 141–147.

Malhotra, S. (1989). Varying risk factors and outcomes: An Indian perspective. In W. Carey & S. McDevitt (Eds.), *Clinical and educational applications of temperament research* (pp. 91–96). Amsterdam: Swets & Zeitlinger.

McCall, R. (1991). So many interactions, so little evidence. Why? In T. D. Wachs & R. Plomin (Eds.). *Conceptualization and measurement of organism–environment interaction* (pp. 142–161). Washington, DC: American Psychological Association.

McClelland, G., & Judd, C. (1993). Statistical difficulties of detecting interactions and moderator effects. *Psychological Bulletin, 114,* 376–390.

Natori, Y., & Oka, T. (1997). Vitamin B$_6$ modulation of gene expression. *Nutrition Research, 7,* 1199–1207.

Park, S., Belsky, J., Putnam, S., & Crnic, K. (1997). Infant emotionality, parenting and 3-year inhibition. *Developmental Psychology, 33,* 218–227.

Plomin, R. (1994). *Genetics and experience.* Thousand Oaks, CA: Sage.

Plomin, R., DeFries, J., & Loehlin, J. (1977). Genotype environment interaction and correlation in the analysis of human development. *Psychological Bulletin, 84,* 309–322.

Rothbart, M. K., & Bates, J. (1998). Temperament. In W. Damon (Series Ed.) & N. Eisenberg (Vol. Ed.), *Handbook of child psychology: Vol. 3. Social, emotional, and personality development* (5th ed., pp. 105–176). New York: Wiley.

Rothbart, M. K, Derryberry, D., & Posner, M. I. (1994). A psychobiological approach to the development of temperament. In J. Bates & T. D. Wachs (Eds.), *Temperament: Individual differences at the interface of biology and behavior* (pp. 82–116). Washington, DC: American Psychological Association .

Rowe, D. (1994). *The limits of family influence.* New York: Guilford.

Rubin, K., Hastings, P., Stewart, S., Henderson, H., & Chen, X. (1997). The consistency and comcomitants of inhibition. *Child Development, 68,* 467–483.

Rutter, M. (1983). Statistical and personal interactions. In D. Magnusson & V. Allen (Eds.), *Human development* (pp. 295–320). New York: Academic Press.

Rutter, M., & Pickles, A. (1991). Person environment interaction. In T. D. Wachs & R. Plomin (Eds.), *Conceptualization and measurement of organism environment interaction* (pp. 105–141). Washington, DC: American Psychological Association.

Sackett, G. (1991). Toward a more temporal view of organism–environment interaction. In T. D. Wachs & R. Plomin (Eds.), *Conceptualization and measurement of organism–environment interaction* (pp.11–28). Washington, DC: American Psychological Association.

Scheper-Hughes, N. (1987). A basic strangeness: Maternal estrangement and infant death. In C. Super (Ed.), *The role of culture in developmental disorder* (pp. 131–153). San Diego: Academic Press.

Strelau, J. (1983). *Temperament, personality, and activity.* New York: Academic Press.

Super, C., & Harkness, S. (1999). The environment as culture in developmental research. In S. Friedman & T. D. Wachs (Eds.),. *Measuring environment across the life span* (pp. 279–323). Washington, DC: American Psychological Association.

Talwar, R., Nitz, K., Lerner, J., & Lerner, R. (1991). The functional significance of organismic individuality. In J. Strelau & A. Angleitner (Eds.), *Explorations in temperament* (pp. 29–42). New York: Plenum.

Thoman, E. (1990). Sleeping and waking states of infants. *Neuroscience and Biobehavioral Reviews, 14,* 93–107.

Thomas, A., Chess, S., & Birch, H. (1968). *Temperament and behavior disorders in children.* New York: New York University Press.

Turkheimer, E. (1991). Individual and group differences in adoption studies of IQ. *Psychological Bulletin, 110,* 392–405.

van den Boom, D., & Hoeksma, J. (1994). The effect of infant irritability on mother–infant interaction. *Developmental Psychology, 30,* 581–590.

Wachs, T. D. (1992). *The nature of nurture.* Newbury Park: Sage.

Wachs, T. D. (1995). Genetic and family influences on individual development: Both necessary, neither sufficient. *Psychological Inquiry, 6,* 161–173.

Wachs, T. D. (1996). Known and potential processes underlying developmental trajectories in childhood and adolescence. *Developmental Psychology, 32,* 796–801.

Wachs, T. D. (1999). Celebrating complexity: Conceptualization and assessment of the environment. In S. Friedman & T. D. Wachs (Eds.), *Measuring the environment across the life span* (pp.357–392). Washington, DC: American Psychological Association.

Wachs, T. D. (2000). *Necessary but not sufficient: The respective roles of individual and multiple influences on individual development.* Washington, DC: American Psychological Association Press.

Wachs, T. D., & Bates, J. (in press). Temperament. In G. Bremner & A. Fogel (Eds.), *Handbook of infant development.* Oxford: Blackwell.

Wachs, T. D., Bishry, Z., Sobhy, A., McCabe, G., Shaheen, F., & Galal, O. (1993). Relation of rearing environment to adaptive behavior of Egyptian toddlers. *Child Development, 67,* 586–604.

Wachs, T. D., & Plomin, R. (1991). *Conceptualization and measurement of organism environment interaction.* Washington, DC: American Psychological Association.

Wachs, T. D., Uzgiris, I., & Hunt, J. M. (1971). Cognitive development in infants of different age levels and different environmental backgrounds: An exploratory study. *Merrill-Palmer Quarterly, 17,* 283–317.

Wahlsten, D. (1990). Insensitivity of the analysis of variance to heredity–environment interaction. *Behavior and Brain Sciences, 13,* 109–161.

Author Index

Subject Index